# PIKE PLACE MARKET
## COOKBOOK

# PIKE PLACE MARKET
## COOKBOOK

*Recipes, Anecdotes, and Personalities from*
*Seattle's Renowned Public Market*

Braiden Rex-Johnson
Illustrations by Spencer Johnson

SASQUATCH BOOKS
Seattle

Typeset by Scribe Typography
Printed in the United States of America

Cover and interior illustrations: Spencer Johnson
Cover design: Eilisha Dermont
Interior design: Lynne Faulk
Cover lettering: Dia Calhoun/Design 26

Library of Congress Cataloging in Publication Data

Rex-Johnson, Braiden, 1956–
Pike Place Market cookbook :
recipes, anecdotes, and personalities
from Seattle's renowned public market /
by Braiden Rex-Johnson ; illustrations by Spencer Johnson.
p.      cm.
Includes index.
ISBN 0-912365-52-8 : $15.95
1. Pike Place Market (Seattle, Wash.)    2. Cookery, American.
3. Cookery—Washington (State)—Seattle.    I. Title.
TX715.R439      1992
641.59797'772—dc20                                        91-44944
                                                                        CIP

Sasquatch Books
1931 Second Avenue
Seattle, Washington  98101
(206) 441-5555

*For Spencer and Bo-Bo,*
*with thanks and love.*

# ACKNOWLEDGMENTS

A project of this size and scope is never done by just one person — it's a team effort, and without the help of the following people, the *Pike Place Market Cookbook* could never have become a reality.

My heartfelt thanks go to Anne Depue, managing editor of Sasquatch Books; Paul Dunn, executive director of the Pike Place Market Merchants Association; Steve Evans, farm program coordinator of the Pike Place Market; Roy Feiring, director of marketing of the Pike Place Market Preservation and Development Authority (PDA); Chad Haight, publisher of Sasquatch Books; Mr. and Mrs. A. C. Johnson; Sue Gilbert Mooers, communications specialist of the PDA; Judith Olney, cookbook author and food editor and restaurant critic of the *Washington Times*; Rebecca Pepper, copy editor; Dr. and Mrs. E. B. Rex; Jeff Smith, The Frugal Gourmet, cookbook author and culinary personality; and Shelly Yapp, executive director of the PDA.

Most especially, I wish to thank all of the contributors who shared not only their recipes but their life stories, tragedies, and happinesses with me.

# CONTENTS

# FOREWORD

I can never decide whether Seattle makes the Market or the Market makes Seattle. Certainly one of the most distinguishing characteristics of our beautiful city-by-the-sea is the Pike Place Market. I travel all over the world and when I mention that I have an office in Seattle, people always ask, "Do you go to the Market?" I know which market they mean. I was born and raised here, so the Market is in my blood. It is in the blood of every true Seattleite.

Indeed, my inception into the food world occurred atop a dill-pickle barrel, right on the Market's Main Arcade. My mother had taken me to the Market when I was very young, but my real interest in food began when I got my first job there in 1955. I was barely sixteen years old when I went to work at the old Rotary Bakery, making donuts and pies. It was great fun to go down to the Market early on a summer morning and start the donut batter. I would drink coffee and watch the Market awake. It was then that I fell in love with those who provide us with our daily bread, our vegetables, even, back then, our horse meat. I have never been the same.

A year later I graduated to Brehm's Delicatessen and was literally adopted by the old German, Ed Roesler, who owned the joint. It was there that my food birth on the pickle barrel took place. Ed knew the Market and he knew his customers. "Give them the best, Smith, and fresh, but charge! Charge as much as you can!" The fifties were tough days, and the old institution that we now call the pride of Seattle was in ruins. But I loved it. Oh God, how I loved it — the vendors, the smells, the noise and affection, the rogues! It has always been *my* Market.

After years in graduate school, and after years in the university chaplaincy, and then years in my own shops in Tacoma, I have come back to where I belong. I have an office and a wonderful test kitchen in the midst of all that you are going to read about in this collection of terrific recipes and delightful characters. Food lovers come from all over the country and tell me that they love the place, and I cannot help but remind them that it really is my Market…but I let other people in on weekdays and weekends.

Enjoy the wonderful diversity that defines the Market and this cookbook. How proud I am that the Grand Old Dame of Seattle, this circus of flavors and flowers, of chaos and cabbages, of sausages and street musicians, still exists. Maybe the old girl is immortal. For the sake of our beloved city, I hope this is true.

JEFF SMITH
THE FRUGAL GOURMET

# PREFACE

Tonight I dined on white King salmon fillets with a ginger–soy sauce glaze, organic baby carrots, and romanesco broccoli. Last night it was ling cod served with a salad of eight greens, and a bowl of plump fall raspberries with a kiss of heavy cream for dessert.

These foods are just a few examples of the delectable bounty harvested in the waters and fields of the Northwest that those of us privileged to live here feast on every day. The *Pike Place Market Cookbook* was inspired by this variety of foods, which I behold on my almost-daily shopping excursions to Seattle's Pike Place Market.

My forays into the Market started shortly after my husband, Spencer, and I moved from Dallas to Seattle in early 1990. Although we didn't know Seattle well, we took an apartment half a block from the Market because we both sensed that just a few steps from our front door lay the heart and soul of the city.

In Dallas we relied entirely on our car as a means to get around, and shopping consisted of weekly trips to the best grocery store in the area. Even so, my main concerns were trying to get fish that hadn't been frozen, chicken that wasn't loaded with antibiotics and hormones, and lettuce that hadn't been sprayed with pesticides. I had a vague sense of seasons and would buy whatever was low in price and reasonably fresh, along with a couple of splurges for Chilean strawberries in the winter or Australian apples during the summer. Everything was shrink-wrapped, the faces behind the seafood case and checkout counter changed regularly, and I was just another anonymous shopper scurrying through the aisles and computerized scanners.

Imagine my awe and wonder when I first strolled through Seattle's Pike Place Market in the summer of 1988. The assortment of fish astounded me — what were all these things gaping at me, and how would a person ever learn to cook them? Wasn't a salmon a salmon — was there really more than one kind? All the different types of berries, their colors and aromas and flavors, amazed me. Live street music, not Muzak, filled my ears; the comforting smells of garlic, basil, and cinnamon hung so heavy in the air that they seemed to linger on my palate; "real" people surged around me.

During that first visit, Spencer and I were typical summer tourists — we bought a pound bag of just-picked Bing cherries and ate them as we walked down Pike Place among the farmers' stalls, spitting the warm pits into the palms of our hands. The next day we promenaded again, and devoured a quart of strawberries straight from the box, grit and all.

But when we finally moved to Seattle, I have to admit that the Market intimidated me. The same spirit of independence that attracts merchants and farmers to the Market can overwhelm those used to the anonymity of the supermarket. I'd pop over to the Market occasionally to buy fish or apples, but perhaps because I'd relied on car trips to the supermarket for so long, it just seemed easier to continue my weekly shopping excursions to Larry's or QFC.

Gradually, both Spencer and I adapted to living downtown. We walked everywhere to do our errands. With the alimentary canal of the city just outside our door, it seemed silly to go elsewhere, and I began to shop at the Market more frequently. Suddenly those men and women who had shouted at me to buy started nodding in my direction as I passed. It wasn't too many weeks before I became recognized as a regular customer. As the warm smiles continued, and the respect flowed in both directions, my inhibitions disappeared.

I started patronizing the farmers' tables, doing a sweep through the Main and North Arcades before deciding what to buy. I discovered the slightly bitter taste of kale; that gooseberries need lots of sugar to sweeten them up; that squash blossoms can be stuffed or deep-fried. Like any good local, I learned that geoducks (pronounced "gooey-ducks") are the largest clams in North America, and that the biggest octopus in the world — the Great Pacific — resides under the surface of Puget Sound. I knew I'd passed a personal milestone when I bought my first Copper River salmon and watched in satisfaction as the fishmonger filleted the huge silver fish with ease.

Going to the Market every day became an adventure I relished. The car stayed in the garage for weeks at a time as I began my journey of discovery. As I approached the fishmongers with their stacks of bright crabs, their tubs of pink singing scallops, and their oozing octopus on ice, I'd ask, "What's fresh today? What should I have for dinner?" "Copper River salmon, or halibut cheeks, or Dungeness crab," they would answer, and we'd banter back and forth about the best way to prepare these delicacies.

It was the same at the farmers' tables, the highstalls, the meat markets, the creamery. That's when I realized there was a wealth of knowledge at the Market just waiting to be tapped, gathered, and organized for other cooks, people like me who were overwhelmed by so many choices, so much variety, and all the hubbub and commotion.

I decided to write a cookbook that featured recipes contributed by the merchants, farmers, and restaurateurs who actually *worked* in the Market, for who better knew blueberries, bok choy, and beef tenderloin and how to prepare them? I had no idea how sophisticated and varied the submissions would be; indeed, I didn't even know if I would receive enough to compile a book. But as I began collecting recipes, testing and perfecting them in my home kitchen, reporting the results to the contributors, and taking around samples, the word got out and momentum grew. Over the months, as I trotted to my mailbox or visited my new-found Market friends, I was continually amazed by the imaginative and inspired offerings I received.

A Market neophyte just a year before, I had now become a member of the Pike Place Market family. As the seasons unfolded, I learned how fleeting certain items are. If you want brilliantly colored emerald tangerines, you have to buy them quickly because they last only two weeks. Abalone is so rare you can find it only once every two or three years. Even the farmers themselves come and go with the seasons — when the majority of them left after the first frost at the end of October, I was terribly depressed; I wouldn't see many of them again until the following March or April.

Today I forgo grocery stores — you can't keep me away from the Market. Each time I visit I discover something that I never noticed before — the King Proteus blossoms in front of

Enchanted Garden that look like earthbound sea anemones, another famous name among the 45,000 tiles that line the floor of the Main and North Arcades, the birds that squawk as you pass by the Parrot Market near the Hillclimb.

The result of my year-long exploration is the cookbook you hold in your hands. It is truly a book of the people, by the people, and for the people, to borrow a phrase, for the Pike Place Market family came through with a collection of recipes as broad and tempting as the cornucopia of items they offer for sale. Within these pages you'll find dishes representing eighteen ethnic groups and everything in between. They range from being easy to prepare to complex, commonplace to exotic, healthy to sinful, nostalgic to cutting-edge.

I hope you enjoy sampling the recipes, sharing the meals with loved ones and friends, and "meeting" the cookbook contributors through their words and Spencer's illustrations. Although I'm sorry to see my work on the book come to an end, I am thrilled to share the results with you. Happy cooking and fond memories from the Pike Place Market!

BRAIDEN REX-JOHNSON
FEBRUARY 1992

*Note: Although I attempted to include in this book everyone who was selling food at the Market in 1991, you may find that a favorite is missing. Every food-related business in the Market was invited to submit a recipe. For various reasons, some chose not to participate. Also, the Market is ever changing; some of the farmers and vendors described here may have moved on, and some of the restaurants and highstalls may have changed hands since this book was written.*

# A WORD ABOUT USING THIS BOOK

I work in a 7- by 10-foot kitchen without fancy pots and pans, expensive knives, or kitchen gadgets (other than a food processor, hand mixer, microwave oven, and blender). Although I use non-stick cookware in my everyday cooking, regular cookware works equally as well. All the recipes have been tested under these normal, everyday conditions and modified to reflect the same.

I take it for granted that readers have an understanding of the fundamentals of cooking, or have a good basic cookbook in which to look up questions that might arise. However, I have included descriptions for a few unusual techniques that might be difficult to find elsewhere.

Where recipes do not specify to the contrary, you should use whole milk, whole-milk yogurt, enriched (white) flour, granulated (white) sugar, white potatoes, large eggs, and unsalted butter or margarine. Softened butter means butter softened to room temperature.

Recent concerns about salmonella poisoning have called into question the use of raw eggs in food preparation. Seven recipes in this book make use of raw eggs: Blackberry Mousse with Lemon Madeleines; Chocolate Cognac Pâté with Crème Anglaise; Deviled Fruit Vinegar Butter; Frosty Strawberry Squares; Sea Beans Orientale; Smoked Chicken, Apple, and Walnut Salad; and Tiramisu. Although I experienced no ill effects during the testing of these recipes, I would encourage all readers to use the freshest eggs available and to thoroughly wash the eggs' outside shells before use. Any individuals with chronic or auto-immune diseases should be informed of the uncooked eggs before sampling these particular recipes.

See the Techniques section on page 227 for more detailed hints on how to use this book.

# Introducing the Market

# Introducing the Market

*What Is the Pike Place Market?*

*History of the Market*

*When to Visit the Market*

# WHAT IS THE PIKE PLACE MARKET? One of

the questions most frequently asked by tourists visiting Seattle is, "Does the Market go on every day?" and, in a way, this innocent question perfectly captures the charms and essence of the Market, which goes on seven days a week.

The tourists' curiosity is prompted by the nature of the Market itself, which is at once part meat, fish, and produce market; part breathtaking panorama of water, mountains, and sky; part vaudeville show; part arts and crafts extravaganza; and part slice of nitty-gritty street life.

In official terms, the Market is a seven-acre National Historic District with more than 250 permanent businesses, nearly 100 farmers, more than 200 artists and craftspeople, and 500 permanent residents. But unofficially, it's much more.

Looking beyond the surface, you might be surprised to find a bed-and-breakfast inn, housing for low-income and elderly people, an improvisational comedy troupe, a hotel, child-care facilities, a medical clinic, a senior center, a dentist, a tarot card reader, a

food bank, a daily rummage sale, a half-price ticket booth, and (perhaps most important with all the temptations available!) a cash machine.

The low metal tables in the Main and North Arcades are the stalls that farmers and crafts-people rent by the day. Craftspeople can sell only items that they make, such as jewelry, cloth-ing, and artwork, except for six "grandfathered" vendors who were selling at the Market before the "handmade only" rule was enacted. Although the "handmade only" rule is strictly enforced by Pike Place Market Preservation and Development Authority (PDA) officials through visits to the artisans' studios, the crafts contingent at the Market has grown into the largest permanent crafts display in the Pacific Northwest, and there's always a long waiting list. The population is surprisingly stable — over 35 percent of the crafts vendors have maintained their businesses in the Market for 10 years or more.

Farmers, who get priority for space, sell their own seasonal farm-fresh fruits and vegeta-bles (often representative of their ethnic origins), as well as farm-made products, such as honey, jam, cheese, and flavored vinegars. When you shop the farm tables (also known as day tables or daystalls), you have the opportunity to become part of the Market's age-old "meet the producer" tradition by buying and learning directly from the producer. If you need advice, don't be bashful about asking the farmers you buy from how to select, store, clean, and cook the produce you buy. They'll be more than happy to suggest ways to use the goods they've planted, weeded, and picked for your enjoyment.

The large permanent fruit and vegetable highstalls (located in the Main and North Arcades and along Pike Place) are run by independent produce sellers who import their goods from all over the world and also sell local produce when in season. While you'll find fresh fruits and vegetables at all 10 of them, each has developed certain specialties to ensure that customers can find exactly what they want throughout the year.

Some highstalls arrange their fruits and vegetables in ornate displays with signs such as, "Don't even THINK of disturbing displays," "Fragile. DO NOT FONDLE," or "AVALANCHE WARNING. Please Ask for Assistance." Woe to the customer who touches an apple or knocks a snow pea out of place. At this type of highstall the clerk will pick out the fruits and vegeta-bles requested from boxes and bins behind the displays. Other highstalls are less formal and allow customers inside to choose their own produce.

But if fruits and vegetables, meat and potatoes, bows and bangles were the only drawing cards of the Market, shoppers might just as easily visit their neighborhood supermarket or mall. The thing that makes the Market unique is its people — low-income seniors, downtown office workers, street people, locals who live in surrounding condominium towers, tourists, parents with children in tow, strippers who work at the peep shows along First Avenue — all shopping, working, and sometimes even living together. Shoppers are drawn here as much to mingle with the crowds, to see and be seen, and to share in the excitement as to buy a tomato or a flank steak.

Judy Duff, an organic farmer from Burien, explains, "We are pulled to the Market because it is the heartbeat of life itself. Children, the elderly, and everyone in between feed the Market's diversity and vibrancy. The Market is where East meets West, where cultures of the world become the ingredients for the All-Star American tossed salad."

In this lively community where women in fur coats and tiaras rub elbows with panhandlers in hand-me-down suits, where hints of perfume collide with whiffs of muscatel, diversity and spirit are encouraged, indeed, almost demanded. The Market just wouldn't be the same if it were transplanted to Bellevue, or Des Moines, or Poughkeepsie.

Sue Verdi, a year-round farmer, adds, "The Market is more than just a building or place of business. It is a community where everyone feels at home. Because of its diversity, the Market has an energy and life of its own. Once you have experienced this, it becomes part of you — in your blood. For those of us who work there, we spend more time at the Market with our Market 'family' than we do at our own homes."

Families with long histories in the Market add to the comforting sense of continuity and timelessness found there. Some of these families go back almost to the start of the Market itself. There are the Genzale and Manzo families among the highstallers; Sol Amon and Gary and David Levy among the fishmongers; Sue Verdi, John D'Ambrosio, and Judy Duff among the farmers.

Judy Duff explains, "My great-grandparents used to bring my grandma to the Market to shop when she was just a girl. Grandma, 89 years still strong, remembers those days and talks of them as if they were yesterday. I'm proud to share in the 'soul of Seattle.' The Market is part of my family heritage and home to my past, present, and future as I work there with my mother, husband, and daughter. Our daughter is growing up amidst the Market and we feel it will help weave a strong fabric for the rest of her life."

Is it any wonder that this microcosm of the world has become the most visited landmark in the Pacific Northwest, enjoyed by more than 9 million locals and tourists each year? In her book, *The Farm Market Cookbook*, Judith Olney says, "Pike Place is probably the most stimulating and sensuously appealing market in America," and those of us who love it would quickly agree.

# HISTORY OF THE MARKET

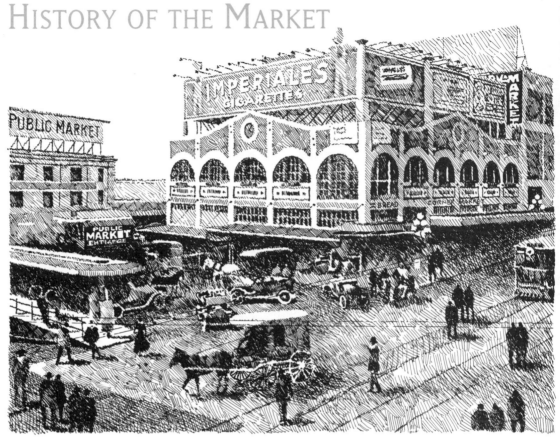

It was unseasonably rainy on the evening of August 16, 1907, and August 17th didn't dawn much better. Rain soaked the cobbled and planked streets of Seattle and turned unpaved roadways into little more than muddy trails.

As H. O. Blanchard, a farmer from Renton, wheeled his wagon over the planks of Western Avenue and up onto Pike Place, he didn't know what would await him — who, if anyone, would be waiting to buy his fresh produce at the newly designated public market, started as an experiment by the Seattle city council because both farmers and consumers were angry over high food prices.

H. O. was not to be disappointed. About 50 shoppers, most of them women, elbowed aside the single policeman stationed to maintain order, stampeded H. O.'s wagon, and bought his entire load before he could even pull to the curb. The following Saturday the crowds were again willing and eager to buy, and the 70 wagons parked on Pike Place sold out their goods within hours. Both Seattle housewives and area farmers embraced the arrangement that provided direct contact between consumer and producer, and, over the years, the Pike Place Market became a city institution.

It reached its heyday during the 1930s, when, during one year, more than 600 farmers were issued permits to sell. Throughout the Depression, the Market provided a welcoming environment to the city's jobless, as well as inexpensive food for the hungry.

During the 1940s, when the Japanese farmers were interned, and many other farmers went to work in defense plants, the Market lost nearly half its independent farmers. Acres of prime farmland were claimed by industry, people moved to the suburbs, and the local supermarket became an accepted convenience. Even the Market's buildings crumbled from neglect; nevertheless, a few hardy farmers hung on and the neighborhood refused to die.

In the 1960s, developers planned to demolish the sagging buildings and put up office and apartment towers on the prime city acreage. But a grassroots citizens' group led by architect and civic leader Victor Steinbrueck formed the "Friends of the Market" to save the beloved landmark. An initiative was put on the ballot on November 2, 1971, and the people of Seattle responded by voting to make the Market a historical district where uses, as well as designs, were preserved.

Strict guidelines were written by the Market Historical Commission, nicknamed the conscience of the Market. According to *The Pike Place Market: People, Politics, and Produce*, the Commission agreed to always consider the following when evaluating applications for use or development:

1. The Market is a place for the farmer to sell his produce.
2. The Market is a place for the sale of every kind of food product.
3. The Market is a place where citizens in the low and moderate income groups can find food, goods and services, and residences.
4. The Market is and will always be a place with the flavor of a widely varied shopping area.

The Commission encouraged 17 specific types of activity, including person-to-person sales; those offering hard-to-find goods; those involving light manufacturing; those catering particularly to the pedestrian; those offering goods for sale in a natural state, as distinguished from prepackaged goods; and those bringing together people of all backgrounds, enriching the quality of life, or relating to historical Market uses or activities.

The seven-acre historical district was placed on the National Register of Historic Places and, in June 1973, the Pike Place Market Preservation and Development Authority (PDA) was mandated by the state to manage the Market in the public's interest. The Authority's mission was and is to purchase, rehabilitate, own, and manage property in the Pike Place Public Market. Over a 15-year period, the PDA renovated or reconstructed every building it owned within the Market Historical District with the help of federal urban-renewal funds and with the philosophy that, "It is generally better to preserve than to repair, better to repair than to restore, better to restore than to reconstruct."

As it was originally built, the Market was designed to emphasize the product, not the architecture, and that remains true to this day. Its unpretentious brick, concrete, and timber structures, marquees, open stalls and tables, cast iron columns, suspended metal lighting fixtures, and tile floors look much as they did during earlier times, and the spirit of the old Market has been preserved.

An example of innovative renovation occurred in the early 1980s, when the Market needed a new floor but did not have the necessary funds. For a $35 donation, Market supporters could have their name or message imprinted on a tile. Today, more than 45,000 tiles cover the floor in the Main and North Arcades.

The consecutive numbers along the outside edge of the walkway are row markers to help locate specific tiles. Look for Ronald and Nancy Reagan's tiles in rows 351 and 352 (just to the south of City Fish), or the tiles imprinted with the prime numbers from one to 100, given by a wife in honor of her mathematician husband (in row 38 in front of DeLaurenti's main entrance).

A less positive chapter in the Market's long history occurred during the early 1990s, when a group of New York City investors who had bought tax credits on the Market's buildings in the early 1980s claimed they owned and could control the buildings when the tax advantages were abolished in the late 1980s. After battling in both Washington State and New York courts, the PDA and citizens' groups wrested control from the investors after agreeing to a $2.25 million settlement. Now that the Market is securely back in public hands, permanent safeguards for the future are being discussed so that nothing similar will endanger it again.

In talking about the future of the Market, Roy Feiring, director of marketing of the PDA, contends that, "By public choice and by law, there can be no expansion of and no change in the Market. It's a matter of keeping it clean, safe, and well maintained, and preserving its traditional uses forever."

# WHEN TO VISIT THE MARKET  Many people want to

know the best time to visit the Market, and I like to answer "any day," for the Market continually changes with the people who visit it, the farmers and craftspeople who attend, the season of the year, and the weather. No two days at the Market have ever, or could ever be alike, which is one of its ineffable charms. As Paul Dunn, executive director of the Pike Place Market Merchants Association says, "You don't need special events at the Market, because the 'regular' Market *is* the event."

However, depending on what you want to buy, certain days of the week are better than others. For the total Market experience, Saturdays during any season of the year are the best overall day, when you'll encounter the biggest crowds and the most activity.

Saturdays in summer (when the sun and Mount Rainier are out) are particularly lively. Visitors armed with video cameras mingle with locals in single-minded pursuit of the choicest flats of raspberries, the sweetest squashes, or the most flavorful basil. Crafts stalls burst out of the North Arcade and run all the way down to Virginia Street. Couples hold hands, t-shirts and cut-offs abound, and music and laughter are in the air.

If you're in search of crafts, Sundays, Mondays, and Tuesdays are good days, for farmers, worn out from busy weekends, generally don't come. Their tables, even up to the Main Arcade, are often populated by artisans selling everything from handmade bathtub toys to hand-painted velvet jackets, sand paintings to hand-stamped leather belts.

If you want to meet lots of farmers with the widest selection of fresh local produce, Wednesdays through Saturdays are your best bets. The farmers' spring crops include arugula, endive, spinach, lettuces, kale, cabbage, leeks, Chinese mustard greens, bok choy, and edible pea vines.

During the summer high season you'll find strawberries, raspberries, blackberries, blueberries, and many other kinds of berries; sugar snap, English shelling, and Chinese snow peas; Kentucky Wonder, Blue Lake, fava, Romano, and *haricots verts* beans; Walla Walla sweet onions; many varieties of corn; tomatoes; zucchini and squashes; and cucumbers on the farmers' tables.

Fall heralds the return of Golden Acorn, Sweet Dumpling, buttercup, butternut, Delicata, and spaghetti squashes; sugar pie, miniature, and full-size pumpkins; apples; gourds; Savoy cabbage; collard greens; kale; and Brussels sprouts.

The winter chill blows in fewer farmers, but those who do come to the Market bring potatoes, beets, chard, kale, turnips, parsnips, carrots, and evergreen wreaths, along with preserved products such as honeys, jams, and jellies. (For a more detailed listing, see the Produce Availability chart, page 229.)

During the winter months the sky can turn a thousand different shades of gray, the air is damp and chill, and a cool, gray light infused with yellow bathes the rain-slicked streets. The crowds are smaller and more local, the Market more solemn and reflective. During this quieter time of the year, the fishmongers, butchers, highstallers, and the few farmers who brave the Market can spend lots of time answering your questions. These can be trying times financially for owner-operated businesses, and by patronizing them during the tough winter months you'll quickly establish yourself as a much-appreciated regular customer.

The winter holidays are an especially beautiful time to visit the Market, when six-foot Noble firs festooned in white lights march across the tops of the tin roofs. With lists in hand, customers rush around in search of the freshest Dungeness crabs, crown roasts of beef, local chestnuts, fresh-killed turkeys, and sumptuous desserts for their holiday dinners, as well as that perfect present for Aunt Polly. Laden with sacks of gifts, food, and wine, they trudge through the Market as Thanksgiving, Chanukah, and Christmas draw near.

Regardless of the day or season of the year you decide to visit the Market, you don't have to get up too early to witness it arising, unlike farmers' markets elsewhere, which begin as early as 3 a.m. Business along Pike Place starts at a more civilized hour. On a clear day, arrive at around 7 a.m. and watch the sun rise on the horizon and Mt. Rainier come out like a big blue cone in the distance, while the soothing sounds of the ferry whistles serenade you.

At this early hour the farmers unload their trucks and set out their produce in elaborate displays, while the fishmongers arrange their slippery charges over ice. The smell of coffee wafts through the air as the restaurants slowly come to life.

Later, around 9 a.m., the craftspeople's roll call takes place at the end of the North Arcade under the direction of the Market Master, Millie Padua, who assigns places based on attendance and seniority. The craftspeople trundle their heavy, loaded carts over the worn brick street and set up shop in their stalls of the day. Grab a latte and pastry at Le Panier for a whiff of Paris and a ringside seat as the activity buzzes around you.

By 10 a.m., the Market is in full swing, its maze of farmers, craftspeople, and small-business owners set up and ready to serve you. Stroll at your leisure, stop to chat, buy a hand-crafted memento, nibble a baklava. Most important, soak up the Market's unique ambience as you partake of its endless bounty.

# *Appetizers*

# Appetizers

Quillisascut Savory Cheesecake

Chicken Livers à la Streisand

Caponata

Grilled and Marinated Eggplant

Mussels and Clams with Roasted Red Pepper Vinaigrette

Salmon Puffs

Piroshky

Tyropitas with Sheep's Milk Cheese

Oven Kebabs

Persian Almonds

# QUILLISASCUT CHEESE COMPANY

Lora Lea and Rick Misterly raise Jersey cows, Alpine goats, Karakul sheep, vegetables, grapevines, and fruit and nut trees on their hilly, 26-acre farm in Rice, in the upper Columbia River valley. "Our farm is an example of what family farms were like before monocropping became the vogue for farmers, back when the pace of life was a little slower and the world seemed smaller," says Lora Lea. "We want to promote the value of rural farm communities. Our goal is to bring our customers handmade, rustic farmstead cheese like the women of my family have been making for generations."

Lora Lea and Rick sold on the farmers' tables in the North Arcade for several years, but now you can buy their lavender-fennel, chipotle chèvre, plain manchego, and maceres goat's milk cheeses at DeLaurenti on Economy Row.

## *Quillisascut Savory Cheesecake*

### QUILLISASCUT CHEESE COMPANY

Because of its tangy taste, this is for true lovers of blue and goat cheese. The crust is fragrant with fresh oregano and crunchy with walnuts. Besides a vegetarian dinner, Savory Cheesecake also makes an elegant appetizer or addition to the buffet table when sliced thinly and served on a pretty platter.

*8 ounces Quillisascut chèvre bleu*

*8 ounces Quillisascut whole goat-milk ricotta*

*½ cup milk*

*2 eggs, beaten*

*3 tablespoons flour*

*Salt and pepper to taste*

CRUMB CRUST
*½ cup bread crumbs*

*¼ cup chopped walnuts*

*1 teaspoon chopped fresh oregano*

*1 clove garlic, chopped*

Preheat oven to 350°F. Get out a 9-inch springform pan and set aside.

Place cheeses in a large mixing bowl and beat with a whisk until blended. Add milk, eggs, flour, and salt and pepper to taste, and whisk until thoroughly blended.

**To prepare crumb crust:** Mix together bread crumbs, walnuts, oregano, and garlic and sprinkle into bottom of springform pan. Add cheese mixture carefully, being sure it spreads to sides of pan evenly.

Bake cheesecake until center is set, about 30 to 35 minutes. Remove sides of springform pan, cut cheesecake into wedges, and serve with a seasonal green salad with vinaigrette dressing.

*Serves 16 as an appetizer, 6 to 8 as an entrée.*

# PATTI SUMMERS

In 1984 vocalist Patti Summers and her husband/bassist, Gary Steele, realized a long-held dream when they got off the lounge circuit and opened Patti Summers, a restaurant, bar, and jazz club in the Corner Market Building at First and Pike. Patti had visions of dressing beautifully, greeting her guests for dinner, singing for them, and hosting famous jazz musicians from all over the country. But day-to-day problems kept getting in the way, from prima donna chefs to drug dealers doing business in the lounge during lunch.

Taking matters in hand, Patti and Gary cleaned up the place and Patti became chef. "I thought Aioli and Calamari were towns in Italy," the flamboyant entertainer with the sparkling eyes says, and chuckles heartily. "If I had known when we bought the restaurant I would end up as the working chef, we never would have bought it. But today, to my knowledge, I run the only restaurant in Seattle where the entertainer and owner is also the chef."

The place has a grotto-like atmosphere, with floating candles, shadowy archways, and a diverse crowd by night. Patti's food leans toward the Italian, and she has a playful time both with her menu, naming the dishes after her favorite enter-tainers, and with her singing, which includes her own and other entertainers' tunes. At least part of the original dream survives intact — Patti and Gary occasionally host such jazz luminaries as Freddie Hubbard, Bobby McFerrin, and Dianne Schurr.

# Chicken Livers à la Streisand

## PATTI SUMMERS

Serve this divine pâté, which is as light as a mousse and slightly sweet, on a bed of green or red leaf lettuce, garnished with baby bagels, cream cheese, cornichons, cherry tomatoes, and thinly sliced sweet onion rings.

*5 tablespoons olive oil*

*1 pound chicken livers*

*⅓ cup minced onion*

*1 clove garlic, minced*

*Pinch of ground mace*

*Pinch of ground allspice*

*Pinch of ground ginger*

*Pinch of dried thyme*

*1 bay leaf*

*½ cup butter*

*½ cup whipping cream*

*2 tablespoons Cognac*

Heat olive oil in a large skillet over medium-high heat and sauté chicken livers 4 minutes, stirring constantly. Turn heat down to low, add onion, garlic, mace, allspice, ginger, thyme, and bay leaf, and cook, stirring constantly, until chicken livers darken and begin to crumble on the surface, about 3 minutes more. Remove bay leaf and place mixture in food processor or blender.

Process mixture until chicken livers are mashed but not smooth, then add butter, whipping cream, and Cognac and process again until mixture reaches desired consistency (you can process until smooth or just until small chunks remain).

Spoon mixture into a 5- by 9-inch loaf pan, smooth top, and chill overnight to let flavors meld. Cut around edges, turn loaf pan upside down, turn pâté out onto a plate, and cut into 1-inch-thick slices. Serve on a bed of lettuce with the garnishes described above.

*Serves 8.*

# LOMBRICI'S ORGANIC FARM

At the age of eight, in a bucolic suburb in California, Katherine Lewis announced to her family and friends that when she grew up she wanted to live on a farm. Today, she and Steve Lospalluto, co-owners of Lombrici's, represent the younger generation of farmers at the Market.

On 10 acres in the Puyallup Valley, about 35 miles south of Seattle, they grow more than 100 varieties of organic vegetables, including a large selection of lettuces, edible flowers, and herbs. Mizuna, arugula, tatsoi, radicchio, frisée, purslane, amaranth, cress, and other greens and herbs make up their seasonal green mix.

They concentrate on the varieties of vegetables that grow best in the Northwest. In early summer these include several types of lettuce, beans, beets, and summer squash; arugula; radicchio; pepper cress; finocchio fennel; sugar snap peas; turnips; and baby bok choy and tatsoi.

Later summer vegetables include several types of tomatoes, peppers, and cabbage; herbs; romanesco broccoli, a gorgeous pale green vegetable whose geometric patterns look like a medieval labyrinth; and Middle Eastern cucumbers. During the fall you'll find many of the above, plus chard, collards, kale, leeks, mâche, five types of winter squashes, celery root, Jerusalem artichokes, scorzonera (black salsify), a dozen different edible flowers, and several types of potatoes.

Katherine and Steve began business in the Market as Martin's Farm, a project of the Martin Luther King, Jr. Ecumenical Center in Tacoma. A major focus of Martin's Farm was donating food to low-income people in Tacoma. When that project ended and Katherine and Steve took over farming the same piece of land, they continued the tradition by donating to food banks in Puyallup and Tacoma. They chose to name their business Lombrici's because it means "earthworms" in Italian.

When asked why she comes to the Market, Katherine explains, "I see some of my Market customers twice a week, every week, and they're good cooks who like to eat. It's fun to exchange ideas and recipes with them." You'll find Katherine and sometimes Steve in the North Arcade on Wednesdays and Saturdays June through October, and on Saturdays only in November and December.

## *Caponata*

#### — LOMBRICI'S ORGANIC FARM —

Caponata is a Sicilian dish generally served at room temperature as a salad, side dish, or relish. Katherine suggests serving caponata over pasta, pizza, or slices of good, crusty bread. It also freezes well.

*1 cup olive oil (divided use)*

*3 pounds eggplant, scrubbed but unpeeled, cut into ½-inch cubes*

*1 pound red bell peppers, chopped*

*4 medium yellow onions, chopped*

1 bulb fennel, diced

3 cloves garlic, minced

2 tablespoons capers

¼ cup pitted green olives stuffed with
   pimentos, diced

3 pounds Roma tomatoes, chopped

½ cup balsamic vinegar

In a large skillet heat ½ cup of the olive oil
over medium heat. Add eggplant and sauté
until it turns golden and is medium-tender,
about 10 to 15 minutes. Stir occasionally so
that eggplant doesn't stick. Add peppers and
cook for another 15 minutes, stirring occasionally. Remove from heat.

Meanwhile, pour remaining ½ cup olive
oil into a large Dutch oven and place over
low heat. Add onion, fennel, and garlic and
sauté until wilted and tender, 15 minutes,
stirring often so that onions do not brown.

Add capers, olives, and chopped tomatoes to the onion mixture in the Dutch oven
and sauté 10 minutes more, stirring occasionally. Add the balsamic vinegar and the
sautéed eggplant mixture from the skillet to
the onion mixture in the Dutch oven and
stir thoroughly.

Continue cooking the combined mixture
until all ingredients are soft and flavors are
melded, about 10 minutes more.

*Makes 3 quarts.*

# Grilled and Marinated Eggplant

— CUCINA FRESCA —

This unusual appetizer or side dish
has a firm texture, wonderful smoky
flavor, and a tangy aftertaste. You will
need a gas stove and stovetop grill, or an outdoor barbecue, to make this dish properly.

2 medium eggplants

½ cup white wine

½ cup olive oil

½ cup red wine vinegar

3 cloves garlic, chopped

Salt and pepper to taste

Preheat oven to 450°F. Take out a cookie
sheet and set aside.

Slice off tops and bottoms of eggplants,
peel four 1-inch strips lengthwise down eggplants, then slice into ¾-inch rounds. Place
eggplant rounds on cookie sheet and bake
for 10 minutes.

Grill eggplant rounds over open flame
just until grill marks show on each side,
then layer in a large glass baking dish.

**To make marinade:** Combine white
wine, olive oil, red wine vinegar, garlic, and
salt and pepper to taste, and mix well. Pour
over layered eggplant and refrigerate at least
2 hours, and preferably overnight, to blend
flavors. Serve slices cold as an appetizer or a
side dish.

*Serves 6 to 8.*

# DU JOUR

At du jour, with its whitewashed walls, pastel posters under glass, and a huge bay window with a view of the Sound, you could almost imagine you were on a mini-vacation instead of on busy First Avenue enjoying breakfast, lunch, or a late-afternoon snack.

The food, served cafeteria-style, matches the setting. Spicy Manhattan clam chowder full of red potato chunks, tomato pieces, and clams will warm you on a cold day. Bread, salad, soup, entrée, and dessert selections change daily, and are available to eat in or take out. A wide selection of espresso drinks, wine, beer, soft drinks, and mineral waters round out the offerings here. This is thoughtfully prepared comfort food for foodies, and the lunchtime crowds tend toward the beautiful, just like the view outside the bay window.

## *Mussels and Clams with Roasted Red Pepper Vinaigrette*

### DU JOUR

This sophisticated treatment of Pacific Northwest shellfish is as tasty as it is pleasing to the eye. For a fancy appetizer for a sit-down dinner party, return clams and mussels to their shells (rinsed clean), place six mussels and six clams over a bed of greens, radicchio, or sea beans, and drizzle with any remaining vinaigrette.

*1 bulb garlic, left whole*

*½ cup dry vermouth*

*½ cup Champagne vinegar*

*1 pound Penn Cove clams, scrubbed*

*1 pound Penn Cove mussels, scrubbed and debearded*

*Juice of 1 lime*

*2 teaspoons freshly ground black pepper*

*1 teaspoon salt*

*2 red bell peppers, roasted, peeled, and seeded (see Techniques section)*

*1 cup extra-virgin olive oil*

*1 cup chopped fresh purple basil*

Preheat oven to 400°F.

Cut the top off the bulb of garlic and place in a covered baking dish to roast, about 30 to 40 minutes. While garlic is roasting, place vermouth and vinegar in a large saucepan, add clams, place over medium heat, cover, and steam until clams open halfway, about 3 to 5 minutes.

Add mussels and steam until mussels open, about 3 minutes more. Remove from heat and cool shellfish in its steaming liquid. When cool, splash cooled steaming liquid into clams to remove any grit. Remove clams and mussels from their shells and set aside to cool. Strain the steaming liquid through cheesecloth and reduce in pan over medium heat to ½ cup. Cool.

Garlic is roasted when it is soft and cloves are pushing their way out of their peels. Squeeze out six cloves and set aside.

Place reduced steaming liquid, the six reserved roasted garlic cloves, lime juice, pepper, salt, and roasted red peppers in food processor and purée. With motor running, drizzle in olive oil until emulsified. Taste vinaigrette and correct seasoning.

Sprinkle basil over mussels and clams, add vinaigrette, and toss. Serve over a bed of greens or radicchio, or serve as an appetizer and spear with toothpicks.

*Serves 4.*

*Note:* When selecting mussels, look for tightly closed and undamaged shells (gaping shells should close when tapped lightly). The mussels should have a mild, fresh smell. As soon as possible after purchasing, store your mussels in an open area or container in your refrigerator, covered with damp paper towels or cloths. Never submerge mussels in fresh water or place them under ice, or in airtight containers or plastic bags, or they will die. Shortly before cooking (and not earlier) scrub the mussels under cold, running water and remove the beards by pulling them out in one firm, snapping motion.

# Salmon Puffs

## TOTEM SMOKEHOUSE

Your guests will think you've slaved for hours over these salmon puff appetizers, when they're really quite simple to make. The puffs can even be prepared ahead and frozen, then crisped and filled just before serving.

*2 cans (6½ oz each) Totem Smokehouse smoked salmon or other smoked salmon*

*1 cup grated sharp Cheddar cheese*

*1 cup diced celery*

*¼ cup chopped green onion*

*⅔ cup mayonnaise*

*¼ cup catsup*

*½ teaspoon dried dill weed*

COCKTAIL PUFFS

*1 cup water*

*½ cup butter or margarine*

*1 tablespoon soy sauce*

*1 cup flour*

*¼ teaspoon salt*

*4 eggs*

Drain salmon, remove skin (if desired), and flake. Mix salmon with cheese, celery, green onion, mayonnaise, catsup, and dill weed, and mix well.

Make Cocktail Puffs.

Just before serving appetizers, split Cocktail Puffs with a serrated knife and fill with about 1 teaspoon of the salmon mixture. If desired, puffs can be baked ahead and frozen until ready to use. Before filling, crisp at 375°F for 2 to 3 minutes.

**Cocktail Puffs:** Preheat oven to 400°F. Lightly grease two baking sheets, and set aside. Bring water, butter or margarine, and soy sauce to a boil in a medium saucepan. Stir in flour and salt and continue to stir over heat until mixture leaves sides of pan and forms a ball, about 1 or 2 minutes. Remove from heat, then cool to lukewarm, about ½ hour. Whisk in eggs, one at a time, beating well after each addition. Drop by teaspoonfuls onto baking sheets, bake for 20 to 25 minutes, and cool. Do not use more than a teaspoon of dough to make puffs, or they'll fall under their own weight and deflate when removed from oven.

*Makes 4 dozen puffs.*

# THE KALEENKA

With its starched red tablecloths, yellow curtains on the storefront windows, dulcimer music in the evenings, and authentic food from all regions of the former Soviet Union, the Kaleenka on First Avenue captures the atmosphere of the mother country without all the turmoil and food shortages.

Food is never in short supply here. Start your meal with a steaming bowl of seven-vegetable borscht (a Ukrainian specialty), served with a dollop of sour cream and a basket of black bread, then move on to *piroshky* (light yeast dough filled with meat and cheese and baked or deep-fried). Entrées include a bursting-with-butter chicken Kiev and chicken Tabaka, a Georgian dish reputed to be Stalin's favorite, in which a marinated chicken breast is pan-fried under a weight.

The Kaleenka started in 1977 as a little espresso cafe, then gradually added piroshky, borscht, salads, and dinner. Named after a tart, bitter berry that grows profusely in Eastern Europe and the former Soviet Union, Kaleenka is also the name of a popular Russian folk song, and its image is often found imprinted on spoons, dolls, plates, and other knickknacks.

During more threatening times between the United States and the Soviet Union, owner Lydia Venichenko Barrett chose the name because it was harmless and nonpolitical. Despite the growing awareness between the two superpowers, Lydia (a native of the Ukraine who has been in Seattle over 30 years) finds it amusing that people sometimes come in and ask her to recount what her country was like during the time of the czars!

# *Piroshky*

## THE KALEENKA

You'll love *piroshky* for appetizers, lunch, or quick snacks — the light, yeasty roll surrounds a spicy ground-beef-and-onion filling. Plus, they're as much fun to make as they are to eat! You can also try filling them with chicken, cheese, vegetables, and fruits for different variations on a theme.

*1½ packages active dry yeast*

*¼ cup warm water*

*4 to 5 cups flour*

*2 tablespoons sugar*

*1 teaspoon salt*

*1½ cups milk*

*1 egg*

*¼ cup light vegetable oil or melted butter*

*1 medium onion, chopped*

*1 clove garlic, minced*

*1 teaspoon olive or light vegetable oil*

*2 pounds ground round*

*Salt and pepper to taste*

*1 egg, beaten*

Get out two cookie sheets and set aside.

Dissolve yeast in the water and let stand 10 minutes. In a large mixing bowl combine flour, sugar, and salt. In a medium mixing bowl place milk, egg, and the ¼ cup oil or butter, and mix well. Make a well in flour, add wet ingredients, and combine to make a soft dough. Knead about 10 minutes, adding additional flour as your hands or bread board become sticky. Grease a large mixing bowl, add dough, turn once to grease dough, cover with a dishcloth, and let rise in a warm place until doubled in volume, about 1 to 1½ hours.

In a small skillet brown onion and garlic in the 1 teaspoon olive or vegetable oil over medium heat. In a separate pan, brown ground beef. Season meat with salt and pepper, and add cooked garlic and onion. Cool meat mixture in refrigerator, and remove any solidified fat.

Punch down dough and let rest 10 minutes. Pinch a golf-ball-sized piece of dough, and flatten with fingers or roll out to ⅛-inch thickness. Place 2 tablespoons filling in center and bring opposite edges of circle together. Pinch securely to thoroughly enclose filling, and place seam side down on cookie sheets.

Let piroshky rise in warm place until puffed, about 30 minutes. Preheat oven to 350°F. Brush piroshky with the 1 beaten egg and bake until light brown in color, about 15 to 20 minutes. The piroshky may also be deep-fried.

*Makes 3 dozen piroshky.*

# *Tyropitas with Sheep's Milk Cheese*

#### GLENCORRA FARM

These easy-to-prepare, healthy appetizers are real showstoppers, and are sure to be the most popular finger food at your next party. Sheep's milk is the most easily digested of all milks and is considered to make the finest cheese and smoothest yogurt. One ounce contains 45 calories, 3 grams of fat, and 65 milligrams of sodium.

*6 sheets filo dough*

*¼ cup butter, melted*

*1 package (8 oz) Glencorra Farm Island White sheep's milk or French Montrachet cheese*

*1 small jar (3 oz) sun-dried tomatoes packed in oil*

*12 large fresh basil leaves or 24 small fresh basil leaves*

Preheat broiler. Take out a cookie sheet and set aside.

Cut filo dough sheets in half widthwise and set aside under damp cloth or paper towel so that edges won't dry out.

To assemble appetizers, separate one sheet of dough, place on bread board, and brush with some of the melted butter. Fold sheet into thirds lengthwise and place 1 tablespoon cheese in corner of rectangle. Layer cheese with a sun-dried tomato and a fresh basil leaf (or 2 small leaves) and fold corner up repeatedly to form a triangle, beginning at end with filling in it. Brush with additional butter and place on cookie sheet.

Repeat with remaining sheets of filo dough, then broil appetizers on cookie sheet until golden brown, about 5 to 7 minutes. Serve warm.

*Makes 1 dozen appetizers.*

# Oven Kebabs

─────── THE SOUK ───────

This is the Pakistani twist on the good ol' American-style hamburger, and can be served as an appetizer or entrée.

2 pounds lean ground beef

¼ teaspoon ground cloves

¼ teaspoon ground cardamom

¼ teaspoon ground black pepper

¼ teaspoon ground cumin

¼ teaspoon ground ginger

¼ teaspoon ground cayenne pepper

1 tablespoon plain yogurt

1 large onion, diced

Salt to taste

Preheat broiler and adjust oven racks so that top rack is about 3 inches from heat source. Take out two cookie sheets and set aside.

Mix all ingredients thoroughly and form into small balls or flatten into 3-inch patties about 1 inch thick. Arrange on cookie sheets and broil about 3 to 5 minutes on each side, depending on desired doneness.

Serve like Swedish meatballs as an appetizer with a spicy dipping sauce (or try the Apricot Sweet-and-Sour Sauce under Garbanzo Bean and Potato Patties, page 62), or as a main course with Pea Pullao (see page 70) and a green salad.

Serves 12 to 16 as an appetizer, 8 as a main dish.

# Persian Almonds

─────── STACKHOUSE BROTHERS' ORCHARDS ───────

Enjoy these salted almonds with a glass of sherry, cherry Gourmandise cheese, and freshly sliced Washington-grown apples for a satisfying combination of colors, flavors, and textures.

¼ cup water

1 tablespoon sea salt

2 pounds raw almonds

Get out a rimmed cookie sheet or shallow baking pan and set aside for later use. Place water and sea salt in a small, glass measuring bowl (for microwave heating) or a small saucepan (for stovetop heating), and stir until salt is almost completely dissolved.

Place the almonds in a large, dry skillet over medium heat. Stir constantly until nuts begin to crackle, about 10 to 15 minutes.

Just after nuts begin to crackle, heat salted water in microwave oven on HIGH or on top of stove over high heat until water boils, 30 seconds to 1 minute.

Remove nuts from heat and pour salt mixture over them. Stir well until they turn white. Turn almonds out onto cookie sheet and allow them to cool and dry in the open air, about 15 to 30 minutes. Store in an airtight container or zip-top plastic bag until ready to serve.

Makes 6 cups.

# Soups and Salads

## Soups and Salads

*Chestnut Soup*

*Mussel and Pale Ale Bisque with Chive Biscuits*

*Salmon Soup with Aioli Sauce*

*Nona's Chicken Dumpling Soup*

*Taco Soup*

*Carrot Soup*

*Norsk Frukt Suppe*

*Summer Melon Soup*

*Sea Beans Orientale*

*Fruit Salad with Lemon Balm*

*Purple Potato Salad*

*Spicy Noodle Salad*

*Pasta Salad with Smoked Salmon*

*Bread Salad*

*Smoked Chicken, Apple, and Walnut Salad*

# NORTHWEST CHESTNUTS

Upon meeting Annie and Omroa Bhagwandin, you sense that this young couple has a mission far beyond just selling nuts. Omroa explains, "We are confident that chestnuts can be an exciting crop for the farmer and a healthy addition to our diet, as they are in Europe and Asia." All of their products are grown without the use of sprays or chemicals, and a portion of their profits goes toward the promotion of environmentally sound agriculture.

Annie has written and self-published *The Chestnut Cookbook*, which contains 50 chestnut recipes, charming illustrations, and cooking hints, and whose proceeds go toward the promotion of tree crops. In the introduction Annie says, "As I stand in the midst of a small grove of 150-year-old chestnut trees my feelings overwhelm me. The strong smell of autumn pervades as I relish each moment in this protective canopy. The strength and abundance of these trees help me feel whole, human, and very much a part of this earth as I silently thank the people who planted them so many years ago."

Annie and Omroa bring organic chestnuts, shelled black walnuts, chestnut-and-fig conserves, and chestnut and black walnut tree seedlings (by special order) from their farm in Morton to the North Arcade several weekends during November and December.

## *Chestnut Soup*

### NORTHWEST CHESTNUTS

This is a rich, spicy soup that would make a great first course for a traditional Thanksgiving or Christmas dinner. Taken from *The Chestnut Cookbook*, this soup is of English origin.

*2 cups chestnut purée made from fresh, dried and rehydrated, or bottled chestnuts, or canned, unsweetened purée (if you need liquid to add to the purée, use a few tablespoons of the 4 cups stock, not additional water)*

*4 cups poultry (chicken or turkey) stock or broth*

*½ teaspoon ground nutmeg*

*¼ to ½ teaspoon ground cayenne pepper, depending on degree of hotness desired*

*1 cup whipping cream*

*Salt to taste*

*Paprika and minced parsley, for garnish*

Mix purée and stock in a large saucepan, and cook for 30 minutes over medium to medium-high heat, stirring occasionally.

Add nutmeg, cayenne, and cream, and stir well. Do not let soup boil once the cream has been added, or it might curdle.

Serve in mugs, garnished with paprika and parsley.

*Makes 4 cups, 6 servings.*

**To make purée:** If chestnuts are fresh, cut an X in each one and then simmer in water to cover for 15 minutes or roast in the oven 15 to 20 minutes at 375°F. Peel chestnuts and purée, adding a bit of the stock if necessary.

# LIBERTY MALT SUPPLY COMPANY

Liberty Malt Supply Company is among the oldest suppliers of home-brewing and wine-making supplies in the United States. It opened its doors in 1921, two years after the start of national Prohibition. Among the products that Liberty Malt sold during those dry times (Prohibition was finally lifted in 1933) was malt for the brewing of beer and a "wine brick" (concentrated and dried wine must) with the instructions: "Do not add water and yeast to this product or alcoholic wine will result."

Today Liberty Malt offers the largest selection of malt and hops to the 1½ million home brewers in the United States, and its six-hour Home Brew U (university) course, presented by Pike Place brewers, teaches students how to become successful home brewers and beer tasters. The top grade one can earn in the course is an "F" (for fermentation).

The LaSalle Hotel building, built around 1908 and now home to Liberty Malt, also has a colorful history. It was formerly one of Seattle's most famous bordellos, run by Nellie Curtis. Nellie's girls used to hand out business cards to sailors on Elliott Bay that read, "You are but a stranger once at Nellie's." Lines were said to extend all the way from the waterfront to Nellie's front door. Today the building houses low-income and elderly residents on the upper floors.

# PIKE PLACE BREWERY

Like Liberty Malt, Pike Place Brewery (just up the street) is owned by Charles and Rose Ann Finkel. Founded in 1989, the brewery produces Pike Place Pale Ale, Pike Place XXXXX Stout, and Pike Place Old Bawdy Barley Wine (named in honor of Nellie Curtis). Charles, a former wine merchant who now imports rare European brews into the United States and is an expert on matching beer and food, says he and his staff like to work in the Market because, "For anyone with a hunger to expand their knowledge of food, the Market is like a great university. . . . It's a real community, with constant change, but with a history and tradition that act as a cement to hold the Market together."

## *Mussel and Pale Ale Bisque with Chive Biscuits*

LIBERTY MALT SUPPLY COMPANY/PIKE PLACE BREWERY

If you're a Northwest microbrewery fan, you'll enjoy this mussel bisque devised by Kerry Sear, executive chef of The Georgian in the Four Seasons Olympic Hotel. The bisque prominently displays the distinctive flavor of Pike Place Pale Ale, a full-bodied, deep amber brew whose malty palate is balanced with the fresh aroma of hops.

2 teaspoons olive oil

2 cups mixture of chopped onions, leeks, and celery

¼ cup chopped potatoes

½ cup fish stock

4 cups Pike Place Pale Ale or other pale ale (divided use)

*1 cup water*

*Salt and pepper to taste (optional)*

*2 tablespoons butter (divided use)*

*2 teaspoons chopped shallots*

*2 teaspoons fresh thyme, stems removed*

*4 pounds fresh, live mussels*

*2 cups mixture of diced carrots, potatoes, celery, and leeks (peel the carrots and potatoes)*

*2 cups whipping cream*

*Pinch of salt*

*Pinch of pepper*

CHIVE BISCUITS

*1¼ cups all-purpose flour*

*1¼ cups pastry flour*

*1½ teaspoons baking powder*

*½ teaspoon salt*

*½ cup cold butter*

*¾ cup buttermilk*

*1 teaspoon fresh chives*

*1 teaspoon diced onions*

Make Chive Biscuits and keep warm.

**To make the soup base:** Heat a large skillet or saucepan over medium heat and add olive oil. When hot, add onion, leek, and celery mixture, and sauté, stirring constantly. Do not allow vegetables to color. Add potatoes, fish stock, 3 cups of the ale, and the 1 cup water, and bring to a boil. Add salt and pepper to taste, reduce heat, and simmer until potatoes are soft.

Meanwhile, heat a large saucepan and add 1 tablespoon of the butter, shallots, the remaining 1 cup ale, thyme, and mussels. Cover with a lid, bring to a boil, and steam mussels until they open, approximately 5 to 7 minutes. Remove mussel meat from shells and set aside. Discard cooking liquid.

In a large saucepan, cook the carrot, potato, celery, and leek mixture in the remaining 1 tablespoon butter until leeks are clear and soft; do not brown. Add mussel meat and mix together.

Using a blender or food processor, purée the soup base and pour over the mussels. Stir in the cream, add the salt and pepper, and slowly bring to a boil.

Serve bisque in preheated bowls with two warmed Chive Biscuits per serving.

**Chive Biscuits:** Preheat oven to 450°F. Take out two cookie sheets and set aside. Mix together flours, baking powder, and salt. Using a pastry blender or two knives, cut in butter until it resembles small crumbs. Add buttermilk and form into a soft dough. Add the chives and onions and mix well. Turn out onto a floured bread board and knead about a dozen times, then roll out dough to a thickness of ½ inch. Cut out 2-inch biscuits and place on cookie sheets. Bake until biscuits are puffed and tender inside, about 8 to 10 minutes. Makes 16 biscuits.

*Makes 8 cups, 8 servings.*

# EMMETT WATSON'S OYSTER BAR

Tucked back in the Soames-Dunn Building, Emmett Watson's Oyster Bar is named for one of Seattle's most crusty, opinionated journalists. Started in 1976 with 210 square feet, eight bar stools, and some of the best fresh oysters, steamed clams, and beers on tap in town, the restaurant today boasts 1,200 square feet, a larger menu, and a charming, ivy-covered courtyard.

In addition to fresh oysters and 50 kinds of beer, Watson's laid-back waitstaff serves hearty breakfasts, notable soups, true cod fish-and-chips, sandwiches, and seafood entrées to everyone from the suit and silk dress crowd to the t-shirt and tattoo contingent. Its oysters and salmon soup have been written up in newspapers from New York to Canada to London.

# Salmon Soup with Aioli Sauce

## — EMMETT WATSON'S OYSTER BAR —

Salmon Soup with Aioli Sauce is the Northwest's answer to cioppino (Italian fish stew) or bouillabaisse (seafood stew from Provence), with a clam-based broth and salmon fillets substituting for the more common tomato-based broth and mild fish fillets. Salmon Soup is one of Watson's specialties — it is world-renowned and deserves to be, as you'll agree after you try this version devised for home cooks.

1 tablespoon olive oil

2 cloves garlic, minced

1 medium onion, chopped

1 can (46 oz) clam juice

Half a 14½ oz can whole tomatoes, drained and chopped

2½ tablespoons dry white wine (optional)

½ teaspoon dried oregano

Pinch of red pepper flakes

Salt and pepper to taste

Homemade croutons

SEAFOOD MIXTURE (VARY PROPORTIONS ACCORDING TO YOUR TASTE):

1 pound salmon fillets (skinned and cut into bite-size chunks)

½ pound lean fish fillets, such as halibut, cod, or red snapper (cut into bite-size chunks)

½ pound clams (scrubbed)

½ pound mussels (debearded and scrubbed)

AIOLI SAUCE

3 cloves garlic, minced

Half an egg (beat 1 egg and use only half)

4½ teaspoons lemon juice

½ teaspoon salt

¼ teaspoon pepper

½ cup olive oil

Heat the 1 tablespoon olive oil in a large saucepan over medium heat, and sauté garlic and onion until opaque but not browned, about 3 minutes. Add clam juice, tomatoes, white wine (if used), oregano, pepper flakes, salt, and pepper. Bring mixture to a boil, then turn down heat and simmer 30 minutes, stirring occasionally.

Make Aioli Sauce.

Just before serving, add seafood to broth. Cover pan and simmer until fish is done and the shellfish opens, about 5 to 7 minutes.

To serve, place croutons in bottom of soup dish, then place fish and shellfish in bowl and ladle broth over fish. Drizzle about a tablespoon of the Aioli Sauce over the fish and broth. Serve immediately with lots of crusty bread and butter.

**Aioli Sauce:** In a food processor or blender combine garlic, egg, lemon juice, salt, and pepper, and process about 2 minutes. Add oil in a slow stream until emulsified. Store in container with a tight-fitting cover until ready to use.

Makes about 6 cups, 4 servings.

# FRANK'S QUALITY PRODUCE INC.

"As far back as I can remember, the Market has been a part of my life," Frank Genzale, owner of Frank's Quality Produce, says. "My family started at the Market in 1922 as farmers. At the age of five I began helping my grandmother, Angelina, in her stall. I feel that our family has been a part of the success of the Market."

The Genzale family's own success story in Seattle began in 1921 when Frank "Cheech" Genzale, Frank's grandfather, left Italy and started working at his brother's farm in the Rainier Valley. By the late 1920s, Cheech was able to buy 10 acres in Sunnydale, where he grew carrots, beets, onions, lettuce, cabbage, spinach, sweet corn, and celery. In 1929 he returned to Italy for his wife, Angelina, and their son, Tony. The family continued to farm, selling their produce on the farmers' tables at the Market, with Angelina and grandsons Tony, Jr., and Frank doing the selling and Cheech and Tony handling the farming. Cheech died in 1973 at the age of 76, and Angelina died in 1986 at the age of 82.

Frank and Tony, Jr., started a highstall together in 1972, but have since parted ways. Today, Frank still owns five acres of his grandparents' original farm adjacent to Sea-Tac Airport, where he grows Walla Walla sweet onions, radicchio, red leaf lettuce, carrots, and basil and other herbs. He sells those, along with a cornucopia of fruits and vegetables, from his highstall location in the Corner Market Building. Frank's is also well known for its beautiful and delicious fruit baskets.

# Nona's Chicken Dumpling Soup

## FRANK'S QUALITY PRODUCE INC.

**N**ona means "grandmother" in Italian, and this beloved recipe was passed down by Frank's grandmother, Angelina, to Frank's mother, Antoinette (Anne). It's a lengthy recipe to prepare, but the result is comfort food, Italian style, a recipe filled with love.

*6 quarts (24 cups) water*

*1 chicken roaster or fryer (about 4 lb), cut into pieces*

*½ teaspoon salt*

*3 tablespoons chicken bouillon powder or 9 chicken bouillon cubes (1 tsp each)*

*½ cup chopped carrots*

*½ cup chopped celery*

*½ cup chopped onion*

*½ cup chopped leek*

*½ teaspoon ground black pepper (divided use)*

*½ cup pastina*

*½ pound boneless, skinless chicken breasts*

*½ pound boneless, skinless chicken thighs*

*2 eggs*

*½ cup grated Parmesan or Romano cheese*

*½ cup minced fresh parsley*

*¼ teaspoon salt*

*Grated Parmesan or Romano cheese (optional)*

Place water and chicken roaster or fryer in a large stockpot. Add the ½ teapoon salt and chicken bouillon. Bring to a boil and simmer, skimming fatty foam that floats to surface. When chicken is done, 45 minutes to 1 hour, remove from stock, skin, debone, and cut meat into bite-size pieces. Strain stock, then return to stockpot. Save chicken meat for later use.

Bring stock back to a boil and add the carrots, celery, onion, leek, and ¼ teaspoon of the pepper. Reduce heat and simmer until vegetables are tender, 7 to 10 minutes. Strain and reserve stock and vegetables for later use. Meanwhile cook the pastina as package directs, about 4 to 6 minutes. Drain, rinse, and set aside for later use.

Grind chicken breasts and thighs, or process in a food processor. Whisk eggs in a large mixing bowl, then add the ½ cup cheese, parsley, the ¼ teaspoon salt, and the remaining ¼ teaspoon pepper. Mix thoroughly. Heat chicken stock to boiling and drop dumpling mixture by rounded, compacted tablespoonsful into the hot stock. Reduce heat, cover pot, and simmer until dumplings rise to the surface of the stock and are tender, about 5 minutes. Add pastina and vegetables to stock and stir well.

Ladle half a dozen dumplings, about ¼ cup of the reserved chicken pieces, and 2 cups broth into each soup bowl. Sprinkle with additional grated cheese, if desired.

*Makes 12 cups, 6 servings.*

# SHANE'S RESTAURANT

Tucked among the vintage antique stores and Shakespeare and Company Books on the Second Floor Down Under, you'll find a friendly outpost for good home cooking — soups, chili, hot dogs, hamburgers, fish-and-chips, and soft-serve ice cream. Janet and Ron Shane are the couple behind Shane's, and in many ways they epitomize what the Market is all about.

"Everything we serve and make is homemade, and all the fresh ingredients are bought at the Market," Janet explains. "Our restaurant is family-run, a continuation of our home life, so a lot of pride and love go into it." Founded in 1980, Shane's triangular space, with five well-worn booths, five tables, and windows all around, offers a limited view of Puget Sound along with a big dose of love.

## *Taco Soup*

### SHANE'S RESTAURANT

This recipe, devised by Janet Shane, is a favorite of Market merchants, security staff, police, and employees of the Pike Place Market Preservation and Development Authority. Word goes out over the Market radio that "today is taco soup day," and Shane's is inundated with eager customers. It's so thick and rich, it should really be called "taco stew."

*½ pound lean ground beef*

*1 to 3 tablespoons taco seasoning mix, depending on spiciness desired*

*1 can (15 oz) chili with beans or 2 cups homemade chili with beans*

*Half a large onion, chopped, or 3 or 4 green onions, chopped*

*1 ripe tomato, chopped*

*1 flour tortilla, cut in half, then cut into ¼-inch strips*

*4 cups chicken broth*

*1 cup grated Cheddar cheese*

*2 cups crushed tortilla chips*

Brown beef over medium-high heat in Dutch oven and drain off fat. Add taco seasoning to taste and stir well for 1 minute, then add chili, onion, tomato, and flour tortilla strips and bring to a boil, stirring well.

Add chicken broth and bring to a boil, stirring well. Simmer for 10 to 15 minutes, stirring occasionally. Serve in large soup bowls topped with cheese and tortilla chips.

*Makes 6 cups, 4 servings as an entrée, 8 servings as an appetizer.*

# Carrot Soup

This recipe is reprinted with the gracious consent of Elizabeth Tanner, author of *A Cook's Tour of the Pike Place Market*, a charming cookbook that she self-published in the early 1970s. The soup is rich and yummy — more tomatoey than carroty, and vibrant orange-red in color. Elizabeth still volunteers her time several days a week at the Market Foundation.

*½ cup butter*

*5 or 6 medium carrots, diced*

*1 cup chopped celery*

*1 large onion, chopped*

*3 medium, very ripe tomatoes, cut into chunks*

*4 peppercorns*

*3 or 4 sprigs parsley, tied together with kitchen string*

*1 slice toast, finely ground*

*1 cup boiling water*

*1¾ cups chicken broth*

*1 cup tomato juice*

*Salt to taste*

*Sour cream and chives or parsley, for garnish*

Melt the butter in a large Dutch oven over low heat, and add carrots, celery, onion, and tomatoes. Cook, stirring occasionally, until vegetables begin to brown.

Add peppercorns, parsley, toast crumbs, and the boiling water, cover Dutch oven, and simmer until vegetables are very tender, about 30 minutes. Remove cover and quickly reduce the remaining liquid, while stirring, until it is almost absorbed.

Remove parsley sprigs and purée mixture in blender or food mill (today's cooks can also use a food processor). Return vegetable purée to Dutch oven and add chicken broth and tomato juice. Taste for seasoning and add salt if needed.

Heat soup slowly until mixture is nice and creamy, about 10 or 15 minutes. Serve with a dollop of sour cream and a sprinkling of chives or parsley.

*Makes 6 cups, 8 servings.*

# Norsk Frukt Suppe

This recipe is reprinted with the generous consent of Margaret Wherrette, one of the coauthors of *The Market Notebook*, a wonderful source of in-depth information on Market produce, published in 1980. Margaret writes, "Fruit soup is a Scandinavian classic. It makes a wonderful dessert after a heavy, wintertime meal. It is rich, but the fruit makes it seem light. It is also good cold for breakfast or served with sherry late in the afternoon." Raw cream is often available at the Pike Place Market Creamery; if not, whipping cream softly whipped makes an acceptable substitute.

1 cup large pearl tapioca

1 pound dried pitted prunes

¼ pound dried apricots

1 cup raisins

½ cup currants

1 lemon, rind and pith removed, thinly sliced

1 orange, rind and pith removed, thinly sliced

1 cup sugar

1 cinnamon stick (3 inches long)

2 firm, tart apples, such as Granny Smith, cored, quartered, and thinly sliced

1 to 2 cups raw cream or whipping cream


Place tapioca, prunes, apricots, raisins, and currants in a large Dutch oven or stockpot, cover with water, and soak overnight. Drain water and add lemon, orange, sugar, cinnamon stick, and apples to plumped fruit in Dutch oven. Cover fruits with fresh water and place Dutch oven over medium heat. Simmer until apples are tender, about 20 to 30 minutes.

Remove cinnamon stick, and let soup cool. Place in refrigerator and chill for 24 to 48 hours to let flavors develop. Divide cold soup among soup bowls and top with 1 or 2 tablespoons of raw cream per serving.

*Makes 16 cups, 16 servings.*

# DANNY'S PRODUCE

Danny's Produce, owned by Tim Manzo and his wife, Dianna, is one of three Manzo-owned highstalls in the Main Arcade of the Market. (For a more complete family history, see page 72.) Danny's has a good selection of general produce, about evenly divided between vegetables and fruit.

## *Summer Melon Soup*

DANNY'S PRODUCE

Y ou'll welcome this sweet, cool soup during those warm summer months. It's a surprisingly light and healthy yet satisfying dessert with a wonderful fragrance and pink color.

*2 cups summer melon, such as cantaloupe, honeydew, or Crenshaw, cut into 1-inch chunks*

*1½ cups water*

*½ cup red wine, such as Chianti or Beaujolais*

*⅓ cup sugar*

*½ teaspoon cornstarch or arrowroot*

*1 teaspoon lemon juice, freshly squeezed*

*½ cup whipped cream or vanilla yogurt*

Place the melon chunks, water, wine, and sugar in a medium saucepan and cook over low heat until fruit softens, about 15 to 20 minutes. Strain fruit and set aside, then return fruit juice to saucepan.

Add cornstarch or arrowroot to fruit juice, and cook over medium heat until thickened, about

1 minute. Add lemon juice to fruit juice and stir; return fruit to saucepan and cook 1 to 2 minutes.

Chill soup in refrigerator until completely cooled, then ladle into soup bowls and garnish with a dollop of whipped cream or vanilla yogurt.

*Makes 3 cups, 4 servings.*

# Sea Beans Orientale

————— SILVER BAY HERB FARM —————

This unique salad takes great advantage of the salty/crunchy flavor of sea beans, which reach their prime from late May to late August, after which time their quality declines. However, they keep in the refrigerator for up to two weeks. They also freeze beautifully and will last for up to a year — just blanch for 2 minutes, chill in ice water, drain, wrap well, and freeze. If you've never tried them, you should — there's nothing like them!

*2 pounds fresh sea beans, blanched, or*
   *2 pounds frozen sea beans, thawed*

*½ cup sesame oil*

*¼ cup olive oil*

*¼ cup rice wine vinegar*

*¼ cup orange juice*

*2 tablespoons soy sauce*

*½ teaspoon minced fresh ginger root*

*2 eggs*

*Freshly ground white pepper*

*¼ cup toasted sesame seed (see Techniques*
   *section)*

Put sea beans into a large mixing bowl. Mix oils, rice wine vinegar, orange juice, soy sauce, ginger, eggs, and pepper in small mixing bowl and whisk until blended. Stir in sesame seed, then pour over sea beans and chill for at least ½ hour. Serve cold.

*Serves 8 to 12.*

*Note:* Sea beans are a perfect garnish or accompaniment to seafoods of all kinds. Steam or sauté them lighty with herbs and garlic as a side dish; use them as a bed or stuffing for fish; add blanched sea beans to cold seafood, potato, or mixed-vegetable salads; or serve them raw with a creamy herb dip.

# Fruit Salad with Lemon Balm

————— RAIN GARDEN —————

You can use any mixture of fruits you want in this lemony/minty salad; the fruits below are included to spark your imagination. If the mixture seems tart, drizzle with wild blueberry honey.

*2 bananas, sliced into ⅛-inch rounds*

*2 kiwi fruit, sliced into ⅛-inch rounds*

*2 star fruit, sliced into ⅛-inch pieces*

*1 grapefruit, sliced into sections*

*1 peach, sliced into ⅛-inch pieces*

*1 tablespoon minced fresh lemon balm*

*1 tablespoon minced fresh mint*

*Juice of 1 lemon*

Combine fruits in a large mixing bowl. In a small mixing bowl stir together lemon balm, mint, and lemon juice, and pour over fruits. Toss to coat fruits and refrigerate until ready to serve.

*Serves 6 to 8.*

# BARB'S GOURMET DELI

Barb's Gourmet Deli has been owned and operated since 1972 by Louise and Bob Cromwell, who also manage the venerable Athenian Inn a few doors north. You'll find an emphasis on Greek items (feta cheese, several types of olives, filo leaves, baklava) at this old-fashioned, counter-style deli because Barb's supplies the restaurant.

During the 1930s, Barb's Gourmet Deli operated as the Milwaukee Delicatessen, the Market outlet for the local Milwaukee Sausage Co. Perhaps because of its original tie-in with the sausage company, Barb's is one of the few places in Seattle where you can purchase homemade scrapple, a Pennsylvania Dutch dish made from finely chopped scraps of cooked pork and cornmeal formed into a loaf, sliced, fried in butter, and served for breakfast or brunch with lots of maple syrup.

## *Purple Potato Salad*

### — BARB'S GOURMET DELI —

Make this potato salad a real conversation piece by using purple potatoes when in season. No matter what kind of potatoes you use, however, you'll enjoy the rich sauce that covers them, full of mayonnaise and mustard. You can cut down on fat and calories by using one of the new reduced-calorie mayonnaises.

*5 hard-boiled eggs, chopped*

*3 celery stalks, chopped*

*2 tablespoons Dijon mustard*

*½ teaspoon pepper*

*½ tablespoon salt*

*2 cups mayonnaise*

*2 tablespoons bacon bits*

*2½ pounds purple potatoes, boiled until just tender and cut into bite-size chunks*

Combine eggs, celery, mustard, pepper, salt, mayonnaise, and bacon bits in a large mixing bowl with a cover, and stir to blend thoroughly.

Add potatoes and stir gently until all pieces are coated with sauce. Serve immediately, or cover and refrigerate until ready to use.

*Serves 10.*

# GRAVITY BAR

Don't be alarmed — even though it looks like some high-tech space station, you're still firmly planted on Planet Earth when you visit Gravity Bar, a serious but not fanatical health-food restaurant next door to Inn at the Market. Here you'll find vegetable and grain entrées; soups, salads, and sandwiches; baked goods; and yes, even espresso.

Gravity Bar is well known for its fresh fruit and vegetable drinks made to order, especially shot glasses full of freshly squeezed, slime-colored wheatgrass juice. This live, enzymatically active, vitamin- and amino-acid-rich food tastes like a field of fresh-mown grass smells, moving from bitter to sweet over the palate. Aficionados claim it "cleanses and detoxifies the body, interrupting cell mutation and disabling toxins."

Gravity Bar started in 1986, some 300 years after Newton's discovery of gravity. Owner Laurrien Gilman says, "Gravity Bar is food as it really is, for people as they really are. Historically, we are unprecedented — our food and decor are as new as it gets. However, in a broad sense, our food is as old as time, related directly to a simple and commonsense approach to life, food, and health."

Laurrien calls the Market the "alive center" of the city. "It's essential to feel part of the chain of life," she says, "from farmers and growers to eaters."

As the book went to press, I learned that the Gravity Bar would be moving to raison d'etre's former space on First Avenue and Virginia, just half a block from the Market. Laurrien promises more comfortable seating, additional menu items with the same natural-food theme, and a calmer atmosphere.

# Spicy Noodle Salad

GRAVITY BAR

Soba noodles are brownish-gray Japanese noodles made from buckwheat flour. You'll appreciate the wonderful mix of tastes, textures, and colors they lend to this healthful dish. The crushed red pepper flakes give Spicy Noodle Salad a good, hot undertone.

1 package (8.8 oz) 40% buckwheat soba noodles (Eden brand preferred; if unavailable, use 1 package (7 oz) 100% buckwheat soba noodles)

¼ cup dry hiziki seaweed

1 cup water

1 medium carrot, julienned

½ cup broccoli florets

¼ cup shoyu (Japanese soy sauce)

¼ cup Oriental toasted sesame oil

¼ cup chopped green onions

2 tablespoons sesame seed, toasted (see Techniques section)

Half a red pepper, julienned

1 teaspoon crushed red pepper flakes

If using 40% buckwheat soba noodles, heat large pot of water to boiling, add noodles, and stir so they do not stick together. Cook at a low boil until al dente, about 4 minutes. If using 100% buckwheat soba noodles, cook as package directs. Pour noodles into colander, rinse with cold water, and drain. Allow noodles to cool in colander.

Meanwhile, put seaweed and the water in a small saucepan and soak for 15 minutes. Then bring to a boil, reduce heat, and simmer for 10 minutes. Rinse well and drain.

In a vegetable steamer, steam the carrots and broccoli until crisp/tender, about 3 minutes, then rinse them with cold water to stop cooking.

Combine the shoyu sauce, sesame oil, green onions, sesame seed, red pepper, and red pepper flakes in large bowl and whisk to mix thoroughly. Add noodles, seaweed, carrots, and broccoli, toss gently, chill, and serve.

Serves 6.

# TOTEM SMOKEHOUSE

When Don Fleming decided to give up the corporate rat race, he knew he had to move to the Pacific Northwest, and he knew he had to start a business that involved seafood. Fascinated with the spawning rituals of salmon, Don spent countless hours in the University of Washington library researching the fish and the methods the Pacific Northwest Indians used to preserve it.

He spent a year traveling the West Coast from Alaska to Oregon, talking to fishermen, canners, and processors, in search of the best seafood products he could find. Taking some of his own recipes, he worked with fish processors to perfect his smoking techniques. His Pacific sockeye salmon was prepared in the traditional manner of the Northwest Coast Indians, slow-smoked over alderwood fires with no added colors, preservatives, or sugars. Because of careful brining (salt infusion) and packaging, the result was a moist, tender, deep-red smoked salmon.

With their smoked salmon finally refined, Don and his wife, Anne, started a small corporate gift business out of their home. It was a real mom-and-pop operation: They did everything, from gluing on labels to hand-screening wooden boxes. They even took, labeled, packed, and delivered orders.

Don and Anne soon opened a retail store on the waterfront, which relocated to the Market in 1983. Today, in addition to salmon, Totem Smokehouse also smokes clams, oysters, scallops, rainbow trout, sturgeon, and albacore tuna, and cold-smokes King lox.

## *Pasta Salad with Smoked Salmon*

### TOTEM SMOKEHOUSE

This makes a great main course for summertime dining or picnicking, is easy to prepare, and doesn't require you to heat up the stove or oven during those long days when the sun is blazing. The lemon and dill in the dressing really bring out the taste of the salmon.

*1 can (6½ oz) Totem Smokehouse smoked salmon, with 1 tablespoon of liquid reserved*

*½ cup provolone or mozzarella cheese, cut into 2- by ¼-inch strips*

*½ cup minced parsley*

*3 cups rotini pasta, cooked, drained, and cooled*

*Crisp salad greens of your choice*

*Tomato wedges*

*Grated Parmesan cheese*

LEMON DRESSING

*½ cup olive oil*

*2 tablespoons lemon juice*

*1 tablespoon reserved salmon liquid*

*1 clove garlic, minced*

*½ teaspoon dried dill weed*

*½ teaspoon grated lemon rind*

*Pinch of freshly ground black pepper*

*¼ cup grated Parmesan cheese*

Make Lemon Dressing.

Drain salmon, reserving 1 tablespoon liquid, remove skin, if desired, and break into chunks in large mixing bowl. Combine with cheese, parsley, and rotini, add Lemon Dressing, and toss lightly.

Mound salmon/pasta mixture on lettuce-lined platter or over salad greens in a bowl; garnish with tomato wedges. Sprinkle with Parmesan cheese and serve.

**Lemon Dressing:** Place olive oil, lemon juice, salmon liquid, garlic, dill weed, lemon rind, and pepper in a small bowl and mix well. Stir in Parmesan cheese.

*Serves 4 to 6.*

# Bread Salad

SUR LA TABLE

Summertime, when the tomatoes, peppers, onions, and basil are at their prime in taste and are least expensive, is the best time for bread salad!

*1 pound firm-textured bread (Ciro's bread from DeLaurenti Specialty Food Markets is recommended), crusts removed and sliced ¾ inch thick*

*1 large clove garlic, peeled and left whole*

*Olive oil*

*1 yellow pepper, diced*

*4 ripe tomatoes, seeded and diced into pieces about the same size as bread cubes*

*1 small Walla Walla sweet onion, sliced into ⅛-inch rings*

*1 cup fresh basil leaves, kept whole if small, torn into pieces if large*

VINAIGRETTE

*1 clove garlic, minced*

*3 tablespoons red wine vinegar*

*½ cup extra-virgin olive oil*

*Salt to taste*

*Extra basil leaves, for garnish (optional)*

Preheat oven to 350°F. Take out two cookie sheets.

Arrange bread slices on cookie sheets so that slices don't overlap, and toast lightly. While slices are still warm, rub the large whole garlic clove over one side of each bread slice, then brush both sides of bread with olive oil. Cool and cut into cubes. (You should have about 4 cups of bread cubes.)

In a large bowl toss together bread cubes, peppers, tomatoes and their juice, onion, and basil.

**To make the vinaigrette:** Mix together the 1 clove minced garlic and red wine vinegar, then add the ½ cup olive oil in a slow, thin stream, whisking constantly so that the dressing will emulsify. When thoroughly blended, add salt to taste and set aside. Prepare recipe to this point about ½ hour before serving.

To serve, pour two-thirds to all of the vinaigrette over the salad, depending on the juiciness of the tomatoes. Toss and let stand at room temperature until juices have penetrated the bread, about 20 minutes. Be careful not to oversoak the bread.

Serve on salad plates with a fresh basil leaf for garnish, if desired.

*Serves 4.*

# Pure Food Meats

Harry Straw, the butcher, prepares fresh chickens, turkeys, and hams in the smoker, and roasts beefs, chickens, and turkeys in the rotisserie here. Besides the usual cuts of meat, you'll find a wide array of unusual items, such as fresh and pickled beef tongues and pickled pigs' snouts. Around the holidays, look for fresh turkeys and crown roasts of beef.

## Smoked Chicken, Apple, and Walnut Salad

### Pure Food Meats

This is a hearty, main-dish salad that is easy to make and lovely to eat, especially when the weather is warm and you don't feel like heating up the oven or stove.

3 apples, cored and diced

1 tablespoon freshly squeezed lemon juice

4 smoked whole chicken breasts (about 2 lb), skinned and cut into thin strips or 1 whole smoked chicken (about 2 lb), skinned and meat removed from bones

1½ cups chopped celery

4 cups chopped watercress leaves

1 cup Lemon-Mustard Dressing (recipe follows)

Freshly ground pepper, to taste

1¼ cups chopped, toasted walnuts (see Techniques section)

LEMON-MUSTARD DRESSING

4 teaspoons freshly squeezed lemon juice

4 teaspoons Dijon mustard

1 egg yolk

¼ teaspoon salt

¼ teaspoon pepper

1 cup olive oil

In a large salad bowl toss apple chunks with lemon juice, then add chicken strips, celery, and watercress leaves and toss well.

Pour Lemon-Mustard Dressing over meat and greens in salad bowl, sprinkle with freshly ground pepper and walnuts, toss, and serve.

**Lemon-Mustard Dressing:** Combine lemon juice, mustard, egg yolk, salt, and pepper in a food processor or blender. Add olive oil in a slow, steady stream and blend until emulsified. Makes 1¼ cups.

*Serves 4 to 6.*

# Vegetarian Entrées and Side Dishes

## Vegetarian Entrées and Side Dishes

Pasta Con Fagioli

Pasqualina Verdi's Pesto Sauce

Lasagna with Sheep's Milk Cheese

Spanakopita with Lovage

Chipotle Chèvre Garlic Pizza

Microwave Mozzarella Vegetable Pie

Panini Brutti

Pozole

Pike Place Market Stir-Fry

Cheese-Macaroni Asparagus Bake

Vegetarian Couscous with Dates and Almonds

Garbanzo Bean and Potato Patties with Apricot
Sweet-and-Sour Sauce

Apple-Yam Holiday Casserole

Stir-Fried Harvest Medley

Ranch Stuffing

Chutney Hollow Squash

Thanksgiving Stuffing

Raspberry Snap Peas

Pea Pullao

Chinese Asparagus

Pak Choi Surprises

Cheesy Tomatoes

Fun with Fresh Fennel

Greek Rice

# MAGNANO FOODS

You might say that olive oil is in Ann Magnano's blood. Her father imports olive oil, as did his father before him. And Ann carries on the family tradition in her healthy foods store — Magnano Foods — on the Market's Mezzanine Level, sandwiched on the sloping wooden floors between the Main Arcade and the Down Under.

Here you'll find barrels of Italian, Spanish, and Greek olive oils, and drums of safflower, sesame, soy, canola, and peanut oils. Vinegars are also available in bulk, as are tamari sauces, maple syrup, and unsulphured molasses. Bulk rices, flours, grains, beans, and pasta line the floors and walls, and shelled nuts, dried fruits, coffee beans, and herbal teas round out the selection. You can even grind your own peanut or almond butter here.

Appropriately enough, Magnano Foods, which Ann purchased in the mid-1970s, was the original site of Pete's Italian Grocery, which later became DeLaurenti, another Market store with a deep Italian heritage.

## *Pasta Con Fagioli*

— MAGNANO FOODS —

Cannellini beans are creamy-white kidney beans, slightly larger than navy beans and with a fluffier texture. *Pasta con fagioli* (with beans) is a healthy vegetarian entrée, especially good served with a fresh green salad, crusty bread, and a bottle of Chianti.

*½ pound dried cannellini beans*

*8 cups water*

*¼ cup olive oil*

*2 or 3 cloves garlic, chopped*

*¼ cup white wine*

*1 teaspoon capers*

*Pinch of dried oregano*

*1 cup sun-dried tomatoes (not packed in oil)*

*1 pound linguine*

*Fresh Parmesan or Pecorino Romano cheese, grated*

*Fresh basil leaves, for garnish*

Fill a large saucepan with fresh water and bring to a rolling boil. Add cannellini beans and boil 3 to 5 minutes. Drain water and replace with the 8 cups water and bring to a boil again.

Meanwhile, heat olive oil in a skillet over medium heat and add garlic. Cook until garlic becomes soft, then reduce heat to low and add white wine and capers.

Reduce heat to low under the beans, add a pinch of oregano and the sautéed garlic and capers to the saucepan, and let simmer until the beans are soft, about 1 hour. During the last 20 minutes of cooking time, add sun-dried tomatoes.

Meanwhile, heat a large pot of water to boiling for pasta. Add pasta and boil 10 to 15 minutes, until pasta is al dente. Drain pasta, then divide it among dinner plates and spoon the cannellini beans and sun-dried tomatoes on top. Sprinkle with freshly grated Parmesan or Pecorino Romano cheese, and garnish with fresh basil leaves.

*Serves 8.*

# VERDI'S FARM-FRESH PRODUCE

Everyone who knows the least bit about the Market either remembers or has heard stories about Pasqualina Verdi, a squat, feisty, ruddy-cheeked woman dubbed the queen of the Market. In 1949, Pasqualina, then a widow with an eight-year-old son, emigrated from Avellino, Italy, to Seattle to marry Dominic Verdi, a farmer and widower with eight children of his own. They raised zucchini, scallions, and other vegetables on their farm in south Seattle, but when it became apparent that the family could not make a living selling their produce to wholesalers, Pasqualina began coming to the Market in 1955.

She didn't speak a word of English, and at first all Pasqualina knew how to do was count and make change. But over the years she learned an engaging, yet bewildering mix of Italian and English, and managed to teach several generations of Seattleites the secrets of Italian cooking. She was so passionate about her produce that she would often sneak unusual vegetables into the bags of unsuspecting customers in the hopes they would try them.

Pasqualina died in 1991, and with her died a little bit of the Market. However, the teaching tradition and passion live on in daughter-in-law Sue Verdi, who's been selling at the Verdi's spot in the Main Arcade for seven years and is a whole lot easier to understand. She explains, "Over the years we've developed a strong rapport with customers who have been buying from us for their daily and weekly meals. Customers often ask me what they're having for dinner and how they should cook it. And, indeed, I help them plan their menus and instruct them on the cleaning, preparation, and cooking of the produce for their meals!"

Sue and Mike Verdi (Pasqualina and Dominic's son) grow about 120 varieties of vegetables, herbs, and cut flowers on their 50-acre farm in Snohomish and are perhaps best known for their sweet basil, which they sell by the bunch or by the crateful for freezing. They grow a large number of European vegetables and salad greens, such as arugula, radicchio, fava beans, broccoli di rapa, and Romano beans, and are constantly experimenting with new and unusual items, such as tatsoi, mâche, and parsley root. Their winter vegetables from storage include potatoes, onions, and winter squashes. Winter crops fresh from the field might include carrots, beets, parsnips, turnips, kale, collards, cabbages, Brussels sprouts, and chicory. You can buy from Sue year-round, Monday through Saturday from May through November, and two or three days a week during the winter months.

# Pasqualina Verdi's Pesto Sauce

### VERDI'S FARM-FRESH PRODUCE

A few years ago, according to Sue Verdi, sweet basil was unknown to most Seattleites. "We only grew about 30 plants for our own consumption," she explains. "But Pasqualina was determined to teach her customers about pesto and began giving recipes on how to use this herb. Largely due to Pasqualina's persuasive salesmanship and her avid cooking instructions, pesto has become so popular here that we now grow three acres of this versatile herb."

*1 pound pasta of your choice*

*2 tablespoons light vegetable oil (or olive oil for a heavier sauce)*

*2 cups minced sweet basil*

*2 or 3 cloves garlic, minced*

*5 or 6 sprigs Italian parsley, minced*

*1 cup water*

*½ cup grated Parmesan, Romano, or Pecorino Romano cheese (or a combination of all three)*

Heat a large pot of water to boiling for pasta. Add pasta and boil 10 to 15 minutes until pasta is al dente. Drain pasta, then return it to pot and cover.

Heat oil in large skillet over medium heat. Add basil, garlic, and parsley and stir constantly for 2 to 3 minutes. Add water and reduce mixture over low heat, stirring occasionally, until desired consistency is reached.

Toss pesto with hot, cooked pasta. Add cheese(s) and toss again. If desired, and if expense is not important, add ground pine nuts to your pesto. Otherwise, ground walnuts or almonds are reasonably priced alternatives.

*Makes ½ cup sauce, 4 to 6 servings as a pasta entrée.*

*Note:* The Verdis were eating pesto long before blenders or food processors were available. If you wish to use these appliances, it is not necessary to cook your pesto, but limit the water and increase the oil.

Pesto is also good over baby new potatoes, broiled fish, or chicken. Add butter or cream cheese to make a great bread spread or chip/vegetable dip. A couple of tablespoons in your favorite minestrone soup recipe adds an extra-special flavor. Pesto is incredibly versatile. Let your imagination run wild.

# GLENCORRA FARM

Although sheep's milk cheeses and yogurt are common in Europe and the Middle East, Glencorra Farm is one of just a handful of farmstead sheep dairies in the United States. Located on Lopez Island in the San Juan Islands, Glencorra was started in 1988 by Ellen Skillings, Marty Clark, and Teri Linneman.

These three young farmers allow their flocks to graze freely through rolling pastures. No antibiotics or growth hormones are used in raising their animals, and no preservatives, stabilizers, or other artificial additives are used in making their Plain Island White, Dill/Garlic, Pepper, and Star Anise cheeses.

Because of people's unfamiliarity with the product, selling sheep's milk cheese can be an uphill fight. But Teri reports that once people sample her cheese (Fridays and Saturdays from May through December in the North Arcade), they appreciate its delicate, distinctive flavor. A typical exchange with a customer usually runs like this. "I've never had sheep cheese. Is it good? Does it taste like goat cheese? Yummm!"

But there's more behind this sheep's milk farm. Lopez Island has traditionally been a farming community, but development is beginning to take over farm land. Glencorra Farm is trying to encourage more farming by producing a product that is easy to transport and that supports the farmer.

Teri enjoys working at the Market because she likes getting feedback from her customers. "When you work hard all week producing the product," she says, "it feels good to have people try it and like it."

As the book went to press, I learned that Glencorra Farm's flock wasn't producing enough sheep's milk to support the production of cheese. While land costs were escalating, lamb meat and wool prices were spiraling downward and the farm's very survival was in question.

Montrachet cheese (a white *chèvre* from Burgundy with a soft, moist, creamy texture and a slightly tangy flavor) can be substituted for sheep's milk cheese in the following recipe and in Tyropitas (see page 22).

# Lasagna with Sheep's Milk Cheese

## GLENCORRA FARM

This is a refreshingly light, delicate, and delicious lasagna, a healthful change from the traditional lasagna laden with béchamel sauce and heavy cheeses.

1 tablespoon olive oil

2 cloves garlic, crushed

1 medium onion, diced

1 pound fresh mushrooms, sliced

1 can (14½ oz) whole tomatoes, chopped, or 3 large fresh tomatoes, chopped, plus their juice

1 can (8 oz) tomato sauce

2 tablespoons tomato paste

1 bay leaf

5 to 6 fresh basil leaves, minced, or 1½ teaspoons dried basil

1 tablespoon honey

½ teaspoon salt

Pepper to taste

9 lasagna noodles

1 pound fresh spinach, cooked or steamed until just wilted

1 package (8 oz) Glencorra Farm Island White sheep's milk cheese, or 8 oz Montrachet cheese, crumbled

1½ cups (¼ lb) kasseri cheese, grated

1½ cups (¼ lb) Pecorino Romano cheese, grated

1 cup sunflower seed, toasted (see Techniques section)

Take out an 8- by 8-inch pan, grease lightly or spray with nonstick corn-oil or olive-oil spray, and set aside.

**To prepare sauce:** Place olive oil in large noncorrosive skillet or saucepan and heat over medium heat. Add garlic and onion and sauté until onion is translucent. Add mushrooms and cook until tender. Add tomatoes, tomato sauce, tomato paste, bay leaf, basil, honey, salt, and pepper and simmer 1 hour, stirring occasionally.

While sauce is simmering, cook lasagna noodles as directed on package. Drain well and return to pan until ready to use.

**To assemble lasagna:** Preheat oven to 375°F. Layer ingredients in the following order: a third of the sauce, a third of the lasagna noodles, half of the spinach, half of the sheep's milk cheese, a third of the kasseri cheese, a third of the Romano cheese, and half of the sunflower seed. Repeat as above, then layer with a third of the noodles, a third of the sauce, remaining kasseri cheese, and remaining Romano cheese. Don't worry if the tomato sauce doesn't flow to edges of the pan — just dot it on and it will spread during baking. Bake 40 minutes, and let rest 10 minutes before cutting.

Serve with a fresh green salad with vinaigrette, crusty bread, and a good bottle of red wine.

Serves 6.

# SILVER BAY HERB FARM

Several times a month, Mary Preus brings a piece of her Bremerton herb farm to the North Arcade. Green, purple, and Piccolo basil (a mild, small-leafed variety and the sweetest of the three) line her table during basil season (June through October), as well as pickling dill, savory, tarragon, thyme, and many other herbs. During the colder months, you'll find herbal nosegays, heart wreaths, herbal vinegars, and bouquets of everlasting statice.

A thoughtful, bespectacled woman, Mary likes to give expert advice on uses for the fresh herbs and herb vinegars, mustards, and honeys she sells. Be sure to ask her about sea beans (*Salicornia*), a briny vegetable that grows wild in specific marine environments and is harvested by hand. They're her most unique offering, not sold by anyone else in the Market.

Silver Bay Herb Farm, which opened for business in 1981, is a working farm where more than 100 types of herbs are grown organically. Located on the same piece of land where Mary grew up, the farm is bordered by Dyes Inlet (a saltwater lagoon) and a salt marsh (where those sea beans grow), and has a view of the Olympic Mountains. Stone artifacts gathered nearby suggest that the land was once a gathering place for Native Americans. A German family homesteaded the land at the turn of the century and raised dairy cattle on it; later on, Japanese immigrants raised strawberries and oysters.

Mary's memories of the Market go way back. In the early days she was known as the Herb Lady, and her young daughters slept in banana boxes while she sold herbs and daffodils. "I like the vitality of the Market, the fact that all kinds, races, and classes of people shop there — also the feeling of community," Mary says. "Dreams, gardens, business, children, friendships, changes, and the heady blessing of herbs are so richly intertwined — my farm, my life."

## Spanakopita with Lovage

#### — SILVER BAY HERB FARM —

Lovage is a flavorful, easy-to-grow perennial that adds beauty to the garden and interest to the table. Its flavor is similar to celery, with hints of allspice or cardamom. If you've never tried it before, you'll be inspired to experiment with it in other recipes, once you taste the special twist it gives to this Greek-inspired dish.

*2 pounds spinach, cleaned and chopped*

*5 tablespoons olive oil (divided use)*

*1 to 3 large cloves garlic, minced*

*1 cup chopped onion*

*1 cup chopped leeks*

*3 eggs, beaten*

*8 ounces feta cheese, crumbled*

*¾ cup grated Parmesan cheese*

*3 tablespoons chopped fresh lovage*

*Freshly ground black pepper to taste*

*2 tablespoons butter, melted*

*1 package (1 lb) filo dough, thawed*

*Pine nuts (optional)*

Preheat oven to 350°F. Take out an 11½- by 14-inch baking pan and brush lightly with olive oil. Set aside for later use.

Steam spinach in a minimum of water until just wilted. Heat 3 tablespoons of the olive oil in a skillet over medium heat and sauté garlic, onion, and leeks until tender.

In a mixing bowl combine eggs, cheeses, lovage, and pepper, then stir in spinach and sautéed onion mixture.

Mix remaining 2 tablespoons olive oil with the melted butter. One by one, brush 10 sheets of filo dough lightly with the oil mixture and lay them in baking pan. Spread the filo layers with half the filling, then layer with 10 more sheets of oiled filo.

Cover second layer of dough with remaining filling, and finish with 10 more sheets of filo, brushing the top piece well with oil. Be sure to fold and tuck filo to fit the pan. (Alternately, before you start working with the filo layers, you can cut through the whole pile so that the individual leaves fit the pan exactly. This also gives you more flexibility in the size pan you use.) With a sharp knife, score the top in diamond shapes and sprinkle with pine nuts, if desired.

Bake until spanakopita puffs and top layer of filo turns golden, 45 to 50 minutes. Cut into diamond shapes to make appetizers, cut into larger pieces and serve immediately as an entrée, or let cool and serve as a picnic lunch.

*Serves 8 as a main dish, 16 as an appetizer.*

*Note:* In Europe, lovage is added to soups, stews, roasts, and savory dishes. Try using lovage butter on grilled salmon or adding lovage leaves to a fresh green or tuna salad. Stalks of lovage simmered in tomato juice add a delicious flavor. Or use the hollow stems to make "lovage straws" for sipping Bloody Marys.

## *Chipotle Chèvre Garlic Pizza*

### QUILLISASCUT CHEESE COMPANY

You'll appreciate this unusual pizza for its cheesy-garlicky taste. It's also an easy-to-make vegetarian entrée.

Crust to fit 12-inch pizza pan

4 ounces Quillisascut chèvre aged in chipotle chili oil

1 bulb garlic, cloves separated, peeled, and cut in half

Dried or fresh oregano, to taste

1 tablespoon chipotle chili oil (drained from cheese)

2 ounces manchego viejo cheese, grated

Preheat oven to 425°F. Take out a 12-inch pizza pan.

Fit dough for pizza crust into pan. Don't worry about smoothing dough — leave the dimples formed by pressing fingertips into dough to trap oil. Crumble chèvre over crust and sprinkle with garlic cloves. Season with oregano, drizzle chipotle oil over the pizza, and sprinkle with manchego cheese.

Bake until crust is browned, about 10 to 15 minutes, slice, and serve warm with a seasonal green salad with vinaigrette dressing.

*Makes 12 slices.*

# *Microwave Mozzarella Vegetable Pie*

SOSIO'S PRODUCE

You can serve this as a hearty side dish or as a vegetarian meal in itself if served with crusty bread and a substantial salad. If you have any left over, put it on a prebaked pizza crust with some tomato sauce and extra mozzarella cheese, and broil or bake until the cheese melts for a great vegetarian pizza!

*2 tablespoons water*

*2 Japanese eggplants, sliced ¼ inch thick*

*1 green, yellow, red, or purple pepper or a mixture of all four, sliced ⅛ inch thick*

*1 yellow onion, sliced ⅛ inch thick and separated into rings*

*1 tablespoon Johnny's Salad Elegance, Mrs. Dash, or similar herb/spice blend of your choice*

*1 cup grated mozzarella cheese*

Sprinkle the water in the bottom of a 6- by 8-inch microwave-safe baking dish, or similar size dish that is at least 3 inches deep. Layer one-third of eggplant, pepper, and onion slices in bottom of baking dish, sprinkle with 1 teaspoon of herb/spice blend, then sprinkle with ⅓ cup of the cheese. Follow the same order with remaining vegetables, herb/spice blend, and mozzarella, ending with mozzarella on the top.

Cover dish with vented plastic wrap, then microwave on HIGH until vegetables are tender/crisp and cheese is melted, about 5 to 7 minutes. Rotate dish two or three times during cooking time. Cover entire dish with plastic wrap, let stand 2 or 3 minutes more to finish cooking, then serve immediately.

*Serves 4 to 6.*

THE PINK DOOR   Walk down Post Alley past the Glass Eye Gallery, past the courtyard with the haunted plum tree, past Kells. Look for the pink door on your left, the one between the faux Greek columns. If you get to Virginia Street you've gone too far. Open the pink door to find . . . the Pink Door, where fun, funk, and Italian food reign supreme. At lunch here on a summer day you can sit on one of Seattle's most beautiful rooftop terraces while you watch the ferryboats make their runs.

Darkness brings out a completely different ambience: Candles glimmer on the oilcloth-covered tables, and the fountain in the center of the room rumbles good-naturedly along with the animated crowd. A four-course, prix-fixe dinner begins with an appetizer, moves to a plate of pasta, your choice of four entrées (cioppino is always one of the choices), and rounds out with salad. Desserts cost extra and you might want to take them in the bar, where a variety of musical acts come by in the evening, including cabaret singer Julie Cascioppo.

# *Panini Brutti*

## THE PINK DOOR

**P**anini brutti means "ugly sandwiches" in Italian, but how could such a delicious summertime sandwich be so unjustly named? Be creative with the marinade and spices you add to marinate the vegetables. You will need a gas stove and stovetop grill, or an outdoor barbecue, to make this dish properly.

8 slices good-quality, crusty, country-style bread

2 cloves garlic, peeled and halved

3 zucchini, cut into 24 slices, ¼ to ½ inch thick

2 eggplants, cut into 12 slices, ¼ to ½ inch thick

Extra-virgin, first-cold-press olive oil

Red wine vinegar

Fresh mint or fresh or dried thyme

Fresh or dried oregano or minced garlic

24 slices fresh mozzarella cheese

2 or 3 red bell peppers, roasted and cut into 16 strips, ¼ to ½ inch thick (see Techniques section)

Salt

Freshly ground black pepper

Grill bread (preferably over charcoal) on both sides. Rub a garlic half on one side of each slice and set aside.

Grill zucchini and eggplant until tender yet firm. Create a marinade to your taste by mixing the olive oil and the red wine vinegar, and place the eggplant and zucchini in it. Sprinkle the zucchini with mint or thyme. Sprinkle the eggplant with oregano or garlic. Cover and set aside.

Preheat oven to 350°F. Take out a cookie sheet. To assemble panini, place bread on cookie sheet and layer each slice with the following: 1½ slices eggplant, 3 slices zucchini, 3 slices mozzarella cheese, and 2 strips roasted bell pepper placed at a diagonal. Drizzle with additional olive oil. Sprinkle with a generous amount of salt and pepper, and bake until cheese is melted, about 4 to 5 minutes. Serve immediately with a green salad with vinaigrette, if desired.

Serves 8.

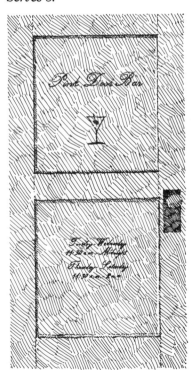

# EL MERCADO LATINO

El Mercado Latino adds lots of spice, both literally and figuratively, to the Market. In the summertime, you'll find boxes brimming with jewel-colored goat's horn, New Mexico Floral Gem, Bulgarian carrot, and Scotch Bonnet peppers, just a few of the more than 25 different varieties stocked by owner Lulu Babas, a warm, friendly woman who seems to call everyone "honey."

At the store's location in the Sanitary Market Building, you'll also encounter *nopales*, the fleshy oval leaves of the prickly pear cactus that have a delicate, slightly tart green-bean flavor, and plantains, a variety of large, firm banana with a mild, almost squashlike flavor. *Cassava* root, whose crisp, white flesh yields a nutritious starch that has become a staple in Africa; *tomatillos*, small, green tomatoes with a parchmentlike covering and unique flavor; and *chayotes*, a gourdlike fruit with white, bland-tasting flesh that can be cooked like summer or acorn squash or used raw in salads, are other interesting possibilities. This is also a reliable place to find a year-round supply of fresh lemon grass.

Inside the store lots of fresh and packaged Caribbean, South and Central American, Spanish, and Creole foods crowd the shelves. Packets of spices from fajita seasoning to menudo mix dangle from revolving racks. Medicinal herbs intended to be brewed into healing teas range from *anis* (anise seed), recommended for upset stomachs, to *zarzaparrilla* (sarsaparilla), a blood purifier and body refresher. Although she stocks quite a wide selection, Lulu will be glad to special-order the more obscure herbs direct from Mexico.

# *Pozole*

EL MERCADO LATINO

Pozole is a mainstay of Mexican cuisine, a pork and hominy soup served with garnishes of lime wedges, crisp pork rinds, avocado pieces, onions, radishes, and whatever else strikes your fancy. And although there are almost as many versions of pozole as there are stewpots in Mexico, most start with *cacahuazincle* corn, and many include beans, ham, and pig's feet. Your kitchen will fill with the wonderful fragrance of corn as the pozole simmers and puffs into tender, flavorful buds. You can adjust the amount of heat and saltiness by the amounts of chile peppers and salt you add.

*½ pound pozole (hominy)*

*3½ quarts water*

*½ to 1 teaspoon salt*

*2 to 4 fresh New Mexico chile peppers or 2 to 4 dried mild red chile pods, chopped*

*1 pound pork or beef steak, cubed*

*⅛ teaspoon dried oregano*

*1 clove garlic, minced*

GARNISHES:
*Chopped onion*

*Shredded cabbage*

*Chopped radishes*

*Salsa*

*Sliced jalapeño peppers*

*Diced avocado*

*Crisp pork rinds*

*Lime wedges*

*Crumbled dried oregano*

*Tortilla chips*

In a Dutch oven, soak pozole in fresh water overnight, then rinse well. Bring the 3½ quarts water to a boil, and add salt and pozole. Cook over medium heat for 2 hours, stirring occasionally.

Add chiles, meat, oregano, and garlic. Cover and simmer for another hour, or until pozole is tender.

To serve, ladle the pozole into soup bowls, place the onion, cabbage, radishes, salsa, jalapeño peppers, avocado, pork rinds, lime wedges, oregano, and tortilla chips in small bowls, and allow your family or guests to serve themselves the garnishes they desire.

*Makes 8 cups, 8 to 10 servings.*

# *Pike Place Market Stir-Fry*

CANTER-BERRY FARMS

Blueberry vinegar is the secret ingredient in this unusual stir-fry side dish. The vinegar leaves an appealing tang that contrasts nicely with the richness of the butter and the crunchiness of the peanuts and vegetables. It would be good served with Chicken Teriyaki, page 98.

½ cup butter

1 bunch green onions, chopped

1 green pepper, chopped

½ pound sugar snap or snow peas, ends with strings removed

1 head bok choy, chopped

½ pound mushrooms, chopped

½ cup unsalted, dry-roasted peanuts

⅓ cup Canter-Berry Farms blueberry vinegar

Heat butter over medium-high heat in a large skillet with a cover, then add green onions and stir-fry 30 seconds. Add green pepper and stir-fry another 30 seconds. Add peas and bok choy and stir-fry 1 minute. Add mushrooms and cook another 30 seconds. Add peanuts and blueberry vinegar, stir well, cover, and cook over medium heat until vegetables are tender, about 3 minutes. Serve immediately.

*Serves 4.*

*Note:* If you're at a loss for other ways to use your blueberry vinegar, try it on fruits, salad greens, green beans or peas, or onions. It also makes a great marinade for mushrooms, pork chops, and chicken. Splash it on fish, or try sautéing scallops, shrimp, Walla Walla onions, or mushrooms in it.

# PIKE PLACE CHEESE

Owner Sean Kavanagh offers cheeses from around the world, along with Washington's own cheeses in his store next to Woodring Orchards in the Main Arcade. Sean has a particularly wide variety of English cheeses, such as Stilton, Double Gloucester, and Cheshire, as well as Scandinavian cheeses, such as Finnish Lappi and Norwegian Nøkkelost.

## *Cheese-Macaroni Asparagus Bake*

— PIKE PLACE CHEESE —

You'll enjoy this hearty macaroni as a side dish, or even as a vegetarian supper if served with crusty whole-grain bread, a green salad, and fresh fruit. It's especially delicious when made with whole wheat macaroni.

*1 tablespoon salt*

*2 cups elbow macaroni, durum or whole wheat*

*3 tablespoons butter or margarine*

*¼ cup chopped onion*

*3 tablespoons flour*

*1¼ teaspoons salt*

*¼ teaspoon pepper*

*½ teaspoon dry mustard*

*1 teaspoon Worcestershire sauce*

*3 cups milk*

*2½ cups grated Swedish fontina or Red Leicester cheese (divided use)*

*1 pound fresh asparagus, cut into ½-inch pieces and cooked or steamed until tender/crisp*

Preheat oven to 400°F. Get out a 1½-quart casserole dish and grease well or spray with nonstick corn-oil or olive-oil spray.

Add salt to a stockpot or Dutch oven filled with 3 quarts of rapidly boiling water, and gradually add macaroni so that water continues to boil. Cook, stirring occasionally, until macaroni is tender. Drain in colander, then return macaroni to pan to keep warm.

Melt butter or margarine in a medium skillet or saucepan over medium heat. Add onion and cook until tender/crisp. Quickly stir in flour, salt, pepper, mustard, and Worcestershire sauce. Gradually add milk, stirring constantly, until mixture begins to boil. Allow to boil until sauce thickens, about 1 to 2 minutes.

Stir in 2 cups of the cheese and continue stirring until cheese melts. Remove from heat and combine with the macaroni and asparagus. Turn into casserole. Sprinkle with remaining ½ cup cheese. Bake until lightly browned and bubbling, about 15 to 20 minutes.

*Serves 6 to 8.*

# PIKE PLACE BAR & GRILL "Market Foods/Market Views"

is the motto of the Pike Place Bar & Grill, where the chef shops the Market daily for fresh seafood, meats, and vegetables. Specialties include "all-you-can-eat" Belgian waffles, daily seafood specials, Cajun selections, and couscous. You can choose from vegetarian, chicken, homemade beef meatball, homemade lamb sausage, lamb marinara, and royale (a little bit of each) couscous each evening. From its location on the second floor of the Corner Market building, this comfortable restaurant has a stellar view of the famous Market clock (reputedly the oldest piece of neon in Seattle, dating from the late twenties or early thirties), and the people and cars bustling about Pike Place.

## Vegetarian Couscous with Dates and Almonds

———————— PIKE PLACE BAR & GRILL ————————

Couscous is a healthy dish, low in fat and quite high in complex carbohydrates. You could easily turn this vegetarian version into a meat-eater's dish — just marinate some lamb or chicken chunks, thread on skewers, roast or broil until done, and serve atop the couscous.

BROTH

*1 tablespoon vegetable oil*

*Half an onion, diced*

*2 cloves garlic, chopped*

*2 ribs celery, diced*

*1 carrot, diced*

*Half a white potato, peeled and diced*

*Half a can (14½ oz) whole tomatoes, plus half the juice (save remaining half can for use in couscous)*

*3 cups water*

*Half a 3-inch cinnamon stick*

*¼-inch piece fresh ginger, peeled and thinly sliced*

*⅛ teaspoon ground cumin*

*¼ teaspoon salt*

COUSCOUS

*½ pound (about 1⅓ cups) couscous*

*½ teaspoon salt (divided use)*

*1 clove garlic, minced*

*¼ teaspoon plus ⅛ teaspoon ground cinnamon*

*¼ teaspoon plus ⅛ teaspoon ground cumin*

*¼ teaspoon ground ginger*

*¼ teaspoon ground cayenne pepper*

*¼ teaspoon paprika*

*1 onion, halved lengthwise and cut into ½-inch chunks*

*1 carrot, halved lengthwise and cut into ½-inch chunks*

*Half a sweet potato, halved lengthwise and cut into ½-inch chunks*

*¼ cup water*

*Half a can (14½ oz) whole tomatoes, chopped (reserve juice in case you need additional liquid for the sauce)*

*Half a zucchini, halved lengthwise and cut into ½-inch chunks*

1 can (8½ oz) garbanzo beans, rinsed and drained

¼ cup golden raisins

½ cup pitted dates, cut into quarters

2 tablespoons slivered, blanched almonds, toasted (see Techniques section)

**To make the broth:** Heat oil in a large Dutch oven over medium heat. Add the onion, garlic, celery, and carrot, and sauté for 5 minutes. Add white potato, tomatoes with their juice, the 3 cups water, cinnamon stick, ginger, cumin, and salt and bring to a boil. Reduce heat and simmer over low heat for 45 minutes, covered. Strain the broth and reserve.

**To make the couscous and vegetables:** Cover the couscous with cold water, swirl, and drain through a fine sieve. Spread out in a large baking pan and let sit for 10 minutes. Rake with your fingers to break up lumps.

Pour the reserved broth into a large Dutch oven, add ¼ teaspoon of the salt, garlic, cinnamon, cumin, ginger, cayenne, and paprika, and bring to a boil. Place the couscous in a large colander that will fit over the liquid. Place a long strip of wet cheesecloth around the rims between the colander and the pan to form a seal and steam, uncovered, over medium heat for 5 minutes.

Remove the colander and place the onion, carrot, and sweet potato into the broth. Replace the cheesecloth and colander and continue steaming, uncovered, for 15 minutes, stirring occasionally with a fork. Remove the pan from the heat. Transfer the couscous to a large baking pan, sprinkle with the ¼ cup water and the remaining ¼ teaspoon of salt, and rake with your fingers to break up any lumps. Let sit for 10 minutes.

Place the pan back on the heat. Add tomatoes, zucchini, garbanzo beans, raisins, and dates, and bring to a boil. Return the couscous to the colander and place the cheesecloth and colander over the liquid and vegetables. Steam, uncovered, over low to medium heat for 20 minutes, stirring occasionally with a fork. If the broth begins to run dry, add the juice left over from the tomatoes mixed with enough water to make ½ to 1 cup of liquid, stir well to mix with vegetables and sauce, and continue to simmer.

To serve, pile couscous into the center of a large serving platter. Make a well in the center. With a slotted spoon, place the vegetables in the well and pour the sauce over all. Garnish with toasted almonds.

*Serves 4 to 6.*

SABRA   Sabra, tucked back in the Soames-Dunn Building, looks out on the courtyard that contains the Market's famous haunted plum tree. Here the ghost of Chief Sealth's daughter, the blue-eyed Angeline of the Orcas Island tribe, supposedly plucks the ripe fruits at night.

Sabra, which means cactus, offers a limited menu of Middle Eastern specialities, including *falafel*, *hummus* (mashed chickpea sauce), *baba ghanoush* (purée of eggplant), and *tabbouleh*, and the courtyard is a great escape from the hubbub of the Market.

## Garbanzo Bean and Potato Patties with Apricot Sweet-and-Sour Sauce

— SABRA —

This makes a delicious side dish or vegetarian entrée when served with a tossed green salad and whole wheat pitas. My husband, an avowed meat eater, said he wouldn't mind eating this once a week instead of meat, it's so tasty and substantial. For better taste and texture, it's worth going to the extra trouble of making your own cooked chickpeas instead of using the canned. Also, you can control the amount of heat and salt you want by the amounts of black pepper and salt you add.

*2 cups cooked chickpeas (about ⅔ cup dried), or 1 can (16 oz) low-sodium garbanzo beans, drained*

*3 medium white potatoes, peeled, boiled, and cubed*

*2 teaspoons flour*

*1 to 1½ teaspoons ground black pepper*

*½ to 1 teaspoon salt*

*1 teaspoon ground cumin*

*½ teaspoon granulated garlic or 1 teaspoon minced garlic*

*½ cup minced parsley*

*1 tablespoon olive oil*

APRICOT SWEET-AND-SOUR SAUCE

*¼ cup low-sugar or regular apricot jam*

*1 tablespoon Dijon mustard*

*4 to 6 drops hot-pepper sauce*

*4 drops Oriental toasted sesame oil*

*¼ teaspoon shoyu (Japanese soy sauce)*

Make Apricot Sweet-and-Sour Sauce and refrigerate overnight.

Mix together beans and potatoes, and mash well with a fork. (If you prefer a less smooth texture, allow some of the garbanzo beans to remain whole.) Add flour, pepper, salt, cumin, garlic, and parsley, and mix well.

Heat olive oil in a large skillet over medium-high heat. Form garbanzo mixture into 2-inch patties, about ½ inch thick, and place in pan. Fry until light brown, about 3 minutes per side. Cook in two batches, adding more olive oil if necessary. Serve with Apricot Sweet-and-Sour Sauce or condiment or sauce of your choice, such as chutney (see recipe for Red Raspberry Chutney, page 191), hot mustard, or cocktail sauce.

**Apricot Sweet-and-Sour Sauce:** Place all ingredients in a small glass mixing bowl or jar with cover and whisk until smooth. Cover and refrigerate overnight to let flavors blend, then serve with Garbanzo Bean and Potato Patties.

*Makes 8 or 9 patties, 2 or 3 servings as an entrée, 4 as a side dish.*

# Apple-Yam Holiday Casserole

— THE JARMINS' 5-M ORCHARD —

This is a simple-to-make addition to the holiday table. If you don't plan to cook it immediately after you make it, mix 1 teaspoon of lemon juice with 1 cup of water, dunk the apple slices in the liquid, and then pat dry with paper towels before adding the apples to the casserole, so that they don't discolor.

*6 yams*

*4 large cooking apples, such as Jonagold, Hawaii, or Melrose, sliced ¼ inch thick*

*¾ cup brown sugar, firmly packed (divided use)*

*¾ cup raisins (divided use)*

*½ cup orange juice*

*1 cup miniature marshmallows*

Preheat oven to 325°F. Take out a 2½-quart casserole dish and grease lightly or spray with nonstick corn-oil spray.

In a large Dutch oven or saucepan, bring to a boil enough water to cover the yams. Add yams and cook until partially tender, about 20 minutes. Drain boiling water from yams and cover with cold water. The skins should peel away easily. Pat yams dry with paper towels, then slice ¼ inch thick.

Layer a third of the yams in the casserole dish, then layer a third of the apples over yams. Sprinkle ¼ cup of the brown sugar and ¼ cup of the raisins over apples. Repeat layers twice more.

Pour orange juice evenly over top of casserole, then bake until sweet potatoes and apples are tender, about 30 to 35 minutes. Heat broiler, sprinkle marshmallows over apples, and broil casserole until marshmallows are lightly browned.

*Serves 12.*

# DUFFIELD ORGANIC FARM

Both Judy and David Duff's families have deep ties to the land. Indeed, on any given Friday or Saturday, you'll find three generations of Judy's family selling in the Main Arcade — Judy Duff, mother Norma Smith, and young daughter Deanna Duff, who, along with her father, decorates Duffield Farm's bags with colorful crayon drawings of ladybugs and flowers and the heartfelt words, "Where Food Comes to Life."

When the Duffs bought their land in Burien they did not buy a farm. Instead, they pieced together acreage in a strictly residential area heavily rooted with cottonwood and pussy willow trees, Scotch broom, and purple clover. Fueled by their vision of working with nature to develop a farm, with loppers and chicken fertilizer in hand, they cleared and primed the unfriendly land.

Judy and David have been selling at the Market since 1986. Specializing in fresh, organic produce, their farm table is always a delight to the eye as well as to the palate, with lacy edible flowers in pastel hues, hand-lettered signs describing the taste and origin of each vegetable, and even stuffed animals and dolls. During the "84th Anniversary of the Market" celebration in 1991, Duffield Farm won first place in the farm table display contest.

The Duffs sell different varieties of *haricots verts*; baby romaine, Oak Leaf, and French Brunia lettuces; fresh herbs; Japanese and Chinese greens; a wide variety of squashes; edible flowers; different varieties of vine-ripened tomatoes; and Middle Eastern cucumbers and cornichons from June through October. Their Edible Secret Baskets are filled with the world's smallest variety of tomato, baby lettuces, purple basil, and edible flowers. The Duffs return to the Market at the end of November through December with fresh herbs and everlasting Christmas wreaths made of dried fruits and vegetables.

Judy, an English major in college, says that reading the works of Emerson, Thoreau, and Frost caused her to want to farm the land herself. The purpose of their endeavor is found in the words of Walt Whitman, who wrote, "In this broad earth of ours,/Amid the measureless grossness and slag,/Enclosed and safe within its central heart,/Nestles the seed perfection." Judy says, "Whitman was right. The seed and all its perfection is, indeed, our hope for tomorrow, but it is rapidly running out of safe places to nestle. It is everyone's responsibility to keep today's seed safe for tomorrow. Duffield Organic Farm is trying its best to do just that."

# *Stir-Fried Harvest Medley*

## DUFFIELD ORGANIC FARM

Foods from different nations, such as France, Italy, Japan, and China, meld to create this eclectic and delicious entrée created by Judy Duff. Vegetables of your choice can be added or substituted in this recipe, for, according to Judy, "the key to farm cooking is creativity, *not* rigidity. Enjoy the harvest!"

*1 tablespoon light vegetable oil, such as safflower, soy, or canola*

*½ cup chopped onion*

*¾ cup broccoli florets*

*1 Sun Drops summer squash, chopped into ½-inch-wide by 1-inch sections*

*1 Sunburst summer squash, chopped into ½-inch-wide by 1-inch sections*

*2 small zucchini, chopped*

*1 cup haricots verts (French-style green beans), cut into 1-inch pieces*

*1 cup chopped mizuna (stems and leaves)*

*½ cup chopped shungiku (stems and leaves)*

*1 cup tah tsai or baby pak choi with whole leaves*

*¼ cup sesame seed, toasted (see Techniques section)*

*8 fresh edible nasturtiums*

In a large skillet or wok, heat oil over medium-high heat until very hot. Add onion and stir-fry 2 minutes. Add broccoli, summer squashes, zucchini, *haricots verts*, mizuna, shungiku, and tah tsai or baby pak choi, and stir-fry to desired doneness, about 3 to 5 minutes. You can add 1 or 2 tablespoons of water while stir-frying if you like your vegetables cooked to a more tender stage.

Place on dinner plates, then sprinkle with sesame seed and artistically arrange nasturtiums on top immediately before serving.

*Serves 4.*

# *Ranch Stuffing*

## — Ranch at the End of the Road —

This is a hearty, sweet stuffing full of fruits, vegetables, whole wheat bread, and that secret ingredient — orange or cherry liqueur. Studded with dried cherries, green peppers, and dark raisins, it would be an appealing addition to any holiday table. If you cannot purchase Black Monukka raisins from Vicky and Scott, they are available in the Pike Place Market at Magnano Foods.

*1 cup butter or margarine*

*1 large onion, chopped*

*1½ cups sliced mushrooms*

*1 cup chopped celery and celery leaves*

*Half a large or 1 small green pepper, chopped*

*2 cups water or chicken stock*

*1½ to 2 cups assorted dried fruits, such as Black Monukka grapes (raisins), Bing or Montmorency cherries, apricots, and apples*

*1 to 1½ loaves (about 8 to 10 cups) day-old whole wheat bread (homemade pre- ferred), cut into cubes and toasted in a 300°F oven until dry, about 10 to 15 minutes*

*½ teaspoon dried thyme*

*½ teaspoon dried sage*

*½ teaspoon salt*

*Pepper to taste*

*¾ cup orange or cherry liqueur*

*½ cup chicken stock, warmed (divided use)*

*1 tin smoked baby oysters (optional)*

Melt butter or margarine in large skillet over medium heat. Add onion, mushrooms, celery, and green pepper and sauté until vegetables are soft and translucent; do not allow to brown. Set aside and allow to cool.

Bring the 2 cups water or chicken stock to a boil in a small saucepan, and add dried fruits. Stir, then remove from heat and let stand until fruits are soft and plumped, about 15 minutes.

Put bread cubes into a large mixing bowl and add thyme, sage, salt, and pepper. Add cooled vegetables and dried fruits, in- cluding any liquid that remains.

Mix liqueur with ¼ cup of the chicken stock. Add oysters (if used), to mixing bowl with bread cubes. Add liqueur and stock mixture, and mix stuffing with hands to desired consistency, adding the remaining ¼ cup stock, if desired.

Stuff turkey and roast as usual, or bake the stuffing separately in a casserole, cov- ered, in a 325°F oven for 35 to 45 minutes or in a 375°F oven for 20 to 30 minutes. Remove from oven and serve with turkey and all the trimmings.

*Makes about 12 cups, 12 to 16 servings.*

# CANTER-BERRY FARMS

Canter-Berry Farms in Auburn was homesteaded in 1870 and bought by Edith and Fred Metzler in 1954 from the grandson of the farm's original settler. The farm was already planted in blueberries, but Edith and Fred planted more, and soon their summertime farm became their permanent residence where they raised their four daughters.

In the early days, U-pick blueberries went for 15 cents a pound, and Fred would entice new customers out to the farm by offering them a piece of Edith's blueberry pie. In 1991 U-pick blueberries were 90 cents a pound ($1.50 to $2.00 a pint in the Market), and Edith was still making her famous pie.

Since 1975 the farm has been operated by the second generation of Metzlers — daughter Clarissa Cross and her husband, Doug. In 1983 the younger generation introduced their popular blueberry products — blueberry jam, vinegar, chutney, syrup, and gift packs. They're an energetic young couple who, in addition to raising blueberries, also breed, raise, show, and sell American Saddlebred horses, hence the name of their farm.

During her childhood, Clarissa remembers her parents telling her that if she ate enough blueberries, her eyes would turn the same gorgeous blue. It must have worked, for today Clarissa's eyes are big, round, navy orbs, just the color of fresh blueberries. You'll find Clarissa of the blueberry eyes or Doug in the North Arcade Fridays and Saturdays all year round, with additional days during the summer months and holidays.

## *Chutney Hollow Squash*

### CANTER-BERRY FARMS

This easy-to-make yet elegant side dish would be a beautiful and tasty addition to any holiday table.

*2 small butternut or acorn squash, split and seeded*

*Salt to taste (optional)*

*¼ cup butter*

*6 tablespoons Canter-Berry Farms blueberry chutney or other fruit chutney*

*Blueberry leaves, for garnish*

Preheat oven to 400°F. Place squash halves in baking dish, sprinkle with salt (if used), cover with aluminum foil, and cook until tender, about 35 to 45 minutes. Alternately, you can cook the squash in a microwave-safe dish, covered with vented plastic wrap, on HIGH until done, about 10 to 12 minutes. Let rest for 2 minutes to finish cooking.

Remove cooked squash from oven and place 1 tablespoon butter in each squash center. Add 1½ tablespoons chutney to each center and return squash to oven until heated through, about 1 minute for conventional ovens and 15 seconds on HIGH for microwave ovens. Garnish each squash half with an autumn-colored blueberry leaf and serve immediately.

*Serves 4.*

# LE PANIER, VERY FRENCH BAKERY

Le Panier is a good place to watch the Market come to life in the early morning, while you munch a freshly baked croissant and sip a mocha capped with whipped cream. In addition to some of the best baguettes in the city, *oignon* (onion) and *pain noix* (walnut bread) are two specialty breads that Le Panier has brought to Seattle. *Oignon* is darkened by the sautéed Walla Walla onions baked into it. *Pain noix* is a large, round, rye-based loaf with a craggy top. Studded with fresh walnuts, it has a chewy consistency. For those with a sweet tooth, the baker's specialty is the *amandine* — fresh, homemade almond paste inside a twice-baked croissant topped with fresh almond paste and sliced almonds.

## *Thanksgiving Stuffing*

LE PANIER, VERY FRENCH BAKERY

This is a simple, fruity stuffing that isn't terribly rich or fatty. Don't wait until Thanksgiving — serve it as a side dish with chicken, ham, or a plate of steamed vegetables any time of the year. In place of classic French bread, use additional *oignon* for a stronger onion flavor, or more *campagne* for a heartier stuffing.

*3½ cups chicken broth*

*1 cup chopped dried apricots*

*¼ cup unsalted butter*

*½ cup chopped yellow onion*

*2 medium Granny Smith apples, cored and cut into ½-inch cubes*

*1 tablespoon dried thyme*

*2 teaspoons dried rubbed sage*

*1 teaspoon freshly ground black pepper*

*3 cups oignon (onion bread), cut into ½-inch cubes and dried overnight*

*3 cups campagne (light rye bread), cut into ½-inch cubes and dried overnight*

*2 cups classic French bread, cut into ½-inch cubes and dried overnight*

*2 cups chopped pecans (optional)*

*1 cup dried currants*

Preheat oven to 350°F. Take out a small casserole dish and set aside.

Bring broth to a boil in medium saucepan and add apricots; remove from heat and set aside. Heat butter in a large skillet. Add onion and sauté lightly over low heat for about 10 minutes. If a more moist stuffing is desired, sauté 1 cup of the cubed onion bread during the last 5 minutes of cooking time.

Add onion, broth and apricots, apples, thyme, sage, and pepper to a large mixing bowl. Gradually add the bread cubes until all bread is moist. Add pecans, if used, and currants. Allow stuffing to cool to room temperature.

Lightly coat interior of turkey with butter. Loosely pack stuffing into cavity and roast as usual. The remaining stuffing can be placed in a casserole dish and baked in a 350°F oven for 20 to 25 minutes.

*Makes 12 cups stuffing, enough for a 16-pound turkey.*

# ALM HILL GARDENS

As a boy, Ben Craft helped his father raise dairy cows on 64 acres of leased land that bordered the Sumas River, near the Washington-Canadian border. In 1963, as a teenager, through the sale of cows and the income from his paper route, Ben (with a little help from his dad) purchased the land in Everson he had grown to love for $12,000.

Ben married Gretchen Hoyt, a Puyallup doctor's daughter with no farming background, and together they've been farming that same piece of land in the foothills of the Cascade Mountains for 20 years. Starting out with just one acre of raspberries that produced fruit six weeks a year, Gretchen and Ben's farm business has since expanded to an almost year-round operation with the addition of new crops and farm-made products.

You'll find Ben, Gretchen, son Joshua, or a representative in the Main or North Arcades from March through December. Beginning with colorful tulips in the spring, they move through the seasons with snap and shelling peas; fresh raspberries, blueberries, and berry vinegars; green beans; tomatoes; fresh flowers; pickling cucumbers; carrots; several varieties of potatoes; chrysanthemums; forced bulbs; and evergreen Christmas wreaths. Gretchen is also perfecting several low-sugar berry jams to add to her line of specialty products, with enticing names like raspberry-currant, blueberry-citrus, and raspberry-lemon.

## *Raspberry Snap Peas*

### ALM HILL GARDENS

This is a low-calorie treat — no butter or olive oil, just the fresh taste of snap peas and raspberry-wine vinegar. Feel free to adjust the amount of raspberry-wine vinegar and sesame seed.

*½ pound snap peas, washed and ends with strings removed*

*3 to 5 tablespoons raspberry-wine vinegar*

*2 to 4 tablespoons sesame seed, toasted (see Techniques section)*

Steam snap peas until tender/crisp. Splash with raspberry-wine vinegar and toss until vinegar coats beans evenly, then sprinkle with sesame seed.

*Serves 2 to 4.*

*Note:* From mid-July through December, Gretchen and Ben sell many unusual varieties of potatoes at their stand in the Market. For a colorful addition to the dinner plate, Gretchen advises making mashed potatoes using her Purple Peruvian potatoes, which are purple throughout and are best boiled rather than baked. The Norwegian Wax potatoes (with a flavor similar to Yukon Golds) are also boiling potatoes, great in traditional hot German potato salads or American picnic potato salads. The Yukon Golds are sturdy, rich, buttery-flavored yellow potatoes with a long shelf life, similar to Finnish potatoes.

# THE SOUK

Webster's dictionary defines the word "souk" as a marketplace in North Africa or the Middle East. For the past 15 years the Soames-Dunn Building has housed its own Souk, a marketplace where silk scarves and Indian movie posters hang in the windows, and where the fragrance of exotic spices permeates the air.

Seattle's Souk is a mecca for Middle Eastern, Indian, and Pakistani delicacies. In the cooler you'll find *halal* meats that have been slaughtered and prepared according to the strict guidelines of the Islam religion. Wooden barrels hold numerous basmati rices, legumes, and lentils available in bulk. Black lemons, piled in a tall jar like shrunken heads, add a distinctive flavor to soups, lamb dishes, or rice.

Dozens of brands of chutneys and pickles; quince, date, eggplant, and fig jams; dried apricot paste from Syria; and even toiletries line the sagging shelves. A final reminder of home for Seattle's Indian and Arabic émigrés are the newspapers and magazines, audio and video tapes with exotic foreign actresses, and calendars written in Arabic as well as in several Indian tongues.

## *Pea Pullao*

THE SOUK

This is a colorful rice casserole made extra-special by the addition of traditional Indian spices.

*2 tablespoons butter or vegetable oil*

*1 small onion, sliced*

*4 black peppercorns*

*4 whole cardamom pods*

*¼ teaspoon ground cumin*

*2 bay leaves*

*1 cinnamon stick (3 inches long)*

*Salt to taste*

*1 cup white rice*

*1½ cups water*

*1 package (9 oz) frozen peas*

Preheat oven to 300°F. Heat butter or oil in a large saucepan over medium-low heat and add onion, peppercorns, cardamom pods, cumin, bay leaves, and cinnamon stick. Cook for 5 minutes, stirring occasionally, then add salt to taste.

Stir in rice and coat rice kernels well with oil, then add the water. Bring to a boil, cover, then reduce heat to low to simmer rice mixture. When about half the water has been absorbed by the rice (about 5 to 7 minutes), add peas and stir to mix thoroughly. Turn heat up to bring mixture to a boil, then cover and reduce heat and simmer.

When most of the water has been absorbed (about 5 minutes longer), cover saucepan and put in oven for 15 minutes, being sure to cover saucepan handle with foil if it is not oven-safe. Remove cardamom pods, bay leaves, and cinnamon stick, fluff, and serve.

*Serves 6.*

# Chinese Asparagus

DANNY'S PRODUCE

This is a simple-to-prepare yet tasty dish that makes good use of the Northwest's wonderful asparagus crop, at its best in April and May.

*2 cups water*

*1 pound baby asparagus, rinsed, trimmed, and cut into 1-inch diagonal pieces*

*¼ cup sesame oil*

*2 to 4 tablespoons sesame seed, toasted (see Techniques section)*

*Sugar to taste*

Boil the water in a medium saucepan, add asparagus, and blanch for 1 to 1½ minutes, until tender/crisp. Drain hot water and rinse asparagus pieces immediately in cold water to stop cooking process.

Remove asparagus from cold water, drain as completely as possible, and place in a medium mixing bowl. Add sesame oil, sesame seed, and sugar to taste. Mix well and serve as a side dish with cold meat or a main-dish salad.

*Serves 4.*

# Pak Choi Surprises

DUFFIELD ORGANIC FARM

Pak Choi Surprises were created by Grandma Smith, Judy Duff's mother, to reward her loved ones after long hours of planting, weeding, and harvesting. They are nutritious, fun, and have become a Duff family tradition over the years, sort of like portable carrot-and-raisin salads. The filling is easy to make, and Pak Choi Surprises are fun to assemble — get the kids to help you — the more the merrier.

*Peanut butter*

*12 baby pak choi leaves, rinsed, separated, and patted dry*

*2 cups shredded carrots*

*½ cup seedless raisins*

*¼ cup miniature marshmallows*

*¼ cup crushed pineapple, well drained*

*Mayonnaise to moisten*

Spread peanut butter on baby pak choi leaves. Combine carrots, raisins, marshmallows, pineapple, and mayonnaise, and spread 1 to 2 tablespoons of mixture on top of peanut butter–covered leaves. Roll leaves jelly-roll fashion and secure with toothpicks. Serve as a snack or entrée accompaniment.

*Serves 6 to 12.*

# SOSIO'S PRODUCE

Sosio's is a friendly highstall where you can pick out your own fruits and vegetables without getting your hands slapped. It specializes in some of the more exotic produce, such as a wide variety of mushrooms (chanterelles, morels, shiitakes, Chicken of the Woods), star fruit, cactus pears, guavas, and French morning melons.

On the south wall of the stall, you'll notice a mural of an elderly man surrounded by boxes of fruits and vegetables. The man is Sosio Manzo, patriarch of the Manzo clan, who was born in Italy in 1889 and came to Seattle at the age of 20. He bought a farm in South Park and began selling at the Market in 1909.

Sosio and his wife had five children. Their two sons, Dan and Fred Manzo, grew up in the Market and, in 1948, Dan gave up farming to set up a highstall, which is still in operation today as Manzo Brothers Produce. One of Dan's sons, Tim, runs Danny's Produce, and another son, Dan, Jr., and wife Susie run Sosio's, so when you're shopping the highstalls in the Main Arcade, you have a better-than-average chance of buying produce from the Manzo family somewhere along the line, continuing a long Market tradition.

## *Cheesy Tomatoes*

— SOSIO'S PRODUCE —

Cheesy Tomatoes is an easy yet elegant side dish that goes well with any sort of simply prepared fish, chicken, or meat.

*6 Roma tomatoes, cored and sliced in half lengthwise*

*Johnny's Salad Elegance, Mrs. Dash, or similar herb/spice blend of your choice*

*1 cup grated mozzarella cheese*

Preheat broiler, place oven rack on second level from top (about 8 inches from heat source), and get out a cookie sheet. Place tomato halves on cookie sheet so that they don't touch or overlap. Sprinkle on herb/spice blend to taste, then sprinkle mozzarella cheese on each tomato half.

Cook under broiler until cheese is bubbly and golden brown, about 5 minutes.

*Serves 4 to 6.*

SANDY'S ACRES   Since 1987, when Sandy Erken bought her farm in Arlington, farming has been her dream. Yet, as a single mother of two teenage boys, Sandy faces a tougher challenge than many of the other farmers at the Market, for she must also work as a legal secretary to support her family.

"My real creative call is to the land," Sandy explains. She completed a 2,200-square-foot solar greenhouse in February 1991 and is now making the transition from office work to full-time farming. Her specialty is everything for the gourmet salad.

Sandy sells "gourmet salad makings," a mix of 40 different kinds of international lettuces, depending on what is in season. Based on *mesclun*, a traditional salad mix prepared in Europe for many years, Sandy's gourmet salad makings contain about 50 percent baby lettuces, 15 percent arugula, 20 percent mustard greens, and 15 percent chicory or endive.

You'll also find edible flowers, fresh herbs (including three types of basil), and herb vinegars (basil and a bright orange-red nasturtium vinegar, with a peppery taste) at Sandy's table in the North Arcade.

Two sizes of decorative edible pots (lightweight pulp pots in which all the plants growing inside can be eaten), make beautiful and useful gifts. Sandy describes them as "cut and come again," because once you cut the lettuces, edible flowers, or herbs, they'll spring up again. The salad bowl garden pot contains several baby lettuces, onions, garlic, spinach, tomatoes, and edible flowers; the fresh tea garden pot holds different kinds of mints, chamomile, and anise hyssop for brewing tea; the herb pot with edible flowers contains fennel, oregano, thyme, parsley, and pansies; and a fall pot features colorful kales for salads and vegetable dishes.

## *Fun with Fresh Fennel*

### SANDY'S ACRES

Fennel is a pale green, celerylike vegetable with bright green, feathery foliage and a mild, sweet anise taste. It's rich in vitamin A and also contains good amounts of calcium, phosphorus, and potassium. Available from fall through spring, it can be served in many different ways, including braised, sautéed, in soups, and as shown below.

Slice, dice, or chop a fresh fennel bulb. Mix well with your favorite salad dressing. Just before serving, sprinkle with your favorite edible flower(s), such as nasturtiums,

pansies, or Johnny-jump-ups, and toss gently. This is a wonderful side dish and great conversation piece at the table.

Add chopped feathery fennel leaves to salads.

Add chopped fennel stalks to Italian dishes.

Wrap fresh fennel leaves around your favorite fish fillets before baking or broiling. You can also stuff the cavities of whole fish with fennel leaves before cooking for added flavor.

# *Greek Rice*

———————— Northwest Chestnuts ————————

Greek Rice is an easy-to-make side dish for chestnut lovers, or it could form the focus of a vegetarian dinner with many contrasting tastes and textures when served with steamed fava beans, turnips, and cabbage.

½ *pound fresh chestnuts or ¼ pound dried chestnuts, rehydrated according to package directions, or 8 ounces bottled chestnuts*

¼ *cup olive oil*

*1 cup white or brown rice, cooked according to package directions*

¼ *cup dried currants or chopped raisins*

*2 tablespoons chopped fresh fennel leaf or 2 teaspoons ground fennel or 2 teaspoons fennel seed*

*Salt and pepper to taste*

½ *cup plain yogurt*

*Fresh fennel leaves and lemon wedges, for garnish*

If using fresh chestnuts, roast, peel, and set aside. If using rehydrated or bottled chestnuts, halve and set aside.

Heat a large skillet over medium heat and add olive oil. When hot, add cooked rice, chestnuts, currants, fennel, and salt and pepper.

Stir well until heated through, about 2 or 3 minutes. Scoop into large serving dish, stir in yogurt, and garnish with fresh fennel leaves and lemon wedges.

*Serves 4 as a main dish, 8 as a side dish.*

*Note:* To roast a chestnut, you must first pierce the shell to allow hot air to escape while cooking. Use a sharp paring knife or a serrated steak knife to cut a slash or an X through the shell, but not into the meat. Once this is done to the nuts, all sides must then be heated thoroughly. When the nuts are roasted, the shell will begin to curl away from the cut. The meat will be yellow, soft, and smell sweet. In a chestnut pan or a dry skillet, roast the chestnuts by shaking in or over medium heat for about 20 minutes. In the microwave oven, place a dozen chestnuts around the outer edge of a paper plate and cook on HIGH for 2 minutes. In the oven, place the chestnuts on a cookie sheet or cake pan, sprinkle generously with water, and bake at 400°F for 15 to 20 minutes. The nuts come out firmer when baked. Peel while still hot.

# Entrées

## Entrées

Braised Eggplant with Pork Spareribs

Barbecued Short Ribs

White Country Loaf

Pork Chops with Cabbage and Potatoes

Ham Basted with Crabapple Jelly

Italian Pepper and Sausage Scramble

Pancit Bihon

Chicken Adobo

Richard's Down-Home Chicken

Chicken with Cherry-Wine Sauce

Zaire Chicken Curry

Northwest Chicken Stir-Fry

Chicken Masala

Chicken Gui with Stir-Fried Vegetables

Cornish Game Hens with Raspberry Gravy

Chicken Teriyaki

Korean Beef Barbecue (Bulgogi)

Roast Beef

Rouladen

Mechado

New Mexico Tamales

Roast Lamb

Irish Stew

# SAIGON RESTAURANT

Lucy Pham Nguyen says that working at the Market reminds her of the open markets in her native Vietnam. She oversees her family-run restaurant in the Soames-Dunn Building with a watchful eye, and reports that Saigon was the first authentic Vietnamese restaurant to open in Seattle, in about 1977.

You can rub elbows with everyone from Seattle cops to briefcase-toting businessmen at the counter here, or choose one of the small tables against the wall. Either way, Saigon's good food and cheap prices more than make up for the no-frills atmosphere.

You might opt for a Saigon salad — beef, chicken, or prawns sautéed with onions and tomatoes, served on a bed of rice noodles, shredded lettuce, bean sprouts, and cucumber with Saigon sweet-and-sour sauce, and topped with shredded carrots and roasted peanuts. They also serve a bowl of chicken soup that, when mixed with a touch of hot pepper sauce, will cure you of a stuffy head cold or at least make you feel a whole lot happier.

## *Braised Eggplant with Pork Spareribs*

— SAIGON RESTAURANT —

You'll be amazed at how the fish sauce, tomatoes, and eggplant cook down to form a deep, rich, brown sauce—a perfect counterpoint to the spareribs in this wonderful Vietnamese recipe.

*2 pounds pork spareribs, trimmed of fat and cut into bite-size pieces*

*¼ cup Vietnamese fish sauce (nuoc mam)*

*1 shallot, sliced ⅛ inch thick*

*6 cups water*

*1 pound ripe tomatoes, sliced*

*1 large eggplant or 4 Japanese eggplants*

*2 quarts water*

*2 tablespoons salt*

*1 bunch green onions, chopped*

Rinse spareribs in several changes of fresh water until water runs clear. Place spareribs in a 4-quart saucepan, pour in fish sauce and shallot, and mix well.

Cook spareribs on medium to medium-high heat for 20 minutes, covered, stirring occasionally. Remove from heat, let spareribs absorb fish sauce for a few minutes, and then add the 6 cups water. (Before adding the water, you can drain off any liquid fat that has accumulated in the bottom of the pan.) Bring mixture to a boil over high heat and skim off any foam that rises to the top. Add tomatoes, reduce heat to low, and simmer for 40 minutes, uncovered.

Meanwhile, prepare the eggplant by chopping off stem(s) and slicing into bite-size pieces. In a large mixing bowl, stir the 2 quarts water with the salt until dissolved, add the eggplant, and soak. When the spareribs are ready, drain salty water from eggplant, rinse eggplant well, and add to pan with spareribs. Simmer another 20 minutes over low to medium heat.

To serve, put spareribs and vegetables on a large platter and sprinkle with green onions.

*Serves 4.*

# DON & JOE'S MEATS

The original Don and Joe were Don Kuzaro, Sr., and his brother-in-law, Joe Darby, who worked together at Dan's Meat Market and dreamed of owning the business. When Dan's left the Market in 1969 to go wholesale, Don and Joe were given first shot at buying the retail store, and Don & Joe's Meats was born.

Today's owner, Don Kuzaro, Jr., bought the business from his father around 1985. He enjoys being in an open-air market, being able to walk out of his shop and see the bay and the ships and feel the wind in his face. "I'm also thankful I had a chance to work with my dad, a friendly, honest, hard-working man, whom I've tried to be like in running my business," Don explains. "Also, my father-in-law, Curly Hanada, was a Market farmer and I used to watch him sell and talk to his customers. They are both gone now, but not forgotten."

Don, a boyish-looking man with a crew cut, white cap, and apron, has another reminder of Curly Hanada close at hand, because he married Curly's daughter, Diana. The two met at the Market when they were both in high school. Organic farmer Curly set up his produce stand across from Don & Joe's meat market, and, while helping out their dads on Saturdays, Diana and Don met. After lots of furtive glances and shy advances, the two teenagers fell in love and later married.

The modern-day Don & Joe's, still located under the Market's famous clock, is a full-service meat market featuring a complete selection of beef, lamb, veal, pork, and poultry. Their smoked hams, fresh turkeys, and lamb chops are long-time favorites. They make their own Italian sausage, links, and bratwurst, and also sell the less traditional "cuts," such as brains, sweetbreads, and lamb tongues.

# *Barbecued Short Ribs*

## Don & Joe's Meats

Barbecued short ribs are about as all-American as the Fourth of July, yet this variation takes on Japanese overtones when served with its dark, sweet sauce over steamy white or brown rice. The recipe is a variation of a recipe found in *Roundup of Beef Cookery*, edited by Demetria Taylor and prepared in collaboration with the American National CowBelles. Don's wife, Diana, likes it because it's "easy and delicious!" It can be cooked on top of the stove or in the oven.

*2 tablespoons fat or light vegetable oil, such as corn, soy, or canola*

*3 pounds beef short ribs, cut into portion-size pieces, if necessary*

*1 onion, chopped*

*½ cup celery, sliced ¼ inch thick*

*⅓ cup distilled white vinegar*

*⅔ cup sugar*

*½ cup water*

*3 tablespoons Worcestershire sauce*

*1 teaspoon prepared mustard*

*Dash of salt*

If cooking in oven, preheat oven to 350°F and take out a large Dutch oven.

Heat fat or oil in large skillet over medium-high heat, then add short ribs and brown on all sides. Add onion and celery to skillet and cook until vegetables are tender.

Combine vinegar, sugar, water, Worcestershire sauce, mustard, and salt in small mixing bowl. Pour over ribs and vegetables. To cook on stove top, cover and simmer until tender (bones should come off easily), about 1½ to 2 hours. You can add a little water if the sauce becomes too thick during cooking. To cook in oven, transfer the ribs, vegetables, and sauce to a Dutch oven and cook until tender, about 1½ to 2 hours.

Before serving, remove bones and any excess fat that is floating on top and serve with hot rice and horseradish (fresh or prepared).

*Serves 4.*

# LOUIE'S ON THE PIKE

Right next door to the infamous Champion Party store window, which was decorated with severed monster heads, tombstones, snakes, and the Grim Reaper on a recent visit, you'll find Louie's on the Pike, your friendly neighborhood mom-and-pop grocery store and specialty gourmet shop all rolled into one. Mediterranean and Northwest food items pack the store that at various times has housed a meat market and a taxi stand.

Here you'll find one of the largest selections of Northwest microbrewery products in the city, a large number of Northwest wines and French Champagnes, a deli, products from Dean & DeLuca in New York City, Lotto tickets, and video rentals. The staff, dressed in maroon aprons, is friendly and knowledgeable, especially Chris Hem in the beer department and Jim Just in wines.

## *White Country Loaf*

— LOUIE'S ON THE PIKE —

Because of its great taste, wonderful texture, and versatility, this is one of my favorite recipes in the book. Serve it straight from the oven, like meatloaf; cold at picnics or tailgate parties, like pâté; grilled; or crumbled into spaghetti sauce. Any way you serve it, it's healthy, delicious, and appealing. The sun-dried tomatoes contrast nicely against the pale meat — this dish would look beautiful on a holiday buffet table.

*1 tablespoon olive oil*

*1 tablespoon oil drained from sun-dried tomatoes (see below)*

*1 cup minced onion*

*3 cloves garlic, minced*

*1 pound ground chicken*

*1 pound ground veal or pork*

*2 eggs*

*1 cup bread crumbs*

*1 tablespoon balsamic vinegar*

*1 teaspoon salt*

*1 teaspoon ground pepper*

*1 teaspoon ground cumin*

*1 teaspoon dried oregano*

*1 teaspoon ground fennel or fennel seed*

*2½ tablespoons diced sun-dried tomatoes, packed in oil*

Preheat oven to 350°F. Take out a 5- by 9-inch loaf pan.

Heat a medium skillet over medium heat and add oils. When hot, sauté onion and garlic until transparent. Let cool, saving cooking oil.

Mix ground chicken, ground veal or pork, eggs, bread crumbs, balsamic vinegar, salt, pepper, cumin, oregano, and fennel together in a bowl with your hands or a large spoon, then add the sun-dried tomatoes and onions and garlic and their cooking oil and mix thoroughly.

Place meat mixture in loaf pan and bake until juices run clear or the internal temperature reaches 140°F, 50 to 60 minutes.

If serving hot, let meat rest for 15 minutes before slicing. If serving cold, place in refrigerator until ready to slice and serve. This dish is great cold, accompanied by a tossed vegetable or pasta salad, fresh fruit, dessert, and wine. Slices of leftover Country Loaf can be sautéed with a little olive oil in a skillet and topped with a good-quality spaghetti sauce, or crumble a couple of slices, mix with spaghetti sauce, heat, and serve over cooked pasta or rice.

*Serves 8 to 10.*

## Pork Chops with Cabbage and Potatoes

PAUL DUNN, EXECUTIVE DIRECTOR, THE MERCHANTS ASSOCIATION

Paul Dunn is a Market resident and executive director of the Pike Place Market Merchants Association, "a nonprofit, membership organization that exists to support, assist, and promote the diverse businesses in the Market area, thereby helping to sustain the vitality and character of the Pike Market Historical District." This was a childhood recipe that Paul enjoyed when he was growing up in Detroit. The dish was popular around the Dunn home not only because of its taste, but because of its expandability when hungry friends came in tow. Now he finds it a great dish on those damp Seattle winter nights, with ingredients picked up on his way home through the Market.

*1 tablespoon light vegetable oil, such as corn or soy oil*

*½ cup chopped onion*

*½ cup chopped green pepper*

*6 pork chops*

*1 head of cabbage, blanched in boiling water about 2 minutes, and with leaves separated*

*2 baking potatoes, sliced ¼ inch thick*

*½ cup milk*

*1 teaspoon caraway seed or other favorite seasoning, such as fennel seed*

*1 tablespoon butter*

Preheat oven to 350°F. Take out a 9- by 13-inch baking pan and grease lightly or spray with nonstick corn-oil or olive-oil spray.

In a large skillet, heat oil over medium heat, add onion and green pepper, and stir for 30 seconds. Push vegetables to the side, add pork chops, and cook on each side until browned, 1 to 2 minutes.

Layer one-half of the cabbage leaves and potato slices in bottom of baking pan, spoon half of the sautéed vegetables over cabbage and potatoes, then place pork chops over vegetables so that they don't overlap. Pour half the milk over pork chops, and sprinkle with half the caraway seed.

For second layer, place remaining half of the cabbage leaves and potato slices over the pork chops, then add the remaining sautéed vegetables. Dot with butter and sprinkle with remaining caraway seed.

Carefully pour remaining milk over top of casserole, cover with foil, and bake until pork chops are tender and done, 1 to 1½ hours.

*Serves 6.*

# RACHEL-DEE HERB FARM

Rachel-Dee Herb Farm, located in the foothills of Mount Rainier, is owned by Ivonne and Eugene Brown, who grow more than 125 different herbs on their five acres, without the use of pesticides or chemicals. When the herbs are at the peak of freshness, Ivonne cuts them and makes small batches of jellies and vinegars, which Eugene brings to the North Arcade several days a week at various times throughout the year.

With his full beard, beret, and half-glasses, Eugene cuts a professorial figure among the live herb plants, jars of dried rosemint tea, and herbal wreaths and swags. He'll be delighted to let you sample all of his and Ivonne's homemade products, from crabapple-spearmint jelly to basil-garlic wine vinegar.

## Ham Basted with Crabapple Jelly

— RACHEL-DEE HERB FARM —

Make your springtime special by serving this tasty glazed ham dusted with hazelnuts.

*1 ham*

*1 jar Rachel-Dee crabapple jelly*

*1 tablespoon water*

*Crushed toasted hazelnuts (see Techniques section)*

Cook ham as desired, then remove from oven and score top. Turn oven to 350°F.

Meanwhile, thin crabapple jelly by placing in small saucepan, adding water, and warming over medium heat, stirring until jelly is dissolved. Remove from heat. With an electric mixer, whip at medium-high speed until jelly turns cloudy and reaches the consistency of heavy syrup, about 3 or 4 minutes.

Baste ham with jelly mixture and heat in oven until browned, about 10 minutes. Sprinkle with crushed hazelnuts during last 5 minutes of baking time. Slice and serve warm or cold.

# SHARKEY'S GARDEN GOODIES

Fred Donofrio has come full circle during his long life. He was born in 1911. His father was a farmer in South Seattle, and Fred started selling produce at the Market when he was a very young boy. During the 1930s, one of his friends at the Market nicknamed him "Sharkey" after Jack Sharkey, a professional fighter. Fred left the farm and the Market in 1947 to work as a truck driver for Associated Grocers until retiring in 1974.

Fred was bored with retirement, and expanded the garden he had always kept in his backyard in Kent, near the Green River. When his family gave him a rotary tiller for Father's Day, he expanded his garden to over an acre, and grew so much produce the family couldn't use it all. He tried selling the extra produce on the street outside his house, but when someone suggested he return to the Market, he agreed, and named his business Sharkey's Garden Goodies.

Fred and his wife, Isabel, have continued selling Golden Jubilee corn, beans, tomatoes, acorn squash, red and white potatoes, and hot peppers on Saturdays in the Main Arcade during August, September, and October ever since. Isabel says, "Fred farms his garden all by himself and even makes some of his own seed. He lives for his Saturdays at the Market. It brings back many memories of the 1930s and '40s and working in the Market then. We would like to go more often, if we could only raise more products."

## *Italian Pepper and Sausage Scramble*

SHARKEY'S GARDEN GOODIES

This is a recipe from Fred's mother, Ficella Donofrio, who always made it with the first peppers to ripen. Depending on the hotness of the peppers you use, it will be mildly flavored to very hot and spicy.

*1 tablespoon butter or margarine*

*¼ cup olive oil*

*20 small, green, round, hot Italian peppers, stems removed and peppers cut in half*

*4 medium white rose potatoes, scrubbed but not peeled, cut into bite-size cubes*

*1 yellow onion, sliced*

*Garlic powder to taste*

*Seasoning salt to taste*

*1 pound bulk, Italian sausage, either mild or hot style, formed into bite-size chunks*

Place butter and olive oil in a large skillet over medium heat. Add peppers, potatoes, and onion, and stir to coat well with oils, then add garlic powder and seasoning salt to taste. (Be sure to add seasoning at this point, or the sausage will be too salty.) Cook vegetables until almost tender, 15 to 20 minutes, stirring frequently.

Add sausage chunks and stir until sausage is done, about 10 minutes. Remove to dinner plates and serve with catsup or mustard on the side.

*Serves 4.*

# ORIENTAL KITCHENETTE

Paper snakes slither by, woks steam with stir-fried food, and smiling faces greet you in the southwest corner of the Corner Market Building, where the Apostol family has been happily ensconced since 1973. Parents Mila and Manny, daughters Leila and Joy, and sons Edward and Lem operate three synergistic businesses here.

The Oriental Mart is a specialty grocery that stocks a staggering number of sauces, rices, and noodles basic to Filipino, Chinese, Japanese, Thai, Korean, and Indonesian cuisines. The House of Woks & Bowls features Oriental kitchenware, shoes, kimonos, straw bags, and other novelties. The Oriental Kitchenette boasts a demonstration kitchen where customers are encouraged to pull up a stool, sit at the counter, and watch Mila and her family cook the specials of the day chosen from their native Philippines, as well as other Pacific Rim cuisines.

# *Pancit Bihon*

Oriental Kitchenette, Oriental Mart, and the House of Woks & Bowls

*P*ancit Bihon is Oriental Kitchenette's most popular dish. Based on *bihon* noodles (rice noodles made of rice, corn flour, and water), this excellent basic recipe makes tons of steamy stir-fry teeming with crisp vegetables, silky noodles, and garlic. You'll need an extra-large skillet, wok, Dutch oven, or stockpot, or try stir-frying in two batches. It's great reheated for the next day's meal, and you can experiment by adding additional meats, vegetables, or seasonings, such as fresh ginger, five spice powder, or hot peppers.

*1 package (8 oz) Philippine bihon noodles*

*3 tablespoons vegetable oil, such as peanut (preferred) or corn*

*6 cloves garlic, minced*

*1 onion, sliced into ¼-inch rings*

*1 ½ to 2 cups meat, such as chicken strips, shrimp, Chinese sausage, turkey, beef, etc. (if preparing as a main dish, increase meat to 3 to 4 cups)*

*2 carrots, julienned*

*Half a head of cabbage, cut into large squares*

*Half a bunch of green onions, chopped*

*½ cup pea pods (optional)*

*1 teaspoon salt (or to taste)*

*1 teaspoon pepper (or to taste)*

*Soy sauce to taste, approximately 1 to 3 tablespoons (Oriental Kitchenette uses Philippine soy sauce in its recipe, which gives the Pancit Bihon a rich brown color, but Japanese soy sauce is fine also)*

*1½ to 2 cups chicken broth (divided use)*

*Diced green onions and lemon wedges, for garnish*

Soak *bihon* noodles in warm water for 4 minutes or less. Do not oversoak. Drain in colander and set aside.

Heat oil in large skillet, wok, Dutch oven, or stockpot. Add garlic and cook until browned. Add onion and stir-fry 2 minutes. Add meat and stir-fry until meat is done. Add carrots, cabbage, green onions, and pea pods (if used); mix thoroughly.

Sprinkle mixture with salt, pepper, and soy sauce to taste. Stir-fry until vegetables are tender/crisp in texture. Place ½ cup of the chicken broth in a bowl, add drained noodles, and stir. Add noodles to meat and vegetable mixture and mix thoroughly.

Add remaining broth and cook entire mixture a few minutes more. For drier noodles, add less broth. Serve as a main or side dish, garnished with green onions and lemon wedges.

*Serves 4 as a main dish, 8 as a side dish.*

# *Chicken Adobo*

ORIENTAL KITCHENETTE, ORIENTAL MART, AND THE HOUSE OF WOKS & BOWLS

This is a recipe for garlic aficionados — fried garlic sprinkled on top makes a crunchy counterpoint to the rich, brown, garlicky, slightly salty sauce. You'll unabashedly soak up every drop!

*½ cup Philippine coconut vinegar or distilled white vinegar*

*½ cup Philippine soy sauce or Japanese soy sauce*

*½ teaspoon garlic salt*

*3 bay leaves*

*½ teaspoon finely ground black pepper*

*Salt to taste*

*3 or 4 cloves garlic, crushed*

*2 pounds chicken parts (legs, thighs, or breasts with ribs)*

*2 to 3 tablespoons vegetable oil, such as peanut (preferred) or corn (divided use)*

*2 to 3 tablespoons minced garlic*

In a large bowl combine vinegar, soy sauce, garlic salt, bay leaves, black pepper, salt, and the 3 or 4 cloves garlic, add chicken parts, and marinate in refrigerator several hours or (preferably) overnight.

Remove chicken from marinade; reserve marinade. Heat large skillet over medium-high heat and add 1 tablespoon of the oil. When hot, add the 2 or 3 tablespoons minced garlic and stir-fry until brown. Remove fried garlic and save for later use.

Add the remaining 1 or 2 tablespoons oil to skillet and heat over medium heat. Add chicken pieces and brown well on all sides until done, 10 to 20 minutes, depending on size of pieces. (If you're using large chicken breasts, you can cover pan to help speed cooking process.) Remove chicken pieces to a clean platter and set aside.

Add marinade, a little bit at a time, to pan drippings to make gravy, stirring constantly and scraping up bits on bottom of pan. Once all marinade is added, reduce sauce to desired consistency. Add chicken to gravy, stir thoroughly, and heat through. Divide chicken and gravy among dinner plates, then garnish with fried garlic. Serve with Pancit Bihon (see page 85) and steamed rice, if desired.

*Serves 4 to 6 as a main dish, 6 to 8 if served with Pancit Bihon (page 85) and steamed rice.*

# MARKET CAFE

Since 1980 the Market Cafe has been serving American regional food from its home along First Avenue. Here you'll find breakfast served all day; fresh, grilled foods; and soups and salads. The *huevos rancheros* have been mentioned in *Let's Go USA* for several years running, and the cafe offers a substantial discount to senior citizens.

Owner Richard Van Noord describes his restaurant's philosophy as "slow service with a personal touch," so be patient. Nonetheless, this appealing dinerlike space, with its black-and-white tiles, crowded counter, and cramped booths, is a favorite of Metro bus drivers, hungry journalists, and Market personalities.

## Richard's Down-Home Chicken

### MARKET CAFE

This is a delicious, healthy, gumbolike chicken stew that can be served in numerous ways — most simply over rice with corn tortillas, or with freshly baked corn bread and black beans. It also freezes well and is a nice dish to have on hand for unexpected guests.

1 tablespoon olive oil

1 medium onion, minced

2 cloves garlic, minced

4 celery stalks, minced

2 carrots, minced

7 or 8 tomatillos, minced (to cut down on preparation time, and if a food processor is available, the onion, garlic, celery, carrots, and tomatillos may be chopped together with the chopping blade to a fine dice, then sautéed in the olive oil all at once)

2 teaspoons ground cumin

Pinch of ground cayenne pepper (optional)

1 can (4 oz) green chile peppers, minced

5 cups water, divided use

4 boneless chicken breasts (about 6 oz each), cut into bite-size chunks

½ cup minced cilantro

Salt to taste

1 tomato, seeded and diced

Sour cream

Heat the olive oil in a large Dutch oven over medium heat. Add onion and garlic and cook 1 minute, stirring constantly. Add celery, carrots, and tomatillos and cook until vegetables are tender/crisp, about 3 minutes, stirring constantly. Add cumin, cayenne (if used), and green chile peppers, and stir well to blend. Add 4 cups of the water, bring to a boil, reduce heat, and simmer until almost all the liquid evaporates and a pale green sauce forms, about 15 to 20 minutes.

Add chicken and cilantro, stir well, then add remaining 1 cup water. Bring to a boil, reduce heat, and simmer until chicken is tender and cooked through, about 20 to 25 minutes, or until desired consistency. Stir occasionally while cooking. Add salt to taste, cook 2 minutes more, then serve.

Serve in one of the ways described above, topped with diced tomato and a dollop of sour cream.

*Makes about 4 cups, 6 servings.*

# CHUKAR CHERRY COMPANY

"The year 'round cherry company" was founded in 1986 and has since gone on to win two national specialty-food awards. Chukar Cherries makes dried, pitted sweet Bing, honey-golden Rainier, and Mont-morency tart cherries; dried cranberries and blueberries; chocolate-coated cherries and blueber-ries (coated with Guittard chocolate); cherry pre-serves, sauces, and condiments; cherry herb tea; and Bing cherry scone mix. At its permanent space in the Main Arcade, you'll find fresh cherries during the season, and free samples of their dried products every day of the week.

Founder Pamela Auld explains that Chukar Cherry Company was named after the beguil-ing and swift-flying chukar bird because its image reflects the characteristics of Northwest cherries — tempting and sweet, fleeting in season, and challenging to capture. It can take from three to eight pounds of fresh fruit to make one pound of the dried, and the shelf life of the dried fruit ranges from 3 to 18 months. The dried fruits are good in bread puddings, stuffings, wine sauces, fruit soups, salads, and baked goods, and as a healthy, portable snack food to eat right out of your hand.

# Chicken with Cherry-Wine Sauce

CHUKAR CHERRY COMPANY

This is a recipe I know I'll make time and again because it's easy, delicious, healthy, and showy enough for guests. It uses a fine Washington State–produced Merlot or Cabernet and the wonderful sugar- and preservative-free dried Bing cherries grown in the Yakima Valley of eastern Washington state.

*1 to 2 cups white, brown, or wild rice*

*1 bottle (750 ml) good-quality red wine (Washington State Merlot or Cabernet recommended)*

*1 cup Chukar Cherry Company dried Bing cherries*

*6 boneless, skinless chicken breasts, cut into 1-inch chunks*

*1 to 2 teaspoons olive oil*

*1 tablespoon butter*

*Pinch of sugar*

*Salt, pepper, and dried rosemary to taste*

Cook the rice as directed on the package. (Cook 1 or 2 cups, depending on whether you want ½-cup or 1-cup servings.)

While the rice is cooking, pour wine into a large, noncorrosive saucepan and add the dried cherries. Bring to a boil, then turn down heat and simmer the cherry-wine mixture until the liquid is reduced by half and the cherries lose their wrinkles and plump, about 15 minutes.

While the cherries and wine are simmering, sauté the chicken pieces in a large skillet over medium to medium-high heat, using a minimum of olive oil. Chicken pieces should be white and completely cooked throughout, but still tender.

When the cherry-wine mixture is reduced by half, remove it from heat, add butter and pinch of sugar, and swirl until blended.

To serve, place chicken pieces on top of cooked rice and pour the cherry-wine sauce over the top. Season to taste with salt, pepper, and rosemary (you can do this in the kitchen, or your family or guests can do it themselves at the table). To change the aroma, add a bit of fresh rosemary and white pepper to the finished dish. If your guests are vegetarians, the sauce is delicious by itself served over rice and with lots of steamed or sautéed vegetables.

*Serves 6 to 8.*

# KITCHEN BASICS

Located in the Sanitary Market Building in a space that once housed the American Pie Co., the name says it all at Kitchen Basics, where you'll find lots of basic cookware for beginning cooks. Utility is the watchword here; the store is packed with unique gadgets, old-fashioned meat grinders, potato ricers, *spaetzle* (German noodle and dumpling) makers, cookie molds, baking pans, roasters, food storage sets, tea kettles, and coffee carafes.

# *Zaire Chicken Curry*

### KITCHEN BASICS

This curry is not the usual yellow, creamy type you might find at an Indian restaurant — instead, it's low-fat, hot, and sweet, swimming with currants and red and green peppers. A nice change and definitely worth a try!

*2 tablespoons olive oil*

*1 frying chicken (3½ lb), skinned and cut into large pieces, or 6 chicken breasts, skinned, but with ribs left intact, if you prefer white meat only*

*1½ cups water*

*1 teaspoon salt*

*1 teaspoon black pepper*

*3 or 4 tablespoons curry powder*

*1 teaspoon dried oregano*

*1 teaspoon dried summer savory*

*1 clove garlic, minced*

*1 jalapeño pepper, whole (if you prefer your curry the authentic African way) or minced (if you like lots of extra heat) or a few drops of hot-pepper sauce*

*½ cup firmly packed brown sugar*

*1 green pepper, sliced into thin strips*

*Half a red pepper, sliced into thin strips*

*1 large white onion, thinly sliced*

*½ cup dried currants*

*1 cup uncooked brown rice*

*1 cup lowfat yogurt*

*Mango chutney or hot chutney*

Heat oil in large skillet over medium-high heat. Add chicken pieces and brown, turning down heat and cooking in two batches if necessary. Remove chicken pieces and pat dry with paper towels. Drain excess oil from pan and wipe out any remaining oil with a paper towel.

**To make stock:** Place water, salt, black pepper, curry powder, oregano, savory, garlic, and jalapeño pepper in a 4½-quart Dutch oven or stockpot, and simmer for 5 minutes.

**To make stew:** Add chicken pieces to stock in Dutch oven, sprinkle with brown sugar, top with green and red peppers, onion, and currants, and simmer, covered, over very low heat for 45 minutes to 1½ hours, depending on how you like your chicken. Forty-five minutes gives you chicken of normal American-style tenderness; 1½ hours is the authentic African way, with chicken literally falling off the bone.

While chicken is simmering, prepare rice as package directs, timing it so that it will be ready at about the same time as the curry.

Ladle chicken and vegetables into a large serving bowl. Place yogurt in a medium bowl and slowly add stock remaining in Dutch oven or stockpot to yogurt, stirring to mix thoroughly. Place yogurt mixture back in Dutch oven or stockpot and heat *very* slowly, or yogurt could curdle. Pour heated yogurt/stock mixture over chicken and vegetables.

Ladle chicken pieces, vegetables, and yogurt sauce on top of rice, and serve with mango chutney or hot chutney.

*Serves 6.*

# CHICKEN VALLEY

Market families have played a big part in the history of Chicken Valley, which has been around since the 1940s. First known as Sunny Valley, its name changed to Chicken Valley when Dave Shain bought it in 1955. Over the years, he owned two wholesale chicken houses, in addition to three or four chicken places down at the Market, including Pike Place Poultry, Deluxe Bar-B-Que, and Chicken Valley.

Eddie Shain, Dave's son, grew up in the Market and was friends with Pure Food Fish's owner Sol Amon. Eddie, who's now vice-president of Acme Poultry, also brought up his children in the Market, where they (like their father before them) learned a fabulous work ethic and appreciation for all types of people. One of Eddie's children, Martin, stayed in the food business and went on to co-found Winterbrook Seltzer.

In 1968 Lorraine and Al Lebow bought the place, and Chicken Valley's family tradition continued when, in 1986, one of their sons, Stan, purchased Chicken Valley. A personable, fun-loving man, Stan was well known for shouting, "Hot thighs, get your hot thighs here. Juicy breasts, we got 'em!" Stan sold Chicken Valley in 1989 and now owns a successful restaurant in Issaquah.

From his location in the Main Arcade, just north of Rachel the Pig, present owner Sam Lee offers fresh raw chicken that cooks up tender and tasty in all sorts of dishes. Sam's also got ducks, whole capons, Cornish game hens, pheasants, turkeys, quail, squab, partridges, geese, chicken stock, and rabbit that you can cook at home. If you're hungry for a snack to munch as you walk through the Market, Sam's meltingly tender fried chicken has a light, flaky crust, as do his fried mushrooms and chicken corn dogs.

# Northwest Chicken Stir-Fry

CHICKEN VALLEY

This is a tasty, easy-to-prepare, colorful main dish that makes use of Northwest ingredients prepared with a traditional Oriental stir-fry recipe. The dried cherries are available in the Pike Place Market at Chukar Cherry Company.

*1 tablespoon peanut oil*

*3 drops Oriental toasted sesame oil*

*2 cloves garlic, minced*

*1 small yellow onion, sliced into ¼-inch rings*

*¾ pound boneless chicken breasts, cut into ½-inch chunks*

*¼ cup dried Bing or Montmorency (tart) cherries, plumped (see Techniques section)*

*¼ cup toasted, chopped hazelnuts, with skins removed (see Techniques section)*

*1 pound fresh spinach leaves, cleaned and well drained*

*1½ teaspoons balsamic vinegar*

*¼ teaspoon brown sugar*

*½ teaspoon arrowroot*

Heat oils in a large skillet or wok over medium-high heat. Add the garlic and stir-fry for 30 seconds. Add onion and stir-fry 1 minute more. Add chicken and stir-fry until chicken turns white, 1 to 2 minutes.

Add plumped cherries and hazelnuts and stir-fry for 30 seconds. Add spinach leaves and stir-fry, turning leaves gently. When spinach turns bright green and just begins to wilt, remove from heat.

Mix balsamic vinegar with brown sugar and arrowroot and add to skillet. Stir mixture well, cover skillet, and shake back and forth a few times to blend.

Serve over white or brown rice, soba noodles, whole wheat spaghetti, or fresh angel hair pasta, depending on your mood. It looks beautiful served on a plain, white platter or in a large pasta bowl.

*Serves 4.*

# MARKETSPICE

"Spice is the variety of life" at MarketSpice, which started as a small tea and spice shop on one of the lower levels of the Market in 1911. Specializing in more than 100 bulk loose-leaf teas, a huge collection of spices from around the world that changes monthly depending on what is available, and more than 60 types of bulk coffee beans, the shop has added regular and decaffeinated tea bags, herbal and flavored teas, a wide variety of spice blends, and 29 salt-free seasonings to its product line.

MarketSpice is especially well known for its pungent MarketSpice tea, a black tea flavored with spices and essential oils (especially noticeable is the rich flavor of orange), developed in the early 1970s by a former owner. The wife of a pharmacist who was using oils to flavor his medicines, she tried the same method of camouflage to make tea more palatable, and the result has become one of MarketSpice's most popular products. This is the place to come when your recipe calls for an exotic spice that cannot be found elsewhere.

# *Chicken Masala*

— MARKETSPICE —

Garam is the Indian word for "warm" or "hot," and in classic Indian cooking, *garam masala* is the most important of all spice blends, made up of coriander, ginger, cinnamon, and several other spices, depending on the person mixing it. Although I'd cooked many Indian dishes over the years, I'd never tried this particular spice before I made Chicken Masala. It turned out wonderfully tasty, and I can't wait to experiment with garam masala in the future.

*2 to 3 tablespoons light cooking oil, such as canola, corn, or soy, or ghee (clarified butter; see Techniques section)*

*2 large onions, thinly sliced*

*1 teaspoon granulated garlic*

*1 teaspoon salt*

*2 teaspoons ground garam masala (available at specialty markets, gourmet shops, spice shops, or Indian markets)*

*½ teaspoon ground ginger*

*½ teaspoon ground cayenne pepper, or to taste*

*2 pounds boneless, skinless chicken breasts or chicken thighs*

*1 cup water or chicken stock*

*⅓ cup plain yogurt*

Heat oil or ghee in a large skillet over medium heat, and add onion. Cook until onion is lightly browned. Combine granulated garlic, salt, garam masala, ginger, and cayenne, and add to the onion, stirring to blend.

Cut whole chicken breasts into quarters and place in pan. Allow to brown for 1 to 2 minutes, turning once. Add the water or chicken stock and cover, simmering until chicken is barely tender. Add more water or stock if needed, but *do not overcook.*

Remove chicken to a dish or plate and pour remaining sauce into a blender. Allow to cool slightly, and purée until smooth. (If desired, the dish can be made ahead up to this point and reheated.)

Add yogurt to purée mixture and return to pan along with the chicken and heat through. If the sauce is too thick, thin with stock; if too thin, cook over higher heat (remove chicken first), stirring constantly. Do not allow to boil, or sauce could curdle. Serve over white or brown rice.

*Serves 4.*

# GARLIC TREE RESTAURANT   This family-run restaurant

located about half a block east of the North Arcade up Stewart Street is run by Hong Ja Han (just call her "Mom"), who has owned a variety of restaurants in the United States and Korea since 1967. Daughter Soo Han explains, "The recipes at the Garlic Tree are original creations passed on by Momma Han's mother. Some of our special dishes are garlic wings, garlic chicken, and crab rangoons. And no, not everything on the menu has garlic in it!"

## *Chicken Gui with Stir-Fried Vegetables*

#### — GARLIC TREE RESTAURANT —

You'll prepare this versatile dish time and again because of the many different vegetables you can use and the exquisite flavor of the chicken. It's great to make in the summer when you have too many green peppers, Walla Walla onions, and zucchini in the garden.

*⅓ cup water*

*⅓ soy sauce (Kikkoman brand preferred)*

*1½ teaspoons honey*

*1 teaspoon minced garlic*

*½ teaspoon minced fresh ginger*

*¼ teaspoon ground black pepper*

*½ cup chopped green onion*

*1 pound boneless, skinless chicken breasts*

*1 tablespoon light vegetable oil, such as peanut, corn, or canola*

*6 cups of an assortment of any of the following vegetables, cut into bite-size pieces: broccoli, Napa cabbage, bean sprouts, yellow onions (Walla Walla when in season), green onions, carrots, mushrooms, and green bell peppers*

*½ teaspoon cornstarch*

*2 teaspoons water*

*Several drops of Oriental toasted sesame oil*

Combine water, soy sauce, honey, garlic, ginger, black pepper, and the ½ cup green onion in a small mixing bowl. Divide sauce and place half into bowl large enough to hold chicken breasts without crowding. Reserve remaining sauce for vegetables.

Split each chicken breast by making a horizontal cut almost all the way through each one. Fold out so that each breast makes one large, thin piece of chicken. Place chicken breasts in sauce and marinate for at least 1 hour. The chicken can be pan-fried until cooked through, approximately 3 to 6 minutes, or flame-broiled (as is done at the Garlic Tree) until cooked through, approximately 7 to 10 minutes. Keep chicken warm while cooking vegetables.

Heat oil in large skillet or wok over medium-high heat until almost smoking. Add broccoli, if used, and stir-fry for 2 to 3 minutes, then add remaining vegetables and marinade (approximately ⅓ cup), and stir-fry until vegetables are tender/crisp. In a small glass dish, stir cornstarch and water until completely dissolved, and add to vegetables. Stir thoroughly to blend with vegetables, and cook just until sauce thickens, about 1 minute. Add sesame oil, stir again, then serve immediately with chicken breasts and steamed white or brown rice.

*Serves 2 to 3.*

# Cornish Game Hens with Raspberry Gravy

ALM HILL GARDENS

This is an easy yet lusty presentation of Cornish game hen, fancy enough to serve guests. The skin becomes burnished with the color and flavor of raspberries, the succulent meat subtly flavored, the gravy a pale pink.

*¼ cup raspberry vinegar*

*½ cup olive oil*

*3 Cornish game hens, about 1½ pounds each (defrost if necessary)*

*2 cups frozen raspberries*

*2 tablespoons flour*

*Salt and pepper to taste*

Preheat oven to 400°F. Get out a large roasting pan with a rack, oil lightly or spray with nonstick olive-oil spray, and set aside.

With a whisk, combine raspberry vinegar and olive oil in a small mixing bowl until combined.

Rinse Cornish game hens in cold water, then blot inside and out with paper towels and remove any excess fat from cavities. Pack inside of cavities with frozen raspberries. Tie the legs together and arrange hens on rack, breast side up.

Brush about half the vinaigrette evenly over hens. Place in oven and cook for 10 minutes. Remove hens from oven and brush with remaining vinaigrette. Reduce heat to 350°F, and cook hens until skin is crisp and juices run clear when thigh is pierced with a skewer, 40 to 50 minutes more, brushing or basting with pan juices every 10 minutes. Remove hens from rack and set aside.

To make gravy, separate the fat and the raspberry juice left over in the roasting pan. Set aside raspberry juice for later use. Combine 2 tablespoons of the fat with 2 tablespoons flour, stirring until mixture is no longer lumpy. Place fat/flour mixture in a medium skillet and heat over medium heat.

When mixture is heated, slowly add a little of the reserved raspberry juice, stirring constantly so that no lumps form. Continue to add raspberry juice (or water if you run out of the juice) until gravy reaches desired consistency. Add salt and pepper to taste, then cook a few minutes more, adding more water or raspberry juice if needed.

Cut hens in half and put one half on each dinner plate. Serve with white or brown rice and Raspberry Snap Peas, page 69. Serve the gravy in a pitcher or gravy boat.

*Serves 6.*

# DELUXE BAR-B-QUE
The Economy Market was originally the stable for farmers' horses, and got its name because in the early days it was the discount or day-old section of the Market. Today you'll find Deluxe Bar-B-Que along Economy Row, serving fast foods such as fried and teriyaki chicken, cole slaw and macaroni salad, baked beans, and barbecued pork ribs. This is a good place to stop for a quick lunch, for picnic items, or when you don't feel like making dinner.

## *Chicken Teriyaki*

### DELUXE BAR-B-QUE

This is the actual recipe that Deluxe Bar-B-Que uses for its teriyaki chicken, which is always a delicious treat. Make up this large batch for a family get-together or party, or divide it into halves or quarters for smaller gatherings.

*8 cups (2 quarts or ½ gallon) soy sauce*

*4 cups (1 quart or 2 pints) water*

*3 cups sugar*

*3 cloves garlic, minced*

*1 onion, halved*

*1 cup white wine (optional)*

*20 to 30 chicken pieces*

Mix soy sauce, water, sugar, garlic, onion, and white wine (if used) in a large Dutch oven or stockpot until sugar is dissolved and bring to a boil, stirring occasionally. Remove from heat immediately and allow to cool.

Place chicken pieces in marinade and refrigerate overnight. When ready to cook, preheat oven to 350°F. Remove chicken pieces from marinade and place on lightly greased cookie sheets or baking pans and bake until chicken pieces are done, 30 to 45 minutes.

*Serves 12 to 20, depending on chicken pieces used and appetites.*

# Korean Beef Barbecue (Bulgogi)

### DELUXE BAR-B-QUE

Bulgogi is easy to make and delicious, full of ginger and green onions, which is perhaps the reason it's often referred to as the national meat dish of Korea. It's also versatile — if you aren't a beef fan, you can substitute chicken. This is great served with Stir-Fried Harvest Medley, page 65.

*2 tablespoons sugar*

*¼ cup soy sauce*

*¼ cup minced green onion*

*2 teaspoons minced garlic*

*1 teaspoon minced fresh ginger*

*Dash of pepper*

*1 pound rump roast of beef, thinly sliced*

In a bowl large enough to hold beef, mix sugar, soy sauce, green onion, garlic, ginger, and pepper. Add beef and cover. Marinate meat in refrigerator at least 1 hour and preferably overnight to allow flavors to meld.

Preheat broiler and take out a broiler pan large enough to hold beef slices. Place beef slices on broiler pan. When broiler is hot, place pan in oven and broil until beef is desired doneness, turning once, about 6 to 10 minutes. Serve immediately. To make a complete meal, double the proportions of ingredients for the marinade above, divide into two separate containers, and marinate sliced vegetables such as red peppers, cherry tomatoes, mushrooms, and carrots in the liquid for a few hours. Skewer vegetables and broil along with meat. Serve with brown or white rice.

*Serves 4.*

# CRYSTAL MEATS INC.

Delores and Michael Greenblat, owners of Crystal Meats, like to say that they "trim the meat, not the customer," and the Greenblat family has been doing just that since 1947, when Michael's father bought the business. This second generation of butchers specializes in a variety of quality meats, including poultry, beef, pork, deli cuts, and smoked meats. You'll find them in the Corner Market Building near Oriental Kitchenette and Patti Summers.

# *Roast Beef*

Crystal Meats Inc.

Roasting meat has been variously described as an inherited trait, a science, and an art. In the hope that roasting beef is a skill that all of us can learn, here are some tips from the Greenblats.

Start out with a tender roast. This is most important, since roasting cooks by dry heat and will not break down tough meat fibers. A standing rib roast or similar cut will hold its shape better during roasting and will have better flavor if cooked on the bone. Bring the roast to room temperature before you put it in the oven, so that the meat will cook evenly.

Despite what many people think, putting salt and pepper on the meat prior to cooking will not toughen it. Be sure to season just before the roast goes into the hot oven, however. Insert a meat thermometer into the thickest part of the roast, making sure it doesn't touch fat or bone, which would falsify the reading.

The perfect roasting pan is just 1 inch larger all around than the roast itself; a larger pan can burn the pan juices and a smaller one can steam the meat. A rack works well, because it creates a nicely browned exterior, promotes even cooking, and prevents stewing or steaming. Bone-in roasts have their own built-in rack — simply cook bone-side down.

Searing the meat, rather than cooking at one low temperature continuously, produces the best results. To sear a roast, preheat the oven and the empty roasting pan to 500°F. Add the meat and sear for 15 minutes. Turn heat down to 350°F and roast until desired doneness. Your roast will be cooked rare at 120°F, medium-rare at 125°F, medium at 135°F, and well-done at 150°F.

Allow roast beef to rest for about 15 minutes so that its juices will redistribute and the meat will attain a nice uniform red or pink color throughout. Carve and enjoy with freshly grated horseradish and your favorite side dishes, such as Yorkshire pudding and vegetables.

# BAVARIAN MEAT PRODUCTS INC.

As you walk through the double doors, a rush of spicy, refrigerated air from the meat cases washes over you. Slabs of bacon, coils of smoked links, and mottled blood-and-tongue loaf perch behind glass. Black strips of *landjaeger* wait patiently for mountain climbers, who fill their backpacks with the protein-rich, yet easy-to-transport cousin of beef jerky.

But regular customers, those who come in weekly from Everett and Bainbridge Island and converse with the clerks in guttural German, fill their shopping bags with braunschweiger (the most famous of the liverwursts), Westphalian smoked ham (ham produced from pigs raised on acorns in Germany's Westphalia forest), and head cheese (a sausage made from the meaty bits of the head of a calf or pig), along with German mustards, pickles, and rye breads.

During the holiday season, this little corner of Bavaria in the Soames-Dunn Building (just past Seattle Cutlery) imports gingerbread houses, stollen (Germany's traditional Christmas yeast bread), Advent calendars, candles, and pfeffernüsse (German black-pepper-and-spice cookies). German Christmas carols ring through the air, and customers and staff often break into song in the native tongue. If for too brief a time, they are carried back to the Old Country, just as they have been since 1962, the year Bavarian Meats opened its doors.

# *Rouladen*

### BAVARIAN MEAT PRODUCTS INC.

Rouladen is meat cut from the top or bottom round of beef. It is sold at Bavarian Meats trimmed, pounded thin, and ready to stuff and roll for this traditional German recipe.

*4 beef rouladen*

*Salt and pepper to taste*

*Prepared German mustard (the German Lion or Hengstenberg brands are recommended)*

*4 thin slices bacon, uncooked*

*2 tablespoons diced onion*

*2 tablespoons diced dill pickles*

*1 tablespoon butter*

*All-purpose flour or arrowroot*

*Red wine or beef stock*

Lay out one slice of meat on a piece of waxed paper. Sprinkle with salt and pepper to taste, then spread thinly with mustard.

Place one bacon slice lengthwise over meat, then sprinkle ½ tablespoon onion and ½ tablespoon pickles over meat. Roll meat tightly, like a jelly roll, and secure with toothpicks or rouladen rings (available from Bavarian Meats).

Repeat procedure with remaining three pieces of meat, then brown all four rolls in butter in a large skillet over medium heat. Add more butter, if necessary. Add enough water to cover rouladen, cover skillet, turn down heat, and simmer for 45 minutes. Add more water if needed to keep rouladen covered while they cook.

Remove rouladen and, if desired, make a gravy from pan juices by adding white flour or arrowroot mixed with a little red wine or beef stock.

Place rouladen on dinner plates and serve with red cabbage and German *spaetzle* (tiny dumplings or noodles) or roast potatoes.

*Serves 4.*

# Lina's Produce

Lina's Produce in the Main Arcade offers some of the Oriental fruits and vegetables not offered by other highstalls in the Market. Here you'll find bitter melon; Chinese long beans; mustard, collard, and turnip greens; Japanese eggplant; local squashes; and a good selection of fresh herbs and peppers.

Lina Fronda, the woman behind the name, is a Market old-timer. In 1963, when she came to Seattle from Luzon (the chief island in the Philippines), she went straight to work in the Market. When her husband died in 1980, Lina took over their highstall produce stand, and has been hard at it ever since.

# *Mechado*

LINA'S PRODUCE

Cooks in some parts of the Philippines use 7-Up as a marinade ingredient for meats, much like American cooks use wine. An easy-to-make, economical, flavorful stew with an appealing interplay of colors and textures, *mechado* is full of garlic and pepper, like many Philippine main dishes.

*¾ cup 7-Up*

*2½ tablespoons distilled white vinegar*

*1 tablespoon minced garlic*

*½ to 1 tablespoon ground black pepper, depending on hotness desired*

*2 bay leaves*

*1½ tablespoons soy sauce*

*3½ teaspoons brown sugar*

*2 pounds boneless chuck roast, cut into bite-size cubes*

*2 medium potatoes, cut into bite-size cubes*

*1 red pepper, cut into bite-size squares*

*¼ cup light vegetable oil, such as peanut, corn, or canola*

*1½ teaspoons minced garlic*

*Half a green pepper, cut into bite-size cubes*

*½ cup (half an 8 oz can) tomato sauce*

Combine 7-Up, vinegar, the 1 tablespoon garlic, black pepper, bay leaves, soy sauce, and brown sugar in a large Dutch oven or stockpot, and bring to a boil over medium-high heat. Add beef, potatoes, and red pepper, stir well, and cook until beef browns on outside, about 3 minutes, stirring constantly. Cover pan, reduce heat to low, and simmer until meat and potatoes are tender, 20 to 25 minutes, stirring occasionally. Set aside.

After meat is done, place oil in a large skillet and heat over medium-high heat. Add the 1½ teaspoons garlic and stir-fry until it turns light brown, then reduce heat to medium, add green pepper, and cook 3 minutes more, stirring constantly. Add garlic and green pepper mixture to meat and its sauce in the Dutch oven and stir well. Bring to a boil, add tomato sauce, and stir constantly until mixture is warmed through. Serve immediately in large soup bowls over rice or with bread, if desired.

*Serves 4 to 6.*

# THE MEXICAN GROCERY

From five-pound bags of *masa* (a special dough ground from lime-treated corn kernels), to heady vanilla extract imported from Mexico (great for baking), the Mexican Grocery, on Pike Place, is a good shop to explore if you're interested in Mexican cuisine. With their fresh red and green salsas made on the premises, tortilla chips, fresh tortillas, and tamales, you could put together a dinner party for 6 or 60 at a moment's notice, and have lots of fun in the process.

## New Mexico Tamales

#### THE MEXICAN GROCERY

Masa formed the foundation of ancient Mexican cuisine, and is still the heart of Mexican cooking today, used in tortillas, tacos, enchiladas, and tamales. The Mexican Grocery sells some of the best tamales in town, handmade at their store in South Seattle. Yet making tamales is a lot of work. Even in Mexico they're considered party or fiesta food because they're so time-consuming to prepare, often reserved for birthdays, christenings, or New Year celebrations. Tamales can be filled with everything from beef to seafood to beans, or even left unfilled, but pork is the most traditional filling.

*About 40 ojas (corn husks for rolling tamales)*

SHREDDED PORK FILLING FOR TAMALES

*1 yellow onion, quartered*

*2 cloves garlic, sliced*

*1 teaspoon whole cumin seed*

*4 pounds pork butt roast*

SAUCE FOR PORK FILLING FOR TAMALES

*24 New Mexico, ancho, or pasilla chile pods*

*4 cups water*

*1 tablespoon lard or bacon fat*

*2 to 4 cloves garlic, minced*

*1 tablespoon flour*

MASA MIX

*6 cups fresh masa*

*2 cups lard or bacon grease*

*2 teaspoons salt (optional)*

*About 2 cups reserved pork broth*

Remove corn whiskers from ojas. While preparing rest of recipe, soak ojas in cold water until they become soft and begin to separate.

**To make pork filling:** Heat enough water to cover pork in a large Dutch oven. Bring water, onion, the 2 cloves garlic, and cumin seed to a boil; add pork. Reduce heat, cover pot, and simmer pork until meat pulls apart easily with a fork, 3 to 4 hours. Remove meat from Dutch oven, strain broth, and reserve. With fingers or two forks, shred pork into large bowl, discarding any fat, and place in refrigerator until ready to use.

**To make sauce:** Boil chile pods in the water for 20 minutes. Let cool, then whirl pods and liquid in blender on high speed. Pour mixture through a fine sieve, into a glass dish.

In a skillet heat the 1 tablespoon lard or bacon fat and sauté the 2 to 4 cloves minced garlic. Add flour and mix thoroughly, then add chile sauce and stir until well blended. Remove from heat and add to cooked pork. Stir thoroughly, then return pork mixture to refrigerator.

**To prepare masa:** Put masa into a large bowl, add the 2 cups lard or bacon grease, and mix with hands until fat is thoroughly incorporated into masa. Add salt (if used), and slowly add the 2 cups pork broth, mixing well after each addition of broth. You may not have to use all of the broth, depending on the moisture content of the masa. Knead masa until it is light and fluffy.

**To assemble tamales:** Remove ojas from soaking water, and remove any additional corn whiskers that have appeared. Place ojas on a dish towel to keep moist. Take out one oja and lay it out until it is smooth. Spoon about ¼ cup of the masa into the center of the oja, then spread it over the corn husk with the back of a spoon, leaving about 1 inch at sides and 2 inches at top and bottom of oja. Spoon a couple of tablespoons pork mixture over oja and use back of spoon to spread. Fold oja so that masa edges meet, then wrap plain part (side border) of oja around outside of tamale. Fold bottom end of husk over body of tamale, then fold in tip. Alternately, you can roll your tamales and tie at either end with torn strips of ojas.

**To cook tamales:** Boil 2 cups water in a steamer, then place several ojas over bottom of steamer. Place all the tamales over the ojas, then cover tops of tamales with additional ojas. Place a dishcloth over the top of the ojas to catch any condensation that might form, then cover the steamer.

Steam 1 hour. If steamer boils dry, add an additional cup of *hot* water. Tamales are done when they pull apart easily from the ojas. The dough should be spongy and compact and not cling to the husk.

Remove tamales from steamer and place on large platter or put several on each dinner plate. Serve with refried beans and rice. If you have any pork filling left over, you can use it to fill tortillas or tacos and serve with rice and beans.

*Makes about 32 tamales, 8 to 10 servings.*

# VASHON'S OLD-FASHIONED NURSERY   Linda

Swanson's 6½-acre farm on Vashon Island dates from 1933, when two unmarried Slavic brothers began to grow fruit there, and raised some of the best gooseberries and currants in the town of Dockton. When Linda bought the farm in 1977, she kept the figs, wine grapes, and grape leaves that the brothers left behind, but added her main crops of dahlia tubers, lilies, irises, and garlic.

Her garlic is something special. A variety common throughout the Mediterranean but rare in the United States, it is streaked with purple and possesses a much richer flavor, no bitterness when cooked, and longer storage life than standard garlic. It was brought to Dockton in 1925 by a Yugoslavian couple who raised it successfully for years. Neighbors of Linda, they sold their specialty garlic to her when they finally retired at the age of 90, which may speak volumes about the health benefits of the magical bulb.

Linda started in the Market in 1986, and likes to come because "at the Market people want to know about *you* as much as your product. The people who work at the Market are wonderful, too," she continues. "They are all unique, independent, and just the right degree of crazy."

## *Roast Lamb*

### VASHON'S OLD-FASHIONED NURSERY

Once a year Linda's Dockton neighborhood on Vashon Island holds a lamb roast in which a six-month-old lamb is slaughtered, stuffed with thousands of cloves of fresh garlic, onions, and butter, and rotated over madrona coals while it's basted with the same garlic/onion/butter sauce. The lamb feeds 200 hungry people. You can adapt this basic recipe to the number of people you wish to serve. It's mouthwateringly tender and juicy, permeated inside and out with fresh garlic, and swimming in butter. In short, it's hard to beat!

*1 lamb leg or loin roast*

*Garlic cloves, sliced ⅛ inch thick (divided use)*

*Butter*

*Yellow onion, sliced into ⅛-inch rings*

Preheat oven to 350°F. Take out a roasting pan with rack, grease lightly or spray with nonstick olive-oil spray, and set aside. Trim all fat from lamb roast, then rub 1 or 2 garlic cloves over outside of roast. Make 1-inch slits into roast and insert slices from 2 more garlic cloves.

In a large skillet heat butter over medium heat. When hot, add onion rings and remaining garlic slices and sauté just until onion begins to wilt, 2 or 3 minutes. Add lamb roast and brown lightly on all sides.

Place lamb roast on rack in roasting pan, spread onion and garlic slices over and around it, and place in oven. Cook until lamb is desired doneness, let lamb rest 15 minutes, then slice and serve. It's also great reheated the next day in hot lamb sandwiches.

# Kells Irish Restaurant & Pub

Kells is named after the Book of Kells, the seventh-century illuminated manuscripts of the Gospels, written in Latin and never completed. Even the last four digits — 1916 — of Kells' phone number are significant: 1916 was the year of the famous Easter Rebellion against British rule in Dublin, when Irish Nationalists declared Ireland a republic.

Started in 1983 by Ethna and Joe McAleese (who chose Seattle when they emigrated from Belfast because the rain reminded them of Ireland), Kells serves traditional Irish dishes, Ethna's famous Irish breads (the whole wheat is so rich and moist, it tastes like cake), and fine Guinness Stout, Harp Lager, and Grand Irish Whiskey. With its 100-year-old bar imported from Ireland and the slogan *ceád maít failté* — a thousand welcomes — you'll truly experience a wee bit o' Ireland as Joe escorts you to a table in the dark, intimate dining room.

This is a family affair; Ethna and Joe's daughter, Karen, and sons Charlie, Gerald (who runs the Kells in Portland), Paul, and Patrick Pearse help run the business. There's live music in the bar (through the door on the left) Wednesday through Saturday nights, and if the mood strikes him, the patriarch of the clan will sometimes sing an Irish folk song. The band plays traditional Irish music, and contented patrons often sing along.

## *Irish Stew*

— Kells Irish Restaurant & Pub —

Sometimes the simplest things are the best — you'll love the way the lamb, vegetables, water, and spices cook up into a chunky stew that is best served with slabs of homemade Irish soda bread and a pint of Guinness Stout.

*3 pounds lamb sirloin, cut into ½-inch chunks (if your butcher can give you the lamb bone, add it to the stew for extra flavor)*

*Salt and pepper to taste*

*1 pound onions, cut into ¼-inch chunks*

*1 pound carrots, cut into ¼-inch chunks*

*2½ pounds large white potatoes, well scrubbed and cut into ¼-inch chunks*

*½ teaspoon dried thyme*

Season lamb chunks with salt and pepper. In a large Dutch oven over medium heat, sauté lamb pieces until browned. Add onion, carrots, potatoes, thyme, and additional salt and pepper to taste, if desired. Stir well, then add water to cover.

Bring mixture to a boil, reduce heat to medium-low, and simmer, uncovered, approximately 1¼ hours. Add more water (or lamb stock for extra flavor) if necessary. Ladle into soup bowls and serve.

*Makes about 10 cups, 6 to 8 servings.*

# Seafood Entrées

## Seafood Entrées

*Mushroom Salmon Pie with Gruyère Cheese*

*Roast King Salmon with Pinot Noir Mustard Sauce*

*Barbecued Salmon*

*Grilled Salmon with Roasted Hazelnut Butter*

*Creamed Dungeness Crabmeat Omelet*

*Ling Cod Casserole*

*Sea Bass with Fresh Vegetables*

*Baked Sole with Vegetable Ragout*

*Halibut Cheeks en Papillote*

*Trout à la Grecque*

*Prawns Aglio*

*Shrimp Curry*

*Alf's Cracked Crab*

# QUALITY CHEESE INC.

There's been a cheese shop in the Corner Market Building since before World War II, and present owner Nancy Rentschler has been there for over 10 years. Today Quality Cheese offers more than 130 cheeses, about one-third of them domestic and two-thirds imported from all over the world.

One of Nancy's exclusive lines is Sally Jackson goat cheese, both soft and aged. The sun-dried tomato, basil, and oregano type is especially popular with customers. Nancy also carries about eight low-fat cheeses for those on restricted diets.

A real cheese expert, Nancy, a warm, friendly woman comments, "I have the nicest customers around. Some of the locals come in once or twice a week. They're so cheerful and patient, even when they have to wait in line. The local customer is what built our business, and for that I'm very grateful."

## Mushroom Salmon Pie with Gruyère Cheese

——— QUALITY CHEESE INC. ———

Swiss Gruyère, a moderate-fat cow's milk cheese, has a rich, nutty flavor and a pale yellow color. It's delicious in this sinfully rich and tasty quiche, perfect for an elegant brunch, luncheon, or light dinner.

*1 cup finely grated Gruyère cheese*

*Pastry for 9-inch single pie shell, unbaked*

*1 tablespoon butter*

*¾ pound salmon fillet, cut into 1-inch strips*

*1 cup sliced fresh mushrooms*

*3 eggs*

*1½ cups half-and-half*

*Pinch of dried oregano*

*Pinch of dried thyme*

*¼ teaspoon salt*

*Pinch of pepper*

*Additional whole, sautéed mushrooms (optional)*

*Dried oregano (optional)*

Preheat oven to 350°F. Spread Gruyère evenly over bottom of unbaked pie shell.

Melt butter in large skillet over medium heat. Add salmon and mushrooms and sauté about 3 minutes, turning salmon strips once. Cut salmon into 1-inch chunks, then arrange salmon chunks and mushrooms evenly over pie shell.

Beat eggs with half-and-half, oregano, thyme, salt, and pepper, and pour over salmon and mushrooms. Bake until center is set and top is golden, about 45 to 50 minutes. If pie edges start to brown too much, cover pie loosely with aluminum foil during last 10 to 15 minutes of baking time.

Remove pie from oven, let rest 5 minutes, then slice and serve warm with a fresh green salad or steamed vegetables. If desired, decorate center of pie with additional mushrooms and a sprinkling of oregano before slicing.

*Serves 6.*

# CAFÉ SOPHIE

Beware of friendly ghosts at Café Sophie, for this First Avenue restaurant and bar is located in the original Butterworth Mortuary, in use at the turn of the century (1903). The grand-salon dining room once served as the mortuary's high-ceilinged chapel, and the funereal theme continues in the baroque angels and gargoyles, abundance of gilt and mirrors, and solemn classical music. Tucked in the back is the Library, an intimate dining room with red walls, a fireplace, and an impressive view of Elliott Bay.

Café Sophie's menu, which changes seasonally, emphasizes what the chef calls "post-modern cuisine" — contemporary Northwest cuisine steeped in classical European tradition and with an eye toward health. Desserts are legendary — huge, sweet concoctions stuffed with fresh fruits, berries, mousses, and Bavarian cream, and garnished with ruffles of white and dark chocolate.

A midweek lunch is a good time to try Café Sophie, and the place really fills up on warm summer nights, when you can sit under the stars on the outside patio as the First Avenue crowd flows by.

# *Roast King Salmon with Pinot Noir Mustard Sauce*

CAFÉ SOPHIE

This classically inspired dish uses the Northwest's own ingredients to their best advantage. It's light and healthy, yet completely satisfying because of its contrast of flavors and textures. It's showy enough for guests, yet easy on the cook, because most of the preparation can be done well ahead of time. Black mustard seed is available in the Pike Place Market at the Souk.

*1 cup Pinot Noir or other good-quality red wine*

*¼ cup honey*

*¼ cup black mustard seed*

*½ cup red wine vinegar*

*1 teaspoon chopped shallot*

*½ teaspoon salt*

*2 teaspoons chopped fresh tarragon*

*Ground black pepper to taste*

*2 pounds fresh King salmon, steaks or fillets (about 6 ounces per serving)*

*Salt and freshly ground black pepper to taste*

*2 tablespoons olive oil or melted butter*

*1 bunch fresh arugula, rinsed and well dried*

*1 red pepper, diced*

Place wine in a noncorrosive saucepan over high heat and boil until reduced by half. Remove from heat, add honey, and stir until honey dissolves.

In a small, dry skillet, heat mustard seeds until they begin to pop and release their aroma. Remove from heat and add to the wine/honey mixture. Add red wine vinegar, shallot, salt, tarragon, and pepper. Pour into a jar with a lid, and refrigerate at least 8 hours, or overnight. (Mixture can be made ahead to this point and refrigerated for up to 1 week.)

Preheat oven to 450°F. Place salmon steaks or fillets in a greased baking pan and season with salt and pepper. Brush with olive oil or butter, place in oven, and cook 5 to 7 minutes, or until they reach desired doneness.

Divide arugula among 6 dinner plates. Drizzle each plate of arugula with 2 tablespoons of the sauce, warmed or at room temperature. When salmon is cooked, arrange one steak or fillet over each bed of arugula, top with about one-sixth of the red pepper, and serve immediately.

*Serves 6.*

# PIKE PLACE FISH

At Pike Place Fish, located at the hub of the Market, under the neon clock and behind Rachel the Pig, there's always a festive air. While musician Jonny Hahn bangs away at his piano in one of the prime musician's spots, the Pike Place fishmongers pop shopping bags like rifle shots.

In gravelly voices they urge passersby to stop, stop, stop and buy, buy, buy. While the tourists' video cameras whir, the clerks out front hoist a salmon or a halibut from the icy pile and toss it skyward. Somehow, their cohorts behind the counter (almost) always manage to catch the cold, slippery charges — with a whap — like baseballs in a catcher's mitt.

Meanwhile, a gaggle of schoolchildren stops in its tracks as a fishmonger holds up a yellow-eyed rockfish (orange with a bright yellow eye) and fans its tail as though it were "swimming" through the air. Even locals pause for a stolen moment to gaze at the unsightly monkfish that gapes over ice, its jaws propped open, the better to display jagged rows of teeth; the geoduck with its elephant-trunk neck; and the barnacle-encrusted oysters piled six inches high.

Pike Place Fish was started by two partners in 1930. Present owner Johnny Yokoyama began working at his parents' highstall, Roy's Fruits and Vegetables, at the age of eight and grew up in the Market. In 1965 he bought Pike Place Fish for $3,500, $1,200 less than he spent for the Buick Riviera he bought the same year. Ironically, the highstall produce stand where Johnny grew up was right next to the present-day Pike Place Fish.

# *Barbecued Salmon*

## PIKE PLACE FISH

This is a simple recipe devised by Dick Yokoyama, Johnny's brother, who advises that it is always better to undercook, rather than overcook, a salmon — wise words from an expert on fish.

*1 teaspoon garlic powder*

*1 teaspoon pepper*

*1 teaspoon salt (optional)*

*5 pounds salmon, cut into book fillets*

*1 medium onion, sliced into ¼-inch rounds*

*2 lemons, sliced into ⅛-inch rounds*

Mix garlic powder, pepper, and salt (if used) in a small bowl. Sprinkle spice mixture evenly over flesh side of fish. Place onion and lemon slices evenly over seasonings on flesh side of fish.

Place salmon skin side down on grill (coals should be at 350°F), cover, and cook 15 to 20 minutes, depending on thickness of fish and the way you like it cooked. Dick suggests cooking until salmon just flakes.

If you don't have a barbecue grill, you can still try this dish by baking instead of grilling it. To bake fish, place fish skin side down in a shallow baking pan that has been lightly greased or sprayed with nonstick corn-oil or olive-oil spray. Prepare as above and bake about 10 to 15 minutes without turning, depending on the thickness of the fish.

*Serves 8.*

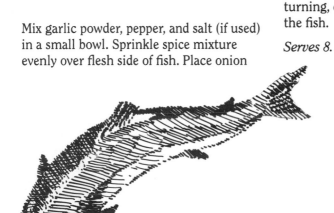

# CUTTERS BAYHOUSE

Cutters Bayhouse* has been a fixture along Western Avenue overlooking the Seattle waterfront since 1983. Wraparound expanses of glass offer panoramic views of the freighters, ferries, and sailboats that ply the Sound. There's animation within the open kitchen, too, as tongues of fire leap from the grill into a sauté pan, or a Caesar salad is tossed skyward by the chefs.

If you're not sure what you want to eat, Cutters is a good restaurant choice, for its menu is wide-ranging, offering simply and often healthfully prepared fish dishes, entrée salads, soups, and pastas prepared using everything from Chinese, to Cajun, to Hawaiian techniques and flavors.

The menu contains a convenient "New in the Market" section that alerts diners to what fish and produce are currently fresh and prime. Cutters is a smoke-free zone, in keeping with its pretty, health-conscious crowd, and the decor is a soothing pale pink, with copper fixtures and mirrors lining the walls. *Just outside of the Market Historic District.

# *Grilled Salmon with Roasted Hazelnut Butter*

CUTTERS BAYHOUSE

A simple and luscious preparation of the Northwest's favorite fish, using the Northwest's favorite nut, this is especially delicious if made on an outdoor barbecue grill with Alaskan Copper River King salmon during their all-too-short run, usually in May or June. For the uninitiated, Copper River is the filet mignon of salmons, a richer, fuller-flavored salmon, red-orange in color, with a large, flaky texture and superior, moist taste.

*2 ounces (about ½ cup) hazelnuts, roasted (see Techniques section)*

*½ cup butter, softened*

*Minced shallots or fresh herbs (optional)*

*Grated lemon rind (optional)*

*4 salmon fillets (8 oz each)*

*2 teaspoons seasoning salt, or salt and pepper (divided use)*

To prepare the hazelnut butter, chop the roasted nuts in a food processor until fine (they should be almost powdery), and set aside. Using a whisk or electric mixer, whip butter until fluffy and light, and fold in the nuts by hand. If desired, add minced shallots and/or lemon rind or other flavorings, such as minced fresh herbs.

To grill fish, preheat a charcoal grill (be sure the grill has been well cleaned with a wire brush to prevent the fish fillets from sticking). Spread 1 tablespoon of the hazelnut butter on the flesh side of each fillet, and place on grill with buttered side down.

Cover the top of each fillet with an additional 1 tablespoon of the hazelnut butter and season with ¼ teaspoon of your preferred seasoning blend, or salt and pepper. Cook for approximately 2 minutes.

Using a long spatula, turn the fish approximately 45 degrees with the flesh side still down, and cook an additional 2 minutes to form diamond-shaped grill marks. Turn fillets over with the spatula so that the skin side is now down. Cook for approximately 1 to 2 more minutes, or until the internal temperature is 140°F.

Just before removing fillets from the grill, top with an additional 1 tablespoon hazelnut butter and ¼ teaspoon seasoning. Serve flesh side up with lemon slices, a fresh vegetable, and either oven-roasted or steamed new potatoes.

*Serves 4.*

*Note:* The hazelnut butter can be made ahead and refrigerated for up to one week, but should be returned to a soft, fluffy consistency before using.

If you do not have a charcoal grill, you can broil your fish. Just place it skin side down on a broiler pan with a rack (grease rack lightly or spray with nonstick corn-oil or olive-oil spray). Place oven rack on first level from top (about 3 inches), place broiler pan under broiler in center of oven, and broil 6 to 10 minutes, depending on thickness of fish and the way you like it done. Rare fish should still be moist and pink in the middle; medium-rare should just flake. If white spots appear, it's overdone.

# ATHENIAN INN

Three Greek brothers started the Athenian Inn over 80 years ago as a bakery, candy shop (the candy was made on the premises), and luncheonette. With its central location in the Main Arcade, the popular Athenian Inn quickly grew from a small restaurant into a restaurant and tavern, and was one of the first Seattle establishments to be granted a liquor license (for beer and wine) in 1933. Bob and Louise Cromwell bought the place in 1966, and their businesses in the Pike Place Market have since grown to include Pure Food Meats and Barb's Gourmet Deli.

Today the Athenian Inn boasts an overflowing menu of ethnically diverse items, such as Scotch Eggs, Rumaki Rickshaw, Dungeness Crab Louie, Sinigang (the Athenian kettle of fish), and Athenian Greek Salad. Beer is important here; they offer more than 16 brews on tap and a selection of bottled beer from all over the world, with exotic names like Lucky Lager, Rattlesnake, and Pete's Wicked Ale. At the front counter you'll find the last 15-cent cup of coffee in Seattle and perhaps the United States, along with the subtle warning, "HOMESTEAD ACT DOES NOT APPLY TO COUNTER."

You can come as you are. Everyone from businessmen to tourists to First Avenue street people stops by for breakfast, lunch, early dinner, a snack, or a drink from 6:30 a.m. to 6:30 p.m. Monday through Saturday. You might want to time your visit based on the rising or setting of the sun, for the waterfront views are outstanding here. Be sure to notice the sign outside the Athenian Inn; it's the original one placed there by those three Greek brothers in 1933.

# *Creamed Dungeness Crabmeat Omelet*

#### — ATHENIAN INN —

This is nostalgia food, the type of breakfast we all used to enjoy before oat bran and guilt came into vogue. If you feel like a splurge, forget the cholesterol and calories and revel in every bite.

*¼ cup butter or margarine*

*¼ cup flour*

*2 cups half-and-half*

*½ teaspoon dry mustard*

*¼ teaspoon paprika*

*¼ teaspoon salt*

*½ tablespoon butter or margarine*

*1 teaspoon grated onion*

*1 cup sliced fresh mushrooms*

*1½ teaspoons sherry*

*4 or 5 eggs*

*1 tablespoon water or milk*

*1 tablespoon butter or margarine*

*¼ cup fresh Dungeness crabmeat*

**To make crabmeat sauce:** Melt the ¼ cup butter or margarine in a large skillet over medium heat, add flour, and then stir until thoroughly blended. Add half-and-half a little at a time until thoroughly incorporated. Add mustard, paprika, and salt, stir well, and reduce heat to low.

Melt the ½ tablespoon butter or margarine in a medium skillet and sauté onion over low heat for 5 minutes. Add mushrooms and sauté just until mushrooms begin to lose their juice, about 2 to 3 minutes, stirring constantly. Remove from heat and add sherry. Add mushroom/sherry mixture to cream sauce, stir until thoroughly blended, and keep warm.

**To make omelet:** Whisk eggs and water or milk until light and foamy. Heat the 1 tablespoon butter or margarine in large skillet over medium to medium-high heat and add egg mixture. Cook until partially done, then turn over and cook other side. Meanwhile, mix crabmeat with sauce, pour crabmeat sauce into middle of omelet, fold omelet in half, and serve immediately. Pour additional crabmeat sauce over top of omelet, if desired. Split in the kitchen or at the table so that omelet serves two people.

*Serves 2.*

# PURE FOOD FISH MARKET

Started around 1917, Pure Food Fish was one of the original fish stores in the Market. And present owner Sol Amon's family has an even longer history of working in the Market. His father, Jack Amon, emigrated from Turkey to Seattle and worked and owned fish markets in the Market beginning in 1911. Jack acquired Pure Food Fish in 1956, and Sol took over in 1959.

Today Pure Food Fish's specialties include fresh Pacific Northwest salmon; alder-smoked, garlic, and cajun-smoked salmon; Dungeness crab; red king crab; and fresh halibut. The company ships seafood all over the world in their reusable insulated coolers with reusable gel-ice cold-packs.

Sol and his clerks, including Harry, Cookie, Jack, and Richard, are quick to offer a smile and a menu suggestion. They know their fish, although Richard loves to tell the tale of one customer who didn't: "This woman called me long distance to tell me that the fish I had shipped her was bad. I asked her what was wrong and she said it was all blue. I realized she had cooked the cold-packs we ship the fish in to keep it fresh and cold!"

## Ling Cod Casserole

### PURE FOOD FISH MARKET

Ling cod has a mild, sweet flavor and firm texture and is very versatile—you can bake, broil, fry, or grill it, or use it in soups and stews. At the height of its popularity it was called "beef of the sea." Nowadays, it's often found smoked. You'll enjoy this low-fat, easy-to-make preparation of fresh ling cod, full of crunchy vegetables.

*1 cup V-8 juice*

*1 cup chopped onion*

*1 cup chopped mushrooms*

*1 cup chopped celery*

*1 cup chopped green or red bell pepper*

*2 cloves garlic, minced*

*Freshly ground pepper to taste*

*1½ pounds ling cod fillets*

*Freshly grated Parmesan cheese*

Preheat oven to 375°F. Take out an 8- by 8-inch baking dish and grease lightly or spray with nonstick olive-oil spray.

In a medium mixing bowl, stir together V-8 juice, onion, mushrooms, celery, bell pepper, garlic, and freshly ground pepper to taste.

Place half of vegetable mixture and juice in baking dish, then place cod over vegetables. Pour rest of vegetable mixture and juice over cod.

Bake 15 to 20 minutes, or until fish and vegetables are desired doneness. Sprinkle top of casserole with Parmesan cheese and bake an additional 3 minutes. Divide fish into four equal portions, place on dinner plates, and serve with lots of crusty bread.

*Serves 4.*

# *Sea Bass with Fresh Vegetables*

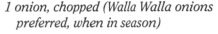

PURE FOOD FISH MARKET

This is an easy-to-make, healthful dish, in which each ingredient complements the whole. Try it served over brown rice or with steamed new potatoes, crusty bread and a bottle of Washington State Chardonnay as a special-occasion dinner for friends or family.

*1 tablespoon olive oil*

*3 cloves garlic, minced*

*1 onion, chopped (Walla Walla onions preferred, when in season)*

*1 green pepper, chopped*

*2 cups (about 6 oz) chopped chanterelle mushrooms*

*2 pounds Chilean sea bass, cut into bite-size chunks*

*½ cup freshly grated Parmesan cheese*

*3 or 4 Roma tomatoes, sliced ⅛ inch thick*

Preheat oven to 375°F. Take out an 8- by 8-inch baking dish or similarly sized casserole dish, grease lightly or spray with non-stick olive-oil spray, and set aside.

Heat olive oil in a large skillet over medium-high heat. Add garlic and cook until soft, about 2 minutes. Reduce heat to medium and add onion, pepper, and mushrooms, and sauté until vegetables are tender/crisp, about 3 minutes.

Add fish chunks and sauté until fish just begins to turn white, stirring occasionally, about 3 or 4 minutes. Spoon fish chunks and vegetables into baking dish, sprinkle with Parmesan cheese, and place tomato slices over the top. Bake until cheese melts, about 15 minutes. Serve as described above.

*Serves 4.*

# CAFE SPORT

Healthy is the watchword at Cafe Sport,* which has been serving up cutting-edge cuisine on Western Avenue since 1984. Next door to the Seattle Club (one of the prime spots for Seattle's Beautiful People, many of whom stop by here for a bite after their workouts), the Art Deco restaurant with its big storefront windows has a rather clubby atmosphere itself, yet the ambience is friendly and warm.

The food makes good use of the freshest Northwest ingredients, with Pacific Rim and New American treatments. Black bean soup, main-course salads with unusual local ingredients, grilled rare yellowfin tuna, crab cakes, and crème caramel (indeed, all the desserts) are menu standouts. An innovative addition is the "Light and Healthy" menu, with selections low in calories, cholesterol, fat, and sodium.

Weekend brunch is a good time to experience Cafe Sport; the selections are varied and outstanding as well as bargain priced. Also enjoy the lively, comfortable bar on a cold Seattle night.

*Just outside of the Market Historic District.

# Baked Sole with Vegetable Ragout

## — CAFE SPORT —

This entrée is one of the offerings from Cafe Sport's "Light & Healthy" menu, and has only 268 calories per serving. It's surprisingly simple to make and so full of flavorful vegetables that it makes a complete meal (no salad, vegetables, potatoes, or pasta needed). Just serve with whole wheat bread and a glass of white wine and you're set for a healthful evening!

*Juice and grated rind of 2 lemons*

*1 tablespoon minced garlic*

*16 ounces petrale or lemon sole, cut into 2-ounce strips*

*2 medium red potatoes, cut in half and sliced ½ inch thick*

*2 carrots, cut in half and sliced diagonally ½ inch thick*

*6 cups chicken stock, homemade or low-sodium storebought variety (Be sure not to substitute a conventional storebought, high-sodium chicken stock. Since the stock is reduced by half, the salt in the stock would become extra-concentrated and the ragout would be much too salty.)*

*2 tablespoons olive oil*

*¼ cup minced shallot*

*1 red bell pepper, cut into ½-inch dice*

*1 yellow bell pepper, cut into ½-inch dice*

*1 cup bread crumbs, homemade or storebought*

*2 zucchini, cut in half and sliced diagonally ¼ inch thick*

*½ pound asparagus, cut diagonally into 1-inch pieces*

*2 tablespoons minced fresh oregano*

*2 tablespoons minced fresh thyme*

*Salt and pepper to taste*

*Lemon wedges, for garnish*

Preheat oven to 475°F. Get out two baking sheets, brush lightly with olive oil, and set aside for later use.

Mix together lemon juice, rind, and garlic, and rub marinade onto sole fillets. Place in glass dish and set aside. Blanch potatoes and carrots in boiling water until cooked al dente, about 1 or 2 minutes. Remove from heat, cool in ice water, and drain.

In a medium saucepan, bring chicken stock to a boil and reduce by half. In a large skillet heat olive oil until just smoking. Add shallot and peppers, and sauté lightly (peppers should still be firm), about 1 or 2 minutes. Add stock and remove from heat.

Dredge sole fillets in bread crumbs. Place fillets on prepared baking sheet, allowing a little space between them. Bake 4 to 5 minutes (the fillets are very thin and will not take long to bake).

Meanwhile, put the shallot/pepper/stock mixture back on the stove on medium-high heat and add the zucchini, asparagus, carrots, and blanched potatoes, and half the oregano and thyme. Bring to a boil and cook until vegetables are al dente, about 5 to 7 minutes, stirring occasionally. Do not allow them to cook too long, or they will become mushy. Season very lightly with salt and pepper.

To serve, divide the ragout between four warmed dinner places, using all the sauce. Layer two pieces of sole on top of each plate. Sprinkle with remaining herbs, garnish with lemon wedges, and serve immediately.

*Serves 4.*

# LOWELL'S RESTAURANT

In 1908 a cup of coffee sold for 2 cents, a pound of coffee went for 30 cents, and Edward and William Manning spent $1,900 to open a coffee cafe in the Market. From this humble beginning grew a chain of 46 West Coast restaurants. Mannings Coffee House was sold in 1957, then sold again to one of its managers, Reid Lowell, who established Lowell's Cafeteria. Now owned by Bill Chatalas, Lowell's Restaurant in the Main Arcade has one of the greatest views of Elliott Bay and one of the tastiest fresh-carved turkey sandwiches in all of Seattle.

Fresh salmon, halibut, shark, oysters, and steamed clams and mussels are on the menu seasonally, and everything is cooked to order. Traditional breakfasts are popular and feature homestyle potatoes, fresh muffins, and fruit. Down-home desserts include apple crisp, carrot cake, and cookies. You can place your order in the cafeteria line on the first floor, or try full-service dining on the second floor. Large portions and good prices are the norm, and, according to General Manager Blake Morrison, "No one ever walks away hungry from Lowell's."

# *Halibut Cheeks en Papillote*

## LOWELL'S RESTAURANT

I n French, *en papillote* means "in paper."
In this elegant dish, choice halibut
cheeks are cooked with fresh vegetables
and dill butter in parchment paper to form
a rich sauce.

*1 carrot*

*1 red onion*

*2 ribs celery*

*1 red pepper*

*1¼ cups butter, softened (divided use)*

*4 tablespoons minced fresh dill (divided
use)*

*¼ cup white wine*

*Juice of 1 lemon wedge (one-sixth of a
lemon)*

*2¼ pounds (36 ounces) halibut cheeks
(about 6 ounces per serving)*

*Salt and pepper to taste*

*White or brown rice, prepared as package
directs*

*Lemon wedges and fresh dill sprigs, for
garnish*

Preheat oven to 375°F. Cut six 12- by
12-inch squares of parchment paper. Fold
squares in half, and cut into half-hearts.
Open and set aside. Get out two cookie
sheets and set aside.

Cut the carrot, onion, celery, and pepper
into matchstick-shaped pieces, approximately
3 inches long.

To make dill butter, place 1 cup (½ pound)
of the butter in a small mixing bowl. Add
3 tablespoons of the minced dill to the butter. Mix thoroughly, then refrigerate.

To make drawn butter, melt remaining
¼ cup butter in small skillet over low heat.
As white foam rises to top, skim and discard.
When only heavy yellow butter remains,
add wine, lemon juice, and the remaining
1 tablespoon of the minced dill, stir well,
and set aside.

Take out one parchment-paper heart.
Using a pastry brush, coat inside with drawn
butter, place about 6 ounces (one-sixth) of
the halibut cheeks along fold, and top with a
mixture of the vegetables. Dot with 1 tablespoon of the dill butter and add salt and
pepper to taste. Do not overstuff parchment,
as it needs room to expand during baking.

Fold half of parchment over fish and
vegetables, then fold over and roll edges of
parchment to seal tightly. It is very important that you form a tight seal all around,
or the parchment could pop open during
baking and the fish and vegetables will not
cook properly. Repeat with remaining pieces
of parchment, fish, and vegetables. (You
may have both leftover vegetables and fish
— if so, make an extra parchment packet
for tomorrow's lunch!)

Place parchment packets on cookie
sheets and bake until slightly puffed, approximately 15 to 20 minutes. As they heat
and if your seals are tight, the parchment
packets will fill with hot air, puff, and make
a buttery dill sauce for the fish.

To serve, place parchment packets on
dinner plates and, with a sharp knife or
kitchen shears, cut open packets in an
x-shaped pattern. Garnish with lemon
wedges and fresh dill sprigs, and serve
with a timbale of rice.

*Serves 6.*

# MR. D'S GREEK DELICACIES

As you walk through the Market, you'll often see hungry pedestrians frantically munching goopy yellow gyro cones before the ingredients all drop on the ground. Gyros, the street snack of Greece, are one of the specialties at Mr. D's Greek Delicacies.

Demetrios Moraitis, with his work-hardened hands and easy smile, is the namesake behind Mr. D's. At the south end of the Triangle Building, you'll often find him entertaining customers and passersby with his bouzouki (Greek mandolin) playing, singing, and dancing. Sometimes he even carves the spinning hunk of gyro meat into likenesses of former U.S. presidents, the Venus de Milo, or Seattle curmudgeon Emmett Watson. "The Market is a great place to express yourself. It has a power, drawing people together," Mr. D says in his thick Greek accent. "I enjoy working in an atmosphere of smiles and laughter, of song and dance. Who wouldn't?"

Mr. D had a successful restaurant in downtown Seattle before opening Mr. D's in the Market. Trout à la Grecque, with its garlic- and thyme-infused marinade, is an adaptation for home cooks of one of his former restaurant's signature dishes.

## *Trout à la Grecque*

— MR. D'S GREEK DELICACIES —

Trout is an economical fish with a delicate flavor, and this recipe uses it to good advantage. Mr. D suggests serving it with a Greek salad (ripe tomatoes, Greek olives, and feta cheese), rice pilaf or French fries, and fresh green vegetables that have been lightly steamed.

*¼ cup olive oil*

*Juice of 1 lemon*

*1 teaspoon dried thyme*

*4 cloves garlic, minced*

*Salt and pepper to taste*

*4 whole trout (about 8 oz each), filleted, and with heads and tails removed*

*½ cup dry white wine*

Preheat broiler. Mix olive oil, lemon juice, thyme, garlic, salt, and pepper in a small glass mixing bowl. Place fish skin side down in a large skillet with an ovenproof handle (or wrap handle in aluminum foil to protect it from heat). Spread fish out so that both halves are open and lie flat in a butterflied position.

Drizzle half the olive oil mixture evenly over fish and place under broiler. Cook about 3 minutes, or until fish is opaque but not done.

Remove skillet from oven and place on stove top over medium heat. Mix wine with remaining half of olive oil mixture. When pan is hot, add wine/olive oil mixture to pan and cook, spooning liquid over fish. Continue cooking and spooning liquid over fish until fish is tender and just begins to flake, about 3 minutes more.

Remove trout to dinner plates and serve immediately.

*Serves 4.*

# IL BISTRO

IL BISTRO Tucked under the Market Theater sign on a cobbled street affectionately known by locals as "Urine Alley," Il Bistro is one of those warm, inviting places that keeps calling you back. A wall full of windows allows light into the almost cavelike subterranean space, with its well-worn oriental rugs, dark furniture, and muted jazz playing in the background.

At lunch the place is almost bright, the food less expensive, the crowd a mixed bag of businessmen and knowledgeable tourists. But the mood changes by night, when a Jaguar or Rolls is invariably parked outside, and lovers celebrate special occasions with goblets of red wine, hearty cioppino, or rack of lamb. The bar is worth trying in and of itself, for it's as atmospheric as the dining room, with a wide selection of coffee drinks, single-malt Scotches, brandies, and cognacs.

## *Prawns Aglio*

### — IL BISTRO —

This dish is so Italian—*aglio* means "garlic" in Italian, and this prawn dish is full of the healthful bulb, along with tomatoes, basil, oregano, and olive oil. Be sure to assemble all the ingredients before cooking, as it cooks very fast, and each ingredient must keep its identity.

1 tablespoon olive oil

12 medium prawns, shrimp, or scampi, cut up back of shell with scissors to devein, but with complete shells left on (if using large scampi, increase cooking time and amount of vermouth added to sauce)

1 tablespoon minced fresh garlic

1 tablespoon minced fresh basil

1 tablespoon fresh oregano or 1 teaspoon dried oregano

2 Roma tomatoes, cored and sliced through center into ⅛-inch rounds

Salt and pepper to taste

Half a lemon

¼ cup dry white vermouth (Boissiere brand preferred)

1 tablespoon butter

Lemon slices and parsley, for garnish

Heat oil in large skillet over medium-high heat (oil should be smoking). Add prawns, garlic, basil, oregano, tomatoes, and salt and pepper to taste. Cook until prawns and garlic are browned, about 1 to 2 minutes.

Squeeze the lemon, add lemon juice and vermouth to skillet, and cook until prawns turn white inside, about 1 to 2 minutes. Remove prawns from skillet and place on four small appetizer plates or one large dinner plate.

Add butter to pan and cook for 1 to 2 minutes, then pour over prawns. Garnish with lemon slices and parsley.

*Serves 1 as a main dish, 4 as an appetizer.*

*Note:* Cooking prawns or shrimp in their shell, instead of shelling completely or leaving just the tails on, keeps them from getting tough.

# Shrimp Curry

#### THE SOUK

This is a simple, satisfying, not-too-spicy curry dish, good for newcomers to Indian food.

¼ cup butter

3 cloves garlic, crushed

2 large onions, sliced

½ teaspoon ground cumin

¼ teaspoon ground black pepper

¼ teaspoon ground cayenne pepper

¼ teaspoon ground turmeric

1 can (14½ oz) whole tomatoes and their juice

Salt to taste

¼ cup warm water (optional)

1 pound shrimp, shelled and cooked

Melt butter in large skillet over medium heat, and add garlic and onions. When onions begin to brown, add cumin, black pepper, cayenne, and turmeric, and cook and stir for 2 minutes.

Reduce heat to low, add tomatoes and their juice and salt to taste, and stir constantly until tomato juice has evaporated. Add shrimp, mix well, and cook for about 5 minutes.

For additional sauce, add ¼ cup warm water before adding shrimp. Serve over rice, or with Pea Pullao (see page 70).

*Serves 4.*

# Alf's Cracked Crab

#### SUR LA TABLE

Shirley Collins, owner of Sur La Table, credits this unusual recipe for freshly cracked crab to her husband, Alf, former restaurant critic for the *Seattle Times*. For variety you can substitute shallots and fennel for the garlic and parsley.

1 large Dungeness crab (about 3 lb), cleaned as described below

½ cup first-press, extra-virgin olive oil

4 cloves garlic, minced

The butter from the crab shell

½ cup finely minced parsley

When crab is in season, ask your fishmonger to clean out the lungs of a large crab but keep the back shell intact. The shell has a creamy yellow pulp on the inside called the "butter." You want to keep the shell so that you can remove the butter and use it in your sauce.

Mix together the olive oil, garlic, butter scraped from the crab shell, and parsley. Rinse the whole crab, then crack gently and marinate in the olive-oil marinade for 30 minutes at room temperature.

Serve one-half crab to each person with lots of coarse country bread and a fresh green salad with vinaigrette dressing.

*Serves 2.*

# Local Chefs
# Cook at the Market

## Local Chefs Cook at the Market

Pork and Clams (Cataplana)

Dungeness Crab Cakes with Orange-Soy Butter

Ragout of Seafood with Herbed Riesling Butter, Served
in a Noodle Basket

Steamed Mussels Pigalle

Shrimp and Shiitake Mushroom Dumplings with Sake Sauce

Chicken with Rhubarb Sauce

# LOCAL CHEFS COOK AT THE MARKET In early

1991, the Merchants Association began a series of cooking demonstrations in which celebrity chefs were invited to come to the Market and use its fresh ingredients to cook their favorite recipes. Market merchants donated the necessary foods and spices, and the chefs prepared their recipes under the famous Market clock, exposed to the elements (often Seattle drizzle and chilling wind) and only inches from the sometimes restive crowds.

Jeff Smith, The Frugal Gourmet, and his culinary assistant, Craig Wollam, inaugurated the promotion. More than 500 people attended, some arriving as early as 10:30 or 11:00 for the demonstration at noon. Many in the crowd had watched Jeff's career skyrocket over the years, and were there to pay him homage—there was lots of handshaking, book autographing, baby kissing, and joy.

Jeff, well known from his nationally syndicated public television show, and the author of (among others) *The Frugal Gourmet*, *The Frugal Gourmet Cooks Three Ancient Cuisines*, *The Frugal Gourmet's Culinary Handbook* (with coauthor Craig Wollam), and *The Frugal Gourmet Celebrates Christmas*, is truly one of Seattle's favorite sons.

Next came Caprial Pence, co-chef de cuisine with her husband, John, at Fullers in the Sheraton Hotel & Towers. "Cappy," a bright, friendly young woman as chipper as her nickname, demonstrated Dungeness Crab Cakes with Orange-Soy Butter. Born in Portland, Caprial graduated from the Culinary Institute of America in Hyde Park, New York, and worked at the Shelburne Inn in Long Beach, Washington, and Dominique's Place in Seattle before joining Fullers.

A rising star among chefs, she won a James Beard Award (like an Oscar for the food and beverage industries) in 1991 as the best chef in the Northwest. She has also won Golden Fork Awards, the Mobil Four-Star Award, and the *Travel-Holiday* Fine Dining Award. She received the first invitation from the former Soviet Union to an American chef and accompanying team, and traveled to Moscow, where she prepared a meal for Soviet officials and the U.S. ambassador to the Soviet Union, and then continued on to the Republic of Georgia, where she demonstrated her skills for Georgian dignitaries.

Barbara Figueroa, executive chef of the Hunt Club at the Sorrento Hotel, appeared in a tomato-red leather bomber jacket and her trademark dangling earrings and cooked three lavish dishes. This Long Island native started out studying to be a physical therapist, but after receiving encouragement from none other than the late James Beard, changed her major and attended the culinary program at New York City Community College.

She apprenticed in France with André Daguin, worked at the Waldorf Astoria, Le Cirque, and Jams in New York City, and tried her hand in Los Angeles at Spago (with Wolfgang Puck) and Camelion before coming to the Sorrento in 1987. Barbara is a contributing editor for *Gastronome,* Chef Guillardin for the Seattle chapter of the Chaine des Rotisseurs, a visiting chef at The Herbfarm, and a member of Save Our Strength, a group of culinary professionals from across the nation whose goal is to help fight hunger.

Next up was Dana Drummond, then chef of Place Pigalle, who cooked one of the restaurant's signature dishes, Steamed Mussels Pigalle, and demonstrated how to work with fresh rabbit. Dana received her B.S. degree in Food Systems Economics and Management from Michigan State University, and graduated from the Culinary Institute of America in 1987.

She worked at Aurora, Aureole, and La Galoise in New York City before moving to the West Coast to "get a life," where she signed on at Place Pigalle as sous chef. She left the restaurant in April 1991, and now works as kitchen manager at the Bagel Oasis in Ravenna. In the future she plans to return to her home state of Michigan and open a healthy foods bakery/soup/salad shop.

Tom Douglas, chef/co-owner (along with his wife, Jackie Cross) of the Dahlia Lounge, cooked one of their popular restaurant's most famous dishes—Dahlia Crab Cakes. A Falstaffian figure with long blond curls, a full beard, and a penchant for the Mariners, Tom hails from Newark, Delaware. Although his only formal culinary training was a high school home economics class, he felt entirely at home cooking in the Market, since for years he was the driving force behind Cafe Sport.

Francois Kissel, chef/owner of Maximilien-in-the-Market, rounded out the cooking demonstrations by preparing four French-inspired dishes. A diminutive yet vibrantly intense man with a deep, husky voice and a thick French accent, Francois was born and raised in Saigon and received his degree in hotel management from L'Ecole Hotelier de Paris, Jean Drouant.

In 1962 he came to the United States and worked at the Fleur de Lys and Trader Vic's in San Francisco. He worked at the Trader Vic's in Seattle and owned the sorely missed Brasserie Pittsbourg in Pioneer Square. He won the gold medal at the Culinary Olympics in Frankfurt in 1976, was knighted by the French government in 1981, and was a founding member of the Pacific Northwest Enological Society. Every year during the holiday season, Francois and his volunteers cook for the homeless. During 1990, between Thanksgiving and New Year's, they cooked 22,000 meals at St. Mark's Cathedral.

The six-week-long series of Thursday afternoon cooking demonstrations was a great success. The demonstrations infused the Market with a special excitement felt by merchants, curious cooks, passersby, and residents alike. It was a pleasure to watch each chef prepare his or her favorite dishes.

Here are Jeff Smith's Pork and Clams, Caprial Pence's Dungeness Crab Cakes, Barbara Figueroa's Ragout of Seafood, Dana Drummond's Steamed Mussels Pigalle, Tom Douglas's Shrimp and Shiitake Mushroom Dumplings (Tom didn't want to reprint his crab cake recipe because of a possible new business venture, so he substituted the dumplings), and Francois Kissel's Chicken with Rhubarb Sauce. The recipes have been devised with the home cook in mind for the enjoyment of family and friends, and all the ingredients are available at the Market.

*Note:* As the book went to press, I learned that Caprial and John were off to Portland to open their own restaurant. Seattle's loss is truly Portland's gain.

# Pork and Clams (Cataplana)

JEFF SMITH, THE FRUGAL GOURMET

The crowds went wild when Jeff Smith cooked this dish of Portuguese origin from his book *The Frugal Gourmet on Our Immigrant Ancestors*. You'll enjoy its hearty, spicy flavor, and its ease of preparation, too.

*2 pounds boneless pork butt, cut into 1-inch cubes*

*1½ cups dry white wine*

*2 cloves garlic, minced*

*Dash of Piri Piri (recipe follows; try about 2 teaspoons to start; more can be added later to taste)*

*1½ teaspoons salt (divided use)*

*½ teaspoon finely ground black pepper (divided use)*

*2 bay leaves*

*¼ cup olive oil (divided use)*

*4 teaspoons paprika*

*2 medium onions, thinly sliced*

*2 pounds small clams, in the shell*

Place pork cubes in a large bowl. Mix together wine, garlic, Piri Piri, 1 teaspoon of the salt, ¼ teaspoon of the pepper, and bay leaves, and pour the mixture over the meat. Allow to marinate 2 hours. Drain meat well, reserving marinade.

Heat 2 tablespoons of the olive oil in a heavy frying pan over medium-high heat and brown pork. Place pork and oil in a heavy 8-quart stovetop casserole dish and add reserved marinade and paprika.

Simmer the meat in the juices, uncovered, until the juices almost evaporate,
about 45 minutes. Skim the fat and discard bay leaves.

Meanwhile, in a deep saucepan, sauté onions in the remaining 2 tablespoons olive oil until tender but not discolored. Add clams, the remaining ½ teaspoon salt, and the remaining ¼ teaspoon pepper. Cook over high heat, covered, for 5 minutes, or until the clams open. Add clams and juice to pork and heat through.

**Piri Piri:** Fill a 1-quart glass canning jar one-third full of tiny, hot, dried red peppers. Add ½ cup whiskey and fill jar with a mixture of half olive oil and half vegetable oil. Cap and let sit one month before using, shaking now and then during curing process. Add more oil as you use up the sauce. This recipe makes 1 quart and can also be cut in half.

*Serves 5 or 6.*

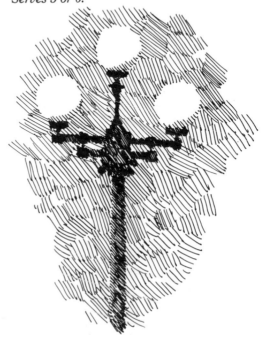

# *Dungeness Crab Cakes with Orange-Soy Butter*

CAPRIAL PENCE, FULLERS, SEATTLE SHERATON HOTEL & TOWERS

These crab cakes are spicy-hot, but the Orange-Soy Butter soothes the burn. Make the Orange-Soy Butter first and hold it until you are ready to serve it with the crab cakes. You can buy *sambal oelek,* Malaysian pepper sauce, in the Pike Place Market at the Souk.

1½ *cups Dungeness crabmeat*

2 *shallots, minced*

3 *cloves garlic, minced*

1 *teaspoon minced fresh ginger*

1 *red pepper, finely diced*

¼ *cup fresh bread crumbs*

⅓ *cup whipping cream*

2 *eggs, slightly beaten*

*Sambal oelek (Malaysian pepper sauce, available at Middle Eastern groceries or specialty spice shops) to taste (try about ½ teaspoon to begin, then add another ½ teaspoon, if desired)*

*Salt and pepper to taste*

*Flour, for dredging*

2 *tablespoons vegetable oil*

ORANGE-SOY BUTTER

½ *cup white wine*

½ *teaspoon rice wine vinegar*

1 *cup orange juice*

2 *shallots, minced*

1 *teaspoon minced fresh ginger*

1 *cup (½ lb) unsalted butter*

1 *teaspoon soy sauce*

*Dash of Oriental sesame oil*

*Salt and pepper*

*Chopped chives, orange zest, and black sesame seed, for garnish*

If crab seems excessively watery, gently squeeze crabmeat to remove as much of the liquid as possible, then place it in a large bowl. Add the shallots, garlic, ginger, red pepper, and bread crumbs, and mix well. Add cream and eggs to mixture and mix well.

Season with *sambal oelek* and salt and pepper. Chill for 30 minutes (do not chill crab cakes more than 30 minutes before cooking, or they may not stick together properly).

Make Orange-Soy Butter. Form crab mixture into eight patties 2 inches in diameter and ¼ inch thick. If crab cakes are too dry to form into patties easily, you can add another egg or a bit more whipping cream. Shape patties, then dredge crab cakes in flour.

Heat oil in a large sauté pan over medium heat until hot, and brown crab cakes well on each side. Drain on paper towels.

To serve, place a circle of Orange-Soy Butter on warmed dinner plates, and place two crab cakes on each plate. Garnish with chives, orange zest, and black sesame seed.

**Orange-Soy Butter:** Place white wine, rice wine vinegar, orange juice, shallots, and ginger in a medium-size saucepan. Cook over high heat until reduced to ¼ cup liquid. Turn heat to low and whisk in butter slowly. Season with soy sauce, sesame oil, and salt and pepper. Strain and keep warm in a warm (not hot) water bath until ready to serve with crab cakes.

*Serves 4.*

# *Ragout of Seafood with Herbed Riesling Butter, Served in a Noodle Basket*

───────── BARBARA FIGUEROA, THE HUNT CLUB AT THE SORRENTO HOTEL ─────────

This is a surprisingly easy dish for such an elegant look and taste; it's great served in a pasta basket as an appetizer, as Chef Figueroa suggests, or over angel hair pasta cooked al dente as an entrée. Whichever way you serve it, you'll want to lap up the sauce with a spoon!

¾ cup Johannisberg Riesling wine

1 teaspoon balsamic vinegar

1 tablespoon chopped shallot

½ cup whipping cream

½ tablespoon butter

½ tablespoon olive oil

1 tablespoon mixture of fresh minced tarragon, chives, and chervil

1 tablespoon peanut oil

8 ounces salmon fillet

5 ounces scallops (singing pink or bay)

5 ounces smoked mussels

2 ounces smoked salmon strips, cut into 1-inch julienne

Vegetable oil, for deep frying

4 ounces fresh angel hair pasta

Fresh herb sprigs, for garnish

Heat the Riesling, vinegar, and shallot in a medium saucepan over high heat and cook until reduced to 2 tablespoons. Add cream; cook until reduced to 3 tablespoons. Whisk in butter and oil. Strain; add herbs.

Heat the peanut oil in a large skillet over medium heat. Add salmon and sauté until tender (do not overcook). Cut salmon into ½-inch cubes. Add scallops to same pan and sauté until almost done. Turn heat to low, add all seafood to pan, and heat gently. Remove from heat and set aside.

Add vegetable oil to a large skillet or saucepan to a depth of 3 or 4 inches and heat to 375°F on a deep-fat thermometer. Press a fourth of the fresh pasta into a small frying basket (2½- or 3½-inch), place another basket on top, press handles together, and fry until crisp. Drain on paper towels (yields four baskets).

To serve, mix seafood with sauce. Place pasta baskets on four appetizer plates, ladle a quarter of seafood ragout into each basket, and garnish with a sprig of fresh herb. If you don't want to go to the trouble of making the pasta baskets but still want to enjoy the sauce, just boil the fresh angel hair pasta until cooked al dente, drain, divide between two dinner plates, and ladle the ragout over the top. Garnish with a sprig of fresh herb and enjoy with a tossed green salad, crusty bread, and a good bottle of white wine (or the rest of the Johannisberg Riesling).

*Serves 4 as an appetizer, 2 as an entrée.*

# Steamed Mussels Pigalle

Dana Drummond, Place Pigalle

This is one of the signature dishes at Place Pigalle (Pig Alley), rich with bacon, celery, and shallots, and infused with a balsamic vinaigrette.

*6 strips smoked bacon, diced*

*2 stalks celery, diced*

*2 tablespoons diced shallots*

*½ teaspoon celery seed*

*1 cup parsley*

*1 tablespoon Dijon mustard*

*1 cup balsamic vinegar (divided use)*

*1½ cups oil (soy, peanut, or olive)*

*2 pounds Penn Cove mussels*

*1 cup white wine*

Heat a medium skillet over medium-high heat and add bacon. After bacon starts releasing its fat, add celery and sauté, stirring occasionally, until bacon turns brown. Drain off excess fat and set aside.

Place shallot, celery seed, parsley, mustard, and ½ cup of the balsamic vinegar in a food processor and process until shallot and parsley are finely chopped. Slowly add oil to form an emulsified vinaigrette.

Place the sautéed bacon/celery mixture, mussels, and white wine in a sauté pan. Cover pan, place over medium heat, and steam the mussels until fully open, about 5 minutes. Discard any mussels that do not open.

Remove mussels from pan, retaining as much of the liquid as possible in the pan. Boil liquid to reduce until almost dry. Add remaining ½ cup balsamic vinegar and reduce until almost dry. Add vinaigrette and warm evenly (be careful not to boil the vinaigrette, or it might break).

Place the mussels in individual serving bowls with the open edges facing up. Pour vinaigrette over mussels, and serve. Be sure to provide an extra bowl for the empty mussel shells, and serve with lots of crusty French bread for soaking up the sauce.

*Serves 4.*

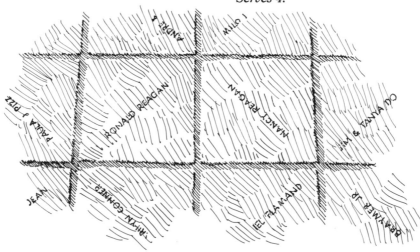

# Shrimp and Shiitake Mushroom Dumplings with Sake Sauce

————— TOM DOUGLAS, DAHLIA LOUNGE —————

This variation on dim sum is an original Tom Douglas recipe, inspired by a meal he enjoyed at a local Chinese restaurant. It makes a great appetizer before an Oriental meal.

*1 pound prawns, peeled and deveined*

*1 green onion, chopped*

*2 tablespoons chopped cilantro*

*2 cups mung bean sprouts*

*2 tablespoons soy sauce*

*½ teaspoon crushed red pepper flakes*

*1 tablespoon sesame seed*

*½ cup coarsely chopped shiitake mushrooms*

*¼ cup peanut oil*

*1 cup chicken stock*

*Additional mung bean sprouts, for garnish*

SAKE SAUCE
*½ cup sake*

*¼ cup soy sauce*

*⅓ cup rice wine vinegar*

*2 tablespoons Vietnamese fish sauce (nuoc mam)*

*1½ teaspoons red chile paste with garlic*

*2 tablespoons sliced green onion*

Purée prawns in food processor. Remove prawns to a large bowl and fold in green onion, cilantro, bean sprouts, soy sauce, red pepper flakes, sesame seed, and shiitake mushrooms. Cover and chill.

Make Sake Sauce. Using a soup spoon, form prawn mixture into 1-inch balls and flatten slightly with the back of a spoon.

Heat peanut oil in a large skillet over medium heat. Fry dumplings in batches until light golden brown on both sides, adding more oil as necessary. When all dumplings have been browned, drain off excess oil and return all dumplings to the pan.

Add chicken stock to the dumplings, bring to a boil, cover pan with a lid or foil, and simmer for 3 to 5 minutes. Dumplings are done when they are springy and firm to the touch — cut one open if in doubt. *Do not overcook*, or dumplings will become rubbery.

Lift dumplings out of stock and arrange on large serving platter or individual appetizer plates. Ladle Sake Sauce over all and garnish with bean sprouts.

**Sake Sauce:** Mix all ingredients together in a small glass dish, cover, and set aside or refrigerate until ready to use.

*Serves 4 to 6.*

# Chicken with Rhubarb Sauce

FRANCOIS KISSEL, MAXIMILIEN-IN-THE-MARKET

This dish is quintessentially French in execution, with a Northwest twist — rhubarb. The rhubarb melds with the butter, leeks, and onions to form a subtle, tasty sauce. You could make it as early as February, when the first crop of hothouse rhubarb comes to the highstalls, or wait until April, May, or June, when outdoor rhubarb (reputed to be more acidic and flavorful) is available on the farmers' tables or in the highstalls.

*1 tablespoon butter*

*1 leek, white part only, washed and chopped into ¼-inch pieces*

*2 teaspoons butter*

*Half an onion, chopped into ¼-inch pieces*

*6-inch stalk of fresh rhubarb, sliced ¼ inch thick*

*2 tablespoons chicken broth or water*

*6 chicken breasts, boned, skinned, and cut into 1-inch pieces*

*Salt or granulated garlic to taste*

*Flour, for dredging chicken pieces*

*2 tablespoons butter*

*1 cup chicken broth*

*Salt and pepper to taste*

*2 tablespoons Triple Sec*

Melt the 1 tablespoon butter in a small skillet over medium heat, and cook the leek until tender. Melt the 2 teaspoons butter in another small skillet over medium heat, and cook the onion until lightly browned.

**To prepare rhubarb purée:** Place rhubarb slices in a small glass dish, add the 2 tablespoons chicken broth or water, cover and vent with plastic wrap, and microwave on HIGH 2 or 3 minutes, or until tender. Put in blender or through ricer and purée. Measure ½ cup of the rhubarb purée and mix together with the leek and onion to make rhubarb sauce. Set aside.

Season chicken pieces with salt (or sprinkle lightly with granulated garlic) and dredge in flour. Melt the 2 tablespoons butter in a large skillet over medium-high heat and cook chicken pieces until lightly browned.

Add rhubarb sauce and the 1 cup chicken broth. Season to taste with salt and pepper. Bring mixture to a boil, cover, and simmer 1 or 2 minutes, or until chicken is fully cooked and tender, but not rubbery. If sauce becomes too thick, add a bit more chicken broth.

When ready to serve, remove from heat and stir in the Triple Sec. Serve with or over rice or pasta with steamed vegetables.

*Serves 6.*

# *Desserts*

## Desserts

Hazelnut Chocolate Chip Cookies

Choco-Coffee Macaroon Cookies

Cappuccino Chip Coffee Bars

Seattle's Best Sour Cream Coffee Cake

Chocolate Cognac Pâté with Crème Anglaise

Tiramisu

Irish Coffee Truffles

Royal Chocolate Truffles

Chocolate Espresso Cheesecake

Lemon Ice

Earl Grey Sorbet

Edith's Blueberry Pie

Blueberry-Peach Cobbler

Blackberry Mousse with Lemon Madeleines

Raspberries with Honey-Almond Cream

Lemon Sponge Pudding

Plum-Walnut Confections

Berry-Filled Squares

Frosty Strawberry Squares

German Apple Cake

Apricot Pie

Hazelnut Cherry Pie

Raspberry Pie

Sour Cream Cranberry Pie

Caramel Corn Lollypops

Jelly Bean Jumble

Holiday Doughnut Trees

# HOLMQUIST HAZELNUT ORCHARD

Holmquist Hazelnut Orchard was founded in 1928 and is owned by Gerald Holmquist, whose grandson is the sixth generation to live on the farm. Located in Lynden, the orchard nudges the Canadian border and has sweeping views of Mount Baker and the Canadian coastal range.

"Washington state grows about 3 percent of the hazelnuts in the United States, compared to Oregon's 97 percent," Gerald explains. "Hazelnuts grow on bushes that are cultivated into trees. When the nuts are ripe, we fly overhead in a helicopter and the air currents from the blades propel the hazelnuts to fall to the ground. The grass under the trees is mowed like a golf-course putting green so that the nuts can be easily gathered."

Holmquist hazelnuts are grown both organically and conventionally and are available in the shell, natural, or roasted. Wednesdays through Saturdays from early spring through summer, you'll find Holmquist hazelnuts in the North Arcade.

## *Hazelnut Chocolate Chip Cookies*

### HOLMQUIST HAZELNUT ORCHARD

These big cookie-jar cookies, brimming with hazelnuts and chocolate, would be great for a lunchbox or after-school snack. If possible, use Holmquist hazelnuts; they're lower in fat and sweeter than normal hazelnuts (more like a cross between an almond and a hazelnut) and make a less greasy, more flavorful cookie.

*2 eggs*

*½ cup granulated sugar*

*1½ cups firmly packed brown sugar*

*2 teaspoons vanilla extract*

*1 cup light vegetable oil, such as canola, corn, or soy*

*2½ cups flour*

*1 teaspoon salt*

*1 teaspoon baking soda*

*1 cup toasted, chopped hazelnuts (see Techniques section)*

*1 cup semisweet chocolate chips*

Preheat oven to 350°F. Take out two cookie sheets and grease lightly or spray with non-stick corn-oil spray. Set aside.

In large mixing bowl beat eggs with whisk until frothy and light. Add sugars and vanilla and whisk until well blended and smooth. Add oil and beat until thoroughly incorporated.

Sift flour with salt and baking soda into wet mixture and mix thoroughly with large spoon (dough will be sticky). Fold in nuts and chocolate chips.

Drop by rounded tablespoons onto cookie sheets, leaving about 2 inches between dough pieces so cookies can spread as they cook. Cook until golden brown around edges, 10 to 12 minutes.

Allow cookies to cool on cookie sheets on wire racks for 1 or 2 minutes, then remove with spatula to wire racks to cool completely.

*Makes 32 cookies.*

# SANO'S ESPRESSO

Sano's Espresso* features espresso drinks made with B & O Special Coffee, scrumptious pastries, Italian sodas, and frozen yogurt. Owner Mazen Elkader, a jovial man originally from Jordan, brings a sense of fun to his espresso bar, with early-morning specials and a late-afternoon happy hour.

Sweet treats are real standouts here, with Uncle Seth's shortbread, oatmeal raisin, and peanut butter cookies; cream cheese and raspberry Danish; plain, blueberry, and raisin scones; *palmiers* (caramelized pastries made of puff pastry dough) and bear claws among the most tempting. In the summer, Mazen puts up tables, chairs, and flower boxes along the sidewalk on First Avenue. In the winter there's an L-shaped counter and a couple of stools inside, a good place to grab a quick espresso and a sinfully rich rum ball.

*Just outside of the Market Historic District.

## *Choco-Coffee Macaroon Cookies*

### SANO'S ESPRESSO

A light, puffy cookie bursting with chocolate, coconut, and a hint of coffee, Choco-Coffee Macaroon Cookies are great for the holidays and freeze well.

½ cup butter, melted

4 squares (1 oz each) unsweetened chocolate, melted

4 eggs

2 teaspoons vanilla extract

2 cups sifted flour

2 teaspoons baking powder

2 cups sugar

½ teaspoon salt

2 cups sweetened coconut (Baker's Angel Flake brand preferred)

½ cup finely chopped walnuts

2 tablespoons dark roast coffee, espresso grind (do not use liquid espresso or instant espresso powder)

½ cup sifted cocoa

½ cup sifted confectioners' sugar

Combine butter and chocolate in a large mixing bowl. With a whisk, beat in eggs and vanilla until thoroughly blended. Add flour, baking powder, sugar, and salt, and mix well. Add coconut, walnuts, and ground coffee, and mix thoroughly (dough will be dry). Cover bowl and place in refrigerator several hours or overnight.

Preheat oven to 375°F. Get out two cookie sheets. In a pie plate or shallow dish, mix together cocoa and confectioners' sugar until thoroughly blended. Working quickly, form dough into golf-ball-sized balls, then roll dough balls in the cocoa/confectioners' sugar mixture.

Place balls on cookie sheets about 2 inches apart and bake until edges are set and cookies are puffy, about 10 to 12 minutes. Remove cookies from oven and let cool on cookie sheets 1 or 2 minutes, then remove cookies to a wire rack to cool completely. Store in an airtight container or freeze for later use.

*Makes 4 dozen cookies.*

# Cappuccino Chip Coffee Bars

### SBC, SEATTLE'S BEST COFFEE

These dessert bars are chock-full of cinnamon, chocolate, and coffee; they're a great pick-me-up with a caffe latte around 3 p.m.

⅓ cup solid vegetable shortening

1 cup firmly packed brown sugar

1 egg

½ cup double-strength hot coffee or espresso

1⅔ cups sifted flour

½ teaspoon baking powder

½ teaspoon baking soda

½ teaspoon salt

½ teaspoon cinnamon

½ cup chocolate chips

¼ cup chopped walnuts

COFFEE GLAZE
1½ cups sifted confectioners' sugar

1 tablespoon butter, softened

1 teaspoon vanilla extract

3 tablespoons strong, hot coffee or espresso

Preheat oven to 375°F. Take out a 9- by 13-inch baking pan and grease lightly or spray with nonstick corn-oil spray.

Cream shortening and brown sugar; blend in egg and the ½ cup coffee. Sift flour with baking powder, baking soda, salt, and cinnamon. Mix well with wet ingredients and stir in chocolate chips and walnuts. Spread batter in baking pan and bake until bars turn golden and toothpick inserted in center comes out clean, 10 to 15 minutes. Cool in baking pan on wire rack.

**To make coffee glaze:** In small mixing bowl blend confectioners' sugar and butter until smooth, then slowly drizzle in vanilla and the 3 tablespoons coffee to make a thin icing (add more coffee if needed). Pour over cooled bars in baking pan and, when icing is set, cut into squares.

*Makes 20 bars.*

# Seattle's Best Sour Cream Coffee Cake

SBC, SEATTLE'S BEST COFFEE

This is a rich, eggy coffee cake you won't be able to resist, and it's not just for breakfast. The hazelnuts throughout the batter, the coffee glaze, and the finely ground coffee on top are unusual touches that make this a recipe to treasure.

½ cup unsalted butter, softened

1 cup granulated sugar

2 eggs

1 tablespoon double-strength coffee or espresso

1 teaspoon vanilla extract

1¾ cups sifted flour

2 teaspoons baking powder

1 teaspoon baking soda

½ teaspoon salt

1 cup sour cream

⅓ cup firmly packed light brown sugar

⅓ cup toasted, chopped hazelnuts (see Techniques section)

½ teaspoon ground nutmeg

COFFEE GLAZE

1 cup confectioners' sugar

3 tablespoons double-strength coffee or espresso

½ teaspoon half-and-half

¼ teaspoon vanilla extract

Confectioners' sugar, sifted

*Pinch of finely ground coffee — Turkish grind (you can use any type coffee you wish in this recipe, as long as it is ground with a Turkish grind, the finest grind of coffee)*

Preheat oven to 350°F. Take out a 12-cup bundt pan, grease lightly or spray with nonstick corn-oil spray, and set aside.

In a large mixing bowl, whisk the butter and sugar together. Beat in the eggs one at a time until well blended. Stir in the 1 tablespoon coffee and the 1 teaspoon vanilla.

Mix together the flour, baking powder, baking soda, and salt and add the flour mixture to the wet ingredients, alternating with the sour cream, until well blended. Combine the brown sugar, hazelnuts, and nutmeg in a small bowl.

Spread one-half of the batter in the bottom of the bundt pan. Sprinkle one-half of the hazelnut mixture over the batter. Pour remaining batter over top, then finish with remaining hazelnut mixture.

Bake until a toothpick inserted in middle of cake comes out clean, 35 to 45 minutes. Let coffee cake cool on wire rack for 15 minutes before removing from pan.

**To make coffee glaze:** Whisk the 1 cup confectioners' sugar, the 3 tablespoons coffee or espresso, half-and-half, and the ¼ teaspoon vanilla in a small bowl and drizzle over cake while still warm. Let cake stand for 15 minutes to absorb glaze. Dust with confectioners' sugar and ground coffee just before cutting and serving.

*Serves 8 to 10.*

# *Chocolate Cognac Pâté with Crème Anglaise*

CAFÉ SOPHIE

This is a great dessert to serve at dinner parties or over the holidays, because the pâté can be made up to a week ahead, then sliced and served when guests arrive. It's even easier if you substitute softly whipped, slightly sweetened whipping cream for the Crème Anglaise. Dried Montmorency cherries are available in the Market at Chukar Cherry Company.

*2 tablespoons Cognac*

*½ cup golden raisins*

*1 tablespoon kirsch (cherry brandy)*

*¼ cup dried Montmorency (tart) cherries*

*1 pound semisweet chocolate, Guittard brand preferred*

*1¼ cups (10 oz) unsalted butter*

*½ cup whipping cream*

*½ cup chopped pecans*

*10 eggs, separated*

CRÈME ANGLAISE

*8 egg yolks*

*1 cup sugar*

*2 cups milk*

*1 vanilla bean*

Line a 4½- by 12½-inch loaf pan with aluminum foil, and set aside.

Get out two small saucepans. In the first combine Cognac and raisins; in the second combine kirsch and dried cherries. Place both over low heat and allow to warm, then remove from heat and set aside.

Break chocolate into small pieces, and melt with butter in a double boiler over low heat. Remove from heat and stir in cream, pecans, raisins, and cherries (plus the juice of the raisins and cherries). Whisk in egg yolks, one at a time, until combined.

With a wire whisk or electric mixer, whip egg whites until soft peaks form. Gently fold in half of the chocolate mixture, then fold in the remaining chocolate mixture.

Pour mixture into prepared loaf pan. Wrap in plastic and refrigerate overnight. (Mixture can be made ahead up to this point and refrigerated, tightly wrapped in plastic, for up to 1 week.)

To serve pour a small pool of chilled Crème Anglaise onto each of 12 dessert plates. Cut the pâté into 12 slices, then place 1 slice on each plate, over the pool of Crème Anglaise.

**Crème Anglaise:** In a large bowl whip together egg yolks and sugar until pale and creamy. Meanwhile, in a saucepan, combine milk and vanilla bean and bring to a boil. Remove bean and set it aside for later use.

Pour hot milk into egg/sugar mixture, stirring constantly. Return mixture to saucepan. Cook over low heat, stirring constantly, until sauce thickens and coats the back of a spoon. Remove from heat.

Over a plate, split vanilla bean with the tip of a sharp knife, add seeds to sauce, and chill until ready to use.

*Serves 12.*

# DeLaurenti Specialty Food Markets

The predominant colors are red, green, and white — the green of the hundreds of bottles of olive oil that fill half a wall, and the red and white of the thousands of cans of tomatoes, tomato pastes, and tomato purées stacked on multiple shelves. The gilded labels of the mustards, capers, olives, and anchovies are like works of art. From the huge bulk rice, bean, and pasta section you can choose any shape, size, or color of pasta imaginable. Chunks of Guittard and Callebaut chocolate, candied violets and rose petals, dried Royal Anne cherries, and sultana raisins make this the logical place to come when holiday baking season rolls around.

In short, if you love food and you have a couple of hours to spend wandering through its narrow aisles, DeLaurenti is a feast for the eyes and the palate. Behind the glass of the refrigerator cases you'll find Spanish chorizo, Hungarian salami, andouille sausage, numerous prosciuttos, and 10 pâtés. Cheese is important here — all sorts of imported and domestic cheeses are available. In the freezer case, you'll find frozen unsalted stocks, manicotti, tortellini, puff pastry, and pizza dough. DeLaurenti has one of the widest selections of Italian wines in the city and also sells Ciro's bread by the pound.

The story of the DeLaurenti family in the Market reaches back to 1928, when Angelina Mustello, an immigrant from Abruzzi, Italy, opened a small store on the Mezzanine Level of the Market (where Magnano Foods is now located). Mama Mustello sold pasta, eggs, butter, and Italian cheeses, and catered to the ethnic communities — Italian, Greek, and Sephardic Jew — that sought out hard-to-find products from their homelands.

Angelina's daughter, Mamie, helped her mother in the store and there met Peter DeLaurenti, a deliveryman for Seattle French Bakery, which has since become Gai's Bakery.

In 1930 Mamie and Peter were married, and shortly thereafter Angelina's store closed due to the Depression.

When Angelina's old store became available in 1948, Mamie and Pete bought it and opened Pete's Italian Grocery. As the store grew and prospered over the years, the site simply became too small to hold all the specialty products and fresh foods it sold.

In 1973 one of Mamie and Pete's sons, Louie, bought the business, changed the name to DeLaurenti, and moved it to its present location at First and Pike. On December 22, 1976, a fire in the Market destroyed the interior of DeLaurenti, and the business closed until March 1977. From January to November 1978, DeLaurenti was temporarily relocated in the Sanitary Market Building during renovation of the Economy Market Building.

Today Louie and his wife, Pat, continue to run DeLaurenti in the Market with the help of their daughter, Vicki. The focus continues to be on Italian products, but the DeLaurentis are always open to new markets, and domestic products, such as Washington cheeses, California tomato products, and dried fruits, are gaining in importance.

# Tiramisu

DeLaurenti Specialty Food Markets

Tiramisu is Italian for "pick me up," and DeLaurenti's definitive version of this classic dessert is guaranteed to do just that!

½ cup sugar

3 eggs, separated

½ pound mascarpone (Italian cream) cheese

2 cups brewed espresso

1 to 3 tablespoons rum, amaretto, Kahlua, Frangelico, or any favorite liqueur (optional)

1 package champagne biscuits (Italian-made ladyfingers), at least 24 to the package

Unsweetened ground cocoa

Small piece of Callebaut semisweet chocolate, shaved

Take out a 9- by 13-inch glass baking dish or pan. Set aside.

In a bowl, whisk together the sugar and egg yolks until they become golden. Gradually add mascarpone and continue stirring until the mixture becomes pale yellow and creamy.

In another bowl, whip the egg whites until stiff, but not dry, peaks form. Fold the meringue thoroughly into the mascarpone mixture.

Place espresso in shallow dish and add liqueur of choice, if desired. Quickly and lightly dip enough biscuits into the brewed espresso to cover the bottom of pan. Cover the biscuits with a layer of the mascarpone mixture, followed by a thorough dusting of cocoa. Repeat this process with up to 3 layers, finishing with the cocoa followed by the shaved chocolate.

After Tiramisu is assembled, shake the pan lightly to settle the ingredients. Chill for at least 2 hours and preferably overnight before serving. Cut and serve.

Serves 6 to 8.

Note: To sift cocoa and avoid lumps, put a few tablespoons of cocoa in a fine-mesh strainer with a handle and hit the side of the strainer with the heel of your hand as you pass it over the top of the mascarpone and egg mixture.

# *Irish Coffee Truffles*

## DILETTANTE CHOCOLATES

Seattle is a city in love with its coffee; hence the inclusion of this recipe for those plagued by double demons — coffee and chocolate. These truffles are also nice and boozy, so be forewarned!

*½ cup espresso or other strong coffee*

*1 pound semisweet chocolate (couverture chocolate preferred), chopped fine*

*1 cup (½ lb) unsalted butter, at room temperature*

*½ cup Irish whiskey*

*1 cup cocoa powder (natural process), for coating*

In a small saucepan, heat the coffee. Pour it into a mixing bowl and cool to 120°F. Melt chocolate in a double boiler to 120°F. With a wire whisk, beat butter into the chocolate bit by bit until the mixture is smooth.

Gradually whisk the chocolate/butter mixture into the coffee, beating until thoroughly blended and creamy. Add whiskey to the mixture. Stir until well incorporated in the batch.

Scrape the mixture onto a cookie sheet and refrigerate until firm, about ½ to 1 hour.

Remove from the refrigerator and form into small balls with a melon-ball scoop. Put on a sheet of waxed paper.

Each time you have formed 6 balls, roll them in cocoa powder, arrange them on a serving plate, and put them back into the refrigerator. If the truffle paste gets too warm to hold its shape well, refrigerate it briefly until it is again firm enough to work with.

When the entire batch is finished and stacked prettily on the serving plate, keep refrigerated until 15 minutes before serving.

*Makes 5 dozen truffles.*

*Note:* To melt chocolate, chop chocolate into small pieces. Pour water into the bottom pot of a double boiler to within 1 inch of the top pot. Bring barely to a simmer and no more. Then put the chocolate in the top part of the double boiler and place it over the warm water. Slowly melt chocolate while stirring constantly.

Make sure that no steam or condensation from the spoon comes in contact with the chocolate at any point. If the natural starch in chocolate combines with water, the mass will thicken, making it lumpy and unusable.

# DILETTANTE CHOCOLATES

Dilettante Chocolates traces its roots back to the turn of the twentieth century, when Julius Rudolph Franzen created pastries for Franz Josef, Emperor of Austria, King of Hungary. While serving the Emperor, Julius obtained the closely guarded formulas of the chocolate confectionery, and later served as master candy maker for Czar Nicholas II at the Imperial Court of Russia.

When he immigrated to the United States around 1914, Julius shared his secret candy-making formulas with his brother-in-law, Earl Davenport. Today Earl's grandson, Dana Davenport, a master confectioner, is continuing the family tradition with Dilettante Chocolates, which are made according to the same formulas that pleased the crowned heads of Europe.

Cafe Dilettante on Post Alley is a dark, romantic place with a cafe menu that includes soups, salads, sandwiches, Dana's superb chocolates, desserts (including Hungarian *rigo janczi*, a chocolate mousse layer cake topped with Dilettante's Chocolate Ephemere Sauce), specially blended coffees, and wine. Chocolate specialties include European-style truffles, toffees, marzipan, buttercreams, caramels, sauces, and toppings.

Dana recounts one funny story about a husband who would come in to buy replacements for the chocolates he'd sneaked out of his wife's hidden box of goodies. Instead of buying his own, he would replace her stash, in what was undoubtedly some sort of daring game to him. But then, people will do anything when it comes to chocolate.

In case you're wondering about the name, "dilettante" is defined as "an admirer or lover of the arts." It was chosen by Dana because, "I consider myself a dilettante in the true sense of the word. I take delight in the arts, and look for the best possible experience to be had from any one of them — including candy making."

# *Royal Chocolate Truffles*

### DILETTANTE CHOCOLATES

This is the truffle for chocoholics who like their vice of choice pure and unadulterated. Nothing beats the deep, dense taste and texture of this basic truffle, which is as easy to make as it is scrumptious to eat.

*⅔ cup whipping cream*

*1 pound semisweet chocolate (couverture chocolate preferred), chopped fine*

*¾ cup cocoa powder (natural process), for coating*

Pour whipping cream into a 3-quart saucepan and bring just to the boil. Remove from heat at once and cool to 120°F. Melt chocolate in a double boiler until it reaches 120°F.

Add the chocolate to the cooled cream (not the cream to the chocolate), and stir until the mixture is smooth. Scrape the mixture onto a cookie sheet, spreading it evenly. Refrigerate for about ½ to 1 hour, or until firm.

Remove from refrigerator and form into small balls with a melon-ball scoop. Put balls on a sheet of waxed paper. After you have formed six balls, roll them in cocoa powder. Arrange them on a handsome serving plate and put them back into the refrigerator. If the truffle paste gets too warm to hold its shape well, refrigerate briefly until it is again firm enough to work with.

When entire batch is finished and stacked prettily on the serving plate, keep refrigerated until 15 minutes before serving.

*Note:* This is a very versatile recipe that can be adapted in many ways to your personal tastes. Add as much as ¼ cup of your favorite liqueur after stirring together the chocolate and cooled cream, then finish as in the master recipe. Use any flavoring extract or oil that appeals to you. Vanilla, almond, and peppermint go well with dark chocolate, but add the flavorings a little at a time, tasting carefully as you go.

If you want a fluffy texture to your Royal Chocolate Truffles, take the mixture out of the refrigerator just before it is set, scrape it into the chilled bowl of an electric mixer, and whip it with a rotary beater until it is fully aerated. Chill thoroughly and it will retain the air you whipped into it. When ready to form it into ball-shape pieces, work with a small portion at a time, keeping the remainder refrigerated. Don't roll in cocoa. When the entire batch is finished, freeze until solid, then dip (in white chocolate if the flavor contrast appeals to you) to keep the air trapped inside the filling. After it has been whipped, do not let the truffle come back to room temperature until it has been dipped and securely protected by a solid shell of coating.

*Makes 5 dozen truffles.*

# THE PIKE PLACE MARKET CREAMERY

Tucked back in the Sanitary Market Building (built in 1910 and so named because it was the only building in the Market where animals were not allowed inside), the Creamery is a place where regular customers can count on a smile, a kind word, and a hug from proprietress and head milkmaid Nancy "Nipples" Douty, who started the Creamery in 1977 and purchased the business in 1978 with the help of a customer who cosigned her loan.

Nancy is one of the healthiest-looking and fittest people in the Market, with her thin yet muscular body, long brown hair, and clear brown eyes, and she can lift a dolly full of milk crates with ease. She's living testament to her philosophy that "eating good food helps you feel good. At the Creamery we also believe in eating food that tastes good."

Nancy specializes in fresh dairy and soy products that you'd never find at your neighborhood grocery store. Among the more unusual offerings are milk in glass bottles, raw goat's milk, rice milk, and soy milk; logs of Jersey butter, similar to rich French butter; and six sizes of eggs from free-running hens, plus quail, duck, goose, and *aracauna* eggs, in season. Devonshire cream, three types of *crème fraîche*, numerous varieties of yogurts, a cornucopia of soy and tofu products, and ice cream and frozen desserts are other tempting options.

Besides buying your milk and other dairy needs here, you can also browse through Nancy's kitschy collection of "Dairy Moo-morabilia" donated by customers and friends, which includes cows and chickens of all makes and models (check out the metal cow in the pearls, straw hat, purple sneakers, and lace socks!), as well as Gary Larson "Far Side" cartoons.

# Chocolate Espresso Cheesecake

## THE PIKE PLACE MARKET CREAMERY

This dessert is a sensuous experience to make, and a celestial experience to eat. Forget the cholesterol and enjoy.

CRUST

*26 chocolate wafer cookies, crushed*

*2 tablespoons sugar*

*1 tablespoon dark roast coffee, espresso grind (do not use liquid espresso or instant espresso powder)*

*¼ cup butter, melted*

FILLING

*3 packages (8 oz each) cream cheese, softened*

*12 ounces semisweet chocolate chips, melted*

*1 cup sugar*

*3 tablespoons flour*

*3 large eggs*

*2 egg yolks*

*¼ cup hot espresso or extra-strength coffee*

*1 cup whipping cream*

*36 dark-chocolate-covered espresso beans (optional)*

*Whipped cream (optional)*

Preheat oven to 350°F. Get out a 9-inch springform pan and grease lightly.

**To make crust:** Place crushed cookies, the 2 tablespoons sugar, ground coffee, and butter in medium mixing bowl. Blend thoroughly and pour into springform pan. Pat crumb mixture on bottom of pan and up sides if enough remains. Chill in refrigerator while you prepare filling. (To save on cleanup, crush cookies in a gallon-size, zip-top plastic bag. Add sugar, coffee, and butter and squeeze outside of bag until mixture is blended. Pour mixture from bag into spring-form pan and use outside of bag to press down crumbs evenly.)

**To make filling:** Place softened cream cheese in large mixing bowl and beat with electric mixer at low to medium speed until creamy. Meanwhile, melt chocolate chips in microwave or top of double boiler, being careful not to scorch chocolate. Set aside for later use.

Add the 1 cup sugar to cream cheese and beat on medium speed until fluffy. Sprinkle flour over cream cheese mixture and blend thoroughly. Add eggs and egg yolks, one at a time, being sure each is thoroughly incorporated. Beat in the melted chocolate, hot espresso, and whipping cream at low speed.

Pour batter over crust and bake for 1 hour. Turn off heat and let cake sit in oven 40 minutes without opening door. Place cheesecake on wire rack and cool completely, then garnish edges of cheesecake with chocolate-covered espresso beans, if desired.

Refrigerate overnight, or preferably for 1 or 2 days to let flavors meld. Slice and serve with whipped cream, if desired.

*Serves 8 to 12.*

*Note:* To melt chocolate in a microwave, put into microwave-safe dish and microwave on LOW for 30 seconds, then stir. Microwave on LOW for another 30 seconds and stir again. If big lumps of chocolate still remain, microwave another 30 seconds. Continue this process until only small lumps remain, then stir to finish melting.

# PROCOPIO GELATERIA

Procopio Gelateria* (Italian ice cream cafe) traces its history back to the 1600s, when Francesco Procopio Dei Coltelli popularized ice cream in Florence, Italy. This master *gelatiere* (ice cream maker) moved to Paris in 1670 and opened the first Parisian cafe, Café Procope. Until this time, ice cream was reserved only for royalty, but Procopio introduced *gelato* (Italian ice cream) to the public and counted Benjamin Franklin, Voltaire, Rousseau, and Napolean among his customers.

The term *gelato* refers to a wide variety of frozen desserts, including fresh fruit ices, cream ices, and *semifreddi*, that are made with pure, fresh ingredients like fruits, nut pastes, cocoa, real liqueurs, milk, and cream. Procopio Gelateria, on the Hillclimb nicknamed "Cardiac Gulch" below the Market, uses the same 300-year-old recipes as Francesco Procopio, and varies the types and flavors of gelato they offer, depending on the season and availability of fresh ingredients. Procopio also serves pastries, light lunches, espresso drinks, and wine in a contemporary European atmosphere.

*Just outside of the Market Historic District.

# Lemon Ice

— PROCOPIO GELATERIA —

You'll enjoy this tart, refreshing ice, as puckery and flavorful as a lemon drop, especially on hot summer days. It's reputed to have been Napoleon's favorite flavor.

2 cups water

¾ cup sugar

¾ cup freshly squeezed lemon juice

2 teaspoons grated lemon rind

2 teaspoons citric acid (available in health food stores under the name C-Crystals or 100% pure crystalline vitamin C)

In a small saucepan, combine water and sugar and heat over medium heat, stirring occasionally, until sugar is dissolved, 2 or 3 minutes. Do not allow to come to a boil. Remove from heat and allow to cool.

Add lemon juice, lemon rind, and citric acid to sugar mixture and stir well to combine. Place in ice cream maker and freeze according to manufacturer's instructions, or place in a glass or metal pan or dish and freeze until mushy, 2 or 3 hours. Stir well and allow to freeze until mushy again, then stir well again. Scrape lemon ice into an airtight plastic freezer container with a lid, cover, and freeze completely. Before serving, allow ice to thaw at room temperature until desired consistency, about 5 minutes.

Makes about 3 cups, 4 servings.

# *Earl Grey Sorbet*

## THE PERENNIAL TEA ROOM

Afternoon tea is credited to Anna, Duchess of Bedford, who found herself fainting from hunger between lunch at noon and dinner at 8 or 9 p.m. She had a maid bring a cup of tea and sandwiches to her room at around 4 p.m. and found she no longer fainted. The Duchess might have enjoyed this refreshing sorbet during the light course of afternoon tea.

*6 cups freshly drawn and boiled water*

*6 teaspoons Perennial Tea Room Earl Grey extra aromatic tea (an extra-strong Earl Grey tea)*

*½ cup superfine (caster) sugar*

*¼ cup vodka (optional)*

Pour freshly boiled water over tea leaves and steep for 3 minutes. Strain tea into a large glass mixing bowl, add sugar, and stir until sugar is completely dissolved.

Pour tea mixture into shallow metal or glass baking pan, mixing bowl, or dish, and set aside to cool completely. If desired, add vodka (the vodka provides a softer texture after freezing).

Freeze mixture until almost hard, which will take several hours. Thaw 5 minutes at room temperature, then mash with fork to a soft consistency or, for a fluffier texture, put in food processor or beat with hand mixer until light and frothy. Store in airtight container in freezer and allow to thaw slightly before serving.

*Makes six 1-cup servings, twelve ½-cup servings.*

*Note:* Many American hotels, department stores, or tea rooms that serve tea refer to it as "high tea" because it sounds more elegant than "afternoon," "Victorian," or "low" tea (developed in the upper class and named for the low chairs in which one sat). However, this is a misconception, for in England "high tea" is anything but elegant; the term refers to a farm or country tea served to heavy laborers at 4 p.m.

It's a major meal of the day, and may include sandwiches on hearty, crusty breads (as opposed to the dainty, crustless breads for "afternoon," "Victorian," or "low" tea); soups; fish; meat pasties; sides of beef; cakes; scones; pies; and countless pots of tea, all served boarding-house style (with all the dishes put on the table at the same time). After "high tea" is served, the workers go back into the fields for several more hours of work.

At 8 p.m. they return to eat the leftovers from "high tea," which are considered a light meal. So don't fall victim to the "high tea" Americanization; "afternoon tea," "Victorian tea," or "low tea" are the proper terms. "Cream tea" refers to any afternoon tea where scones are served with Devonshire clotted cream and jam.

# *Edith's Blueberry Pie*

## CANTER-BERRY FARMS

This is the pie that put Canter-Berry Farms on the map as a U-pick blueberry farm. The simple recipe shows choice blueberries in their most flavorful light. Serve plain or with sweetened whipped cream, ice cream, yogurt, or sour cream.

*Pastry for a 2-crust, 9-inch pie, unbaked*

*4 cups blueberries, fresh or frozen*

*1 cup sugar*

*⅜ teaspoon salt*

*¼ cup flour*

Preheat oven to 400°F. Roll out half of pastry dough and fit into pie pan.

In a large mixing bowl stir together blueberries, sugar, salt, and flour until well mixed. Pour over dough until evenly distributed, then roll out remaining pastry and place over top of berries; crimp edges to seal.

Bake for 15 minutes at 400°F, then reduce heat to 350°F and bake 25 to 30 minutes, about 5 minutes longer if frozen berries are used.

*Serves 8.*

*Note:* When choosing blueberries, search for fresh, plump fruit with a blue-gray bloom. Use fresh berries within a week of picking and store in an aerated container in the refrigerator after removing any moldy or soft fruit. If frozen dry, blueberries won't stick together, and you can dip out the amount needed at a later date.

# *Blueberry-Peach Cobbler*

## BICKFORD ORCHARD

This is a magical dessert. The dough starts out on the bottom of the casserole, then travels to the top during baking. It's full of bubbling-hot fruit and so good it doesn't need a topping.

*½ cup butter or margarine*

*1 cup flour*

*¾ cup sugar*

*2 teaspoons baking powder*

*½ cup milk*

*2 cups sliced peaches*

*1½ to 2 cups blueberries*

*½ cup sugar*

Preheat oven to 350°F. Get out a 2½-quart baking dish.

While the oven preheats, melt butter in the baking dish in the oven, then set aside. Combine flour, the ¾ cup sugar, and baking powder; add milk and stir just until blended. Spoon batter over butter in baking dish, but do not stir.

Combine fruit and the ½ cup sugar. Spoon over batter, but do not stir. Bake until fruit is bubbly and crust is golden brown, 45 to 55 minutes. Serve warm.

*Serves 6 to 8.*

# CHEZ SHEA
Chez Shea is an intimate and appealing 30-seat restaurant located in the historic Corner Market Building (built in 1912). Towering arched windows, twinkling candles, the lights of faraway boats sparkling in Elliott Bay, and the sound of ferry whistles bellowing in the distance create the atmosphere for a romantic, leisurely rendezvous.

Sandy Shea, chef/owner of Chez Shea (which roughly translated means "at Shea's place"), felt fated to claim the unusual space from the moment she moved into an apartment directly across from it. When the space became available in 1983, Sandy bought it. Today she offers four-course, prix-fixe dinners including appetizer, first course, choice of five entrées, and salad, with dessert à la carte. A recent innovation is a two-course dinner offered Tuesdays through Thursdays.

Sandy labels her style of cooking "contemporary regional." It is based on French tradition, with influences drawn from Mediterranean, Mexican, Asian, and American cuisines. She's a Pacific Northwest native, brought up on a farm in Oregon's Hood River valley. Although mostly self-taught, Sandy studied at La Varenne in Paris and closely follows the teachings of the late James Beard, another child of the Pacific Northwest.

## Blackberry Mousse with Lemon Madeleines

—— CHEZ SHEA ——

Unlike many of the other desserts in this book that are decidedly "homey," this is an elegant "restaurant" dessert, yet it is surprisingly easy to make. The Lemon Madeleines are dense, lemony little cakes that are great with the Blackberry Mousse, tea, or coffee. Serve the Blackberry Mousse with Lemon Madeleines, a glass of Champagne, and a silver spoon for a once-in-a-lifetime experience.

*1¼ pounds (about 5 cups) fresh blackberries or unsweetened frozen blackberries, thawed*

*½ cup sugar*

*2 teaspoons unflavored gelatin*

*2 tablespoons water*

*1 egg yolk*

*2 tablespoons sugar*

*1 cup chilled whipping cream*

LEMON MADELEINES

*6 egg yolks*

*½ cup sugar*

*2 tablespoons grated lemon rind*

*1 tablespoon fresh lemon juice*

*1 cup flour, sifted*

*6 tablespoons unsalted butter, melted and cooled to lukewarm*

*Confectioners' sugar*

In a large, heavy saucepan, cook berries and the ½ cup sugar over medium heat, stirring occasionally, until mixture is juicy, about 15 minutes. Transfer mixture to food processor or blender and purée. Strain to remove seeds.

Meanwhile, sprinkle gelatin over the water in a small, heavy saucepan. Let stand until softened, about 10 minutes. Stir over low heat just until melted. Whisk gelatin mixture into hot blackberry purée. Refrigerate, stirring occasionally, until cold but not set, about 45 minutes.

Whisk egg yolk and the 2 tablespoons sugar in a small bowl until thick and pale. Fold into berry mixture. Whip cream in large bowl until soft peaks form. Carefully fold whipped cream into berry mixture. Divide mixture among balloon goblets and chill until set, about 3 hours. Can be prepared 1 day ahead. Cover and refrigerate.

**To make Lemon Madeleines:** Preheat oven to 375°F. Butter 12 madeleine molds and set aside.

Beat egg yolks and sugar with electric mixer until pale yellow and slowly dissolving ribbons form when beaters are lifted, about 5 minutes. Fold in lemon rind and lemon juice. Fold in flour.

Place half of batter in small bowl; fold in butter. Gently fold batters together. Divide batter among madeleine molds and bake until toothpick inserted in center of madeleines comes out clean, about 15 minutes.

Turn madeleines out onto a wire rack and cool completely. Sift confectioners' sugar over madeleines before serving. Madeleines can be prepared 6 hours ahead. Store at room temperature in airtight container until served. Makes 1 dozen.

*Serves 6.*

## Raspberries with Honey-Almond Cream

VALLEY PACKER FARMS

This is a simple yet elegant raspberry dessert. Serve it on your finest china with silver spoons, and pretend you're at a manor house in England.

4 cups (2 pt) red raspberries

2 cups (1 pt) whipping cream

½ teaspoon almond extract

1½ tablespoons good-grade raw honey

Mint leaves

¼ cup toasted, slivered almonds

If using organic raspberries, do not wash; if using nonorganic berries, just sprinkle with water so they do not become mushy.

With rotary mixer, whip cream in a small mixing bowl until it forms a thick liquid. Add almond extract and honey and whip until soft peaks form — do not whip until stiff.

To serve place a fourth of the raspberries on a dessert plate in a circle, then place mint leaf or leaves at the top of the plate. Spoon 2 or 3 dollops of whipped cream on top of the berries and sprinkle with 1 tablespoon of the almonds. Repeat this process with the remaining ingredients. Serve immediately.

*Serves 4.*

# SNOQUALMIE VALLEY HONEY FARM

One summer, Nancy Hutto learned how to say "honey" in 12 different languages at her stand in the Main Arcade. "Honey is such a universally known and appreciated product that people often ask for 'plain honey.' They're amazed at all the flavors created from different flower-nectar sources and the variety of products available. So we educate people about honey," Nancy explains.

Nancy and co-owner Mike Wills oversee 600 colonies of bees, from which they gather and produce 10 local liquid honeys with varying flavors; 12 flavored cream honeys (honeys that have fruit or spice added); beeswax candles; pollen; honeycomb; and a healing balm made with beeswax, royal jelly, oils, herbs, and a natural antibiotic gathered by the bees.

Nancy and Mike's honey farm is located in North Bend, and both come from long lines of beekeepers. "Honey is a neat product because bees take something that wouldn't otherwise be used — nectar — and turn it into a gift of the gods," Nancy says. "And no other plant or animal is killed to make it." You'll find Nancy, Mike, or a representative of Snoqualmie Valley Honey Farm ready to introduce you to the world of honey with free samples, seven days a week.

## *Lemon Sponge Pudding*

— SNOQUALMIE VALLEY HONEY FARM —

This recipe conjures up sweet memories of childhood. The pudding forms two layers as it bakes, and when you turn it out onto a plate, a rich, lemony pudding covers the warm, spongy cake.

½ cup mild-flavored honey, such as fireweed, apple, or lemon cream

¼ cup flour

½ teaspoon salt

2 tablespoons butter, melted

2½ tablespoons lemon juice

Grated rind of 1 lemon

3 egg yolks, beaten

½ cup milk

3 egg whites, beaten until stiff

Fresh berries (optional)

Whipped cream (optional)

Preheat oven to 350°F. Generously butter four custard cups. Get out a baking pan that will comfortably hold all of the custard cups and set aside.

Blend honey, flour, and salt in a large bowl. Add melted butter and stir well. Add lemon juice and lemon rind and blend well. Combine beaten egg yolks and milk, mix well, and stir into honey mixture.

Fold in egg whites, leaving a few lumps. Ladle pudding into custard cups, then place custard cups in baking pan and pour hot water around them, being careful not to splash any water into the custard.

Cook pudding until light brown on top and a toothpick inserted in middle comes out clean, 35 to 40 minutes. To serve, cut around edges, turn puddings out onto dessert plates, and garnish with fresh berries and a dollop of whipped cream, if desired.

*Serves 4.*

# ISLAND MEADOW FARM

Island Meadow Farm on Vashon Island was founded sometime during the 1880s, but many know it as the "Old Nut Farm," because of the personalities and vision of its owners from 1920 to 1974, the Shane brothers. These two bachelor brothers planted walnut and hazelnut varieties from all over the world, and created some of their own by grafting. They also grew unusual nut and fruit trees, such as sweet chestnut, hickory, plumcot, and papaw, or custard fruit.

Present owners Bonnie and Bob Gregson have owned the farm since 1988, and come to the North Arcade in November and December with organic English walnuts, 11 varieties of hazelnuts, sweet chestnuts, and hickory nuts.

## *Plum-Walnut Confections*

ISLAND MEADOW FARM

A nice twist on almond-stuffed dates, these Plum-Walnut Confections are a grown-up treat! The recipe was first presented to members of the Pacific Northwest Food & Wine Symposium.

*1 package (3 oz) cream cheese, softened*

*1 tablespoon grated orange rind*

*1 tablespoon Cointreau, Triple Sec, or Grand Marnier*

*24 dried Italian prune plums (home-dried preferred), cut in half lengthwise (you can substitute storebought pitted prunes, although the flavor and texture will be different)*

*48 walnut halves*

*½ cup sifted confectioners' sugar*

Place cream cheese, orange rind, and liqueur in food processor or blender, and blend until mixture is smooth and pale yellow in color. Place 1 teaspoon of cream-cheese mixture on cut side of each prune plum, then place walnut half on cream-cheese mixture and press down gently. Sprinkle prune plums with confectioners' sugar.

To serve, place each confection in a paper candy cup and place on a serving plate lined with a lacy paper doily.

*Makes 4 dozen confections.*

# Berry-Filled Squares

—————————— THE GRANGER BERRY PATCH ——————————

The not-too-sweet shortcake base of these dessert bars really allows the flavor of the fruit to shine through. My husband, a real shortcake connoisseur, adored them! They would be great served at tea with Earl Grey Sorbet, page 158.

¾ *cup margarine*

½ *cup sugar*

*1 teaspoon vanilla extract*

*1 egg*

*2½ cups sifted flour*

½ *teaspoon baking powder*

*2 cups Granger Berry Patch fruit spread, any flavor, or 2 cups low-sugar or fruit-only jam or jelly*

Preheat oven to 400°F. Take out a 9- by 13-inch baking pan.

With a whisk or mixer, beat the margarine until it's light and fluffy. Gradually add sugar and beat until margarine and sugar are well blended. Add vanilla and egg and beat well.

Sift flour with baking powder and add gradually to creamed mixture, mixing thoroughly after each addition. Press dough lightly over bottom and partway up sides of ungreased baking pan. This is easy if you use the back of an oval soup spoon. Bake until shortbread colors slightly and is no longer soft, about 15 to 20 minutes. Remove from oven and cool on wire rack.

Meanwhile, heat spread in saucepan over medium heat or in microwave until it becomes liquid. Spread hot jam over cooled shortbread. Allow spread to harden before cutting into squares. Store any remaining squares in refrigerator.

*Makes 2 dozen squares.*

THE JARMINS' 5-M ORCHARD Miriam and Marvin Jarmin grow strawberries, blackberries, raspberries, and six kinds of apples (Jonagold, Hawaii, Akane, Melrose, Spartan, and Gala) on their Mount Vernon farm in the Skagit Valley. Marvin comes from a farming family, has a master's degree in landscape design and horticulture from Washington State University, and was a horticulturist for Skagit County until his retirement in 1989. In addition to running the farm, he's now manager of the Washington Red Raspberry Growers Association.

The Jarmins started selling at the Market in 1985 and come to the North Arcade on Saturdays during October, November, and December. During the holiday season, they'll sell you a holly wreath or make up a special holiday gift box for family or friends. In case you're curious about the name, the "5-M" refers to the first names of Miriam and Marvin, and their children Marilee, Michelle, and Matthew. Even the name of their dog, Max, begins with an "m."

# *Frosty Strawberry Squares*

## THE JARMINS' 5-M ORCHARD

A light, smooth, sweet strawberry cream floats over a walnut cookie-crumb crust, making this one of the most delicious desserts in the book. If you want to dress it up for a summertime dinner party, you can divide the crust and filling between two 9-inch pie plates and call it "Mile-High Strawberry Pie."

*1 cup flour*

*¼ cup firmly packed brown sugar*

*½ cup chopped walnuts*

*½ cup butter, melted*

*2 cups fresh, sliced strawberries*

*2 egg whites*

*1 cup granulated sugar*

*2 tablespoons lemon juice*

*1 cup whipping cream, whipped until soft peaks form*

*12 whole fresh strawberries (optional)*

*12 sprigs of mint (optional)*

Preheat oven to 350°F. Take out a 9- by 13-inch baking pan and set aside. Take out a rimmed cookie sheet.

In a medium mixing bowl mix flour, brown sugar, walnuts, and butter. Spread in cookie sheet so that dough is about ¼ inch thick (it will not completely fill pan) and bake until golden brown, 15 to 20 minutes. After first 5 minutes of baking time, chop and turn dough so that it forms pea-sized crumbs. Stir and turn crumbs after every 5 minutes thereafter, so that they brown evenly. Remove from oven and allow to cool.

Sprinkle crumbs over bottom of 9- by 13-inch pan. With electric mixer at low speed beat together strawberries, egg whites, granulated sugar, and lemon juice until strawberries are crushed, then turn mixer to high speed and beat until mixture turns light pink and glossy (it will almost triple in volume) and stiff peaks form, 4 or 5 minutes. Fold in whipped cream.

Pour strawberry filling over crust in pan. Place in freezer until frozen, several hours or overnight. Remove from freezer about 5 minutes before serving, slice, and serve with a whole fresh strawberry and a sprig of mint on the side, if desired.

*Serves 12.*

# German Apple Cake

WOODRING ORCHARDS

Make this moist cake, full of grated apples and walnuts, at the height of apple season and you'll think you've died and gone to heaven. The cream cheese icing is the final, sinful touch, although the cake is plenty delicious, quite satisfying, and decidedly more healthful without it.

2 eggs

2 cups sugar

2 cups flour

2 teaspoons cinnamon

1 teaspoon baking soda

½ teaspoon salt

1 teaspoon vanilla extract

4 cups grated apples, medium grate (about 3 large, firm apples, such as Golden Delicious or Granny Smith)

½ cup chopped walnuts

CREAM CHEESE ICING

2 packages (3 oz each) cream cheese, softened

1 tablespoon margarine, melted

1 teaspoon vanilla extract

1½ cups sifted confectioners' sugar

Preheat oven to 350°F. Take out a 9- by 13-inch baking pan, grease lightly or spray with nonstick corn-oil spray, and set aside.

Beat eggs in large mixing bowl until light and foamy, then add sugar, flour, cinnamon, baking soda, salt, and vanilla. Stir until well blended (dough will appear dry), then add apples and any juice that accumulates during grating. Mix well and add walnuts.

Pour dough into baking pan and bake until cake shrinks from sides of pan and toothpick inserted in middle comes out clean, 35 to 40 minutes. Cool on wire rack.

**To make icing:** Beat cream cheese, margarine, and vanilla with a wire whisk or electric mixer until smooth and fluffy. Add confectioners' sugar a little at a time, until all is incorporated and icing is smooth.

Ice cake, cut into slices, and enjoy.

*Serves 12.*

# STACKHOUSE BROTHERS' ORCHARDS

Stackhouse sells almonds of all sorts, dark and golden raisins the size of your thumbnail, and dried apricot slabs in the North Arcade of the Market seven days a week, all year round. Here you can sample their dried fruit, and natural (raw), BBQ, hickory-smoked, plain-roast, garlic-onion, and orange-honey almonds. The orange-honey almonds are a delight, great to eat out of hand, and exquisite when tossed with a mix of organic lettuces, a shot of olive oil, and a touch of rice wine vinegar.

## *Apricot Pie*

### — STACKHOUSE BROTHERS' ORCHARDS —

This is one fruit pie you can make all year round because it uses dried, instead of fresh, fruit. It's also great for people who like rich, less-sweet desserts — the tart, slightly chewy apricots form a nice contrast to the smooth custard, whipped cream, and flaky crust.

*Pastry for 9-inch single pie shell, unbaked*

*1¾ cups (½ pound) Stackhouse Brothers' Orchards dried apricots, chopped*

*Grand Marnier or Triple Sec*

*1 package (3.4 oz) cooked-style vanilla pudding and pie filling*

*1 teaspoon vanilla extract*

*Pinch of salt*

*2 cups (1 pt) whipping cream*

*Sugar or artificial sweetener to taste*

Bake pie shell and set aside to cool.

Place apricots in a small saucepan and cover with Grand Marnier or Triple Sec. Place over medium heat and bring to a gentle boil, then cover, turn off heat, and leave pan on burner.

Meanwhile, prepare vanilla pudding as package directs, but add the extra vanilla and pinch of salt. Place pudding in pie shell, then spoon apricots over top. Spoon all but 1 tablespoon of the apricot/liqueur liquid over apricots, being careful to avoid crust so that it doesn't become soggy.

Whip cream with sweetener of your choice and remaining 1 tablespoon of apricot/liqueur liquid for extra flavor. Cover apricots with the whipped cream, chill pie a few hours in refrigerator, cut into slices, and enjoy.

*Serves 8.*

# PIKE PLACE NUTS

Mondrian patterns of rectangles and bars outline the selections of raw and roasted nuts at Pike Place Nuts on Economy Row next door to Danny's Wonder Freeze and Art Stall Gallery. Among the more unusual items here are unsalted soy nuts; onion-garlic wheatnuts; a colorful mix of shelled pistachios and dried cranberries (craisins), especially good for salads; pepitas (roasted pumpkin seeds); and toffee peanuts.

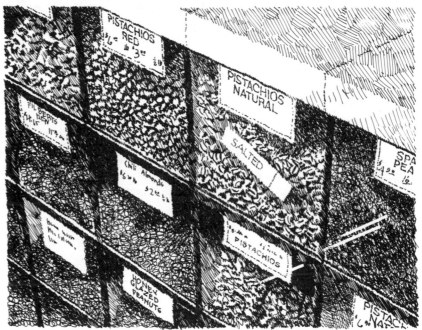

# Hazelnut Cherry Pie

PIKE PLACE NUTS

Washington State produces more sweet cherries than any other state in the union. Mid-June to early August is the time to get your fresh cherries to make this light, easy-to-prepare summertime treat. Choose fruit that is plump, firm, smooth, and bright in color for the best flavor and texture.

*½ cup hazelnuts, toasted, skinned, and finely crushed (see Techniques section)*

*½ cup graham cracker crumbs*

*½ cup flaked coconut*

*2 tablespoons brown sugar*

*1 egg white*

*2 cups fresh, pitted sweet cherries*

*1 package (3.4 oz) vanilla or chocolate pudding and pie filling*

*Whipped cream or whipped topping (optional)*

*Additional crushed hazelnuts and/or cherries (optional)*

Preheat oven to 375°F. Get out a 9-inch pie plate, grease lightly or spray with nonstick corn-oil spray, and set aside.

Place hazelnuts, graham cracker crumbs, coconut, and brown sugar in medium mixing bowl and mix well, making sure there are no lumps in brown sugar.

Beat egg white with electric mixer until stiff but not dry. Fold into nut mixture, blending well. Pat crust into bottom of pie tin and up onto sides if enough remains. Bake pie crust until lightly browned around edges, 5 to 7 minutes. Remove crust from oven and cool on a wire rack.

When crust is cool, spread cherries over it in an even layer. Prepare pudding according to package instructions for pie filling. Pour over cherries in crust and refrigerate. When pudding is thick and creamy, slice pie, and garnish slices with a dollop of whipped cream or whipped topping and additional hazelnuts or cherries, if desired.

*Serves 6 to 8.*

# D'AMBROSIO'S FARM

John D'Ambrosio is a member of one of the oldest farm families in the Market, a family that has sold there in various capacities for over 60 years. John's grandfather and father were truck farmers, his uncle Tony sold on the farm tables, and his uncle John owned one of the highstalls. Today John represents the third generation, and with his wife, Brendan, owns D'Ambrosio's Farm in Burien, which specializes in berries and herbs.

Among their berries you'll find strawberries, blackberries, blueberries, and raspberries. Basil is a favorite herb, but they also sell oregano, marjoram, thyme, tarragon, garlic, and rosemary. Assorted vegetables in season and colorful floral bouquets dot their stall in the Main Arcade six days a week, June through October.

"We like to work in the Market because of all the different people. Every day is different," Brendan says. "Also, it's a nice feeling, raising produce and having happy customers purchase it for their families."

## *Raspberry Pie*

— D'AMBROSIO'S FARM —

This raspberry pie boasts a special filling the D'Ambrosios devised to keep the raspberries from becoming too runny. The trick is a tiny bit of cornstarch. You'll know your pie is done when raspberry juice bubbles out of the slits in the top crust. For an extra light, tasty crust, substitute 2 tablespoons of raspberry vinegar for 2 tablespoons of the water called for in the crust recipe.

*½ cup sugar*

*⅓ cup flour*

*½ teaspoon cinnamon*

*½ teaspoon cornstarch*

*4 cups fresh raspberries*

*2 tablespoons butter or margarine*

PIE CRUST

*⅔ cup plus 2 tablespoons solid vegetable shortening*

*2 cups flour*

*1 teaspoon salt*

*4 to 5 tablespoons cold water*

Preheat oven to 425°F. Prepare pie crust. Take out a 9-inch pie plate and put half of rolled-out crust into it.

Mix sugar, flour, cinnamon, and cornstarch in a large mixing bowl until well blended. Fold in raspberries, being careful not to stir so hard that they become mushy.

Pour raspberries over bottom crust, then dot with margarine or butter. Cover with top crust and crimp edges to seal. Cut a few slits in top crust to allow steam to escape while baking. Bake until crust is light brown and raspberry juice bubbles from the slits in the crust, 40 to 50 minutes. Slice and serve with sweetened whipped cream, vanilla ice cream, or raspberry frozen yogurt.

**Pie Crust:** Place shortening, flour, and salt in a large mixing bowl. With a pastry blender or two knives, cut shortening into flour until the pieces are the size of small peas. Add water (or raspberry vinegar) 1 tablespoon at a time, tossing with a fork after each addition, until pastry holds its shape and forms a ball (you may not need to use all the water called for in the recipe). Divide pastry in half and form into balls. With a rolling pin, roll out each ball into a circle 2 inches larger than 9-inch pie plate.

*Serves 8.*

# Sour Cream Cranberry Pie

## MECH APIARIES

Fresh cranberries come into the Market's highstalls from October through December, and this delicious pie makes a great finale to any fall or holiday meal — a pleasant change from pumpkin and mince pies. The tartness of the cranberries makes a nice contrast to the smooth, sweet, custardy filling.

2 eggs

¾ cup honey

1 cup sour cream

2 tablespoons cranberry juice

¼ teaspoon salt

2 tablespoons flour

1 cup raw cranberries

9-inch pie shell, unbaked

1 cup chopped walnuts

Preheat oven to 425°F.

With an electric mixer, beat the eggs in a small mixing bowl until thick. In a large mixing bowl mix together the honey, sour cream, and cranberry juice. Stir the eggs in carefully by hand.

Mix salt and flour together with cranberries and add to egg mixture, stirring gently. Pour into unbaked pie shell and sprinkle walnuts over the top.

Bake for 10 minutes at 425°F, then turn oven down to 375°F and continue baking for 25 minutes more or until well browned. Cool completely on a rack before cutting.

*Serves 8.*

# POPCORNER

Behind the yellow semicircular counter lurk tempting goodies for the young and the young at heart. Glazed popcorn in neon colors with flavors such as cinnamon spice, fruit salad, peanut butter, and red raspberry offer the ultimate sugar high, while the less adventuresome can feast on small to jumbo-sized bags of fresh, plain popcorn dispensed from a movie-house-style popper. Hot caramel popcorn with nuts (mixed in a stainless steel tray right before your eyes) is another option.

You'll find savory popcorn in plain, cheddar, bacon-and-cheese, and sour-cream flavors, as well as seasonings, popcorn poppers, and decorative tins, great for stuffing with popcorn and giving as gifts. Popcorner is located across the hall from SBC in the Post Alley Market. Its low-calorie, high-fiber popcorn is cooked in 100 percent soybean oil and contains less saturated fat than popcorn fried in coconut oil.

## *Caramel Corn Lollypops*

#### —— POPCORNER ——

For safety's sake, an adult should make this caramel popcorn up until the point where the caramel corn cools, then get the children to butter their hands, shape the lollypops, and decorate them with candy corn, raisins, jelly beans, or nonpareils.

*3 tablespoons vegetable oil, such as canola, corn, or soy*

*⅔ cup unpopped popcorn*

*1 cup firmly packed brown sugar*

*¾ cup water*

*¼ cup light corn syrup*

*2 drops food coloring (optional)*

*12 wooden popsicle sticks*

Preheat oven to 300°F. Heat the oil in a large, heavy saucepan or Dutch oven until it sizzles. Pour in the popcorn, cover saucepan, and allow popcorn to pop completely, shaking occasionally. Pour popped popcorn into a large bowl, remove any unpopped kernels, and place in oven to keep warm.

In a medium saucepan combine brown sugar, water, corn syrup, and food coloring (if used). Stir over medium heat until mixture boils. Reduce heat to low and continue cooking until temperature registers 250°F on a candy thermometer (until it forms a barely hard but still pliable ball when dropped in cold water), about 15 to 20 minutes after it starts to boil. Pour caramel over popcorn while tossing with a large spoon. *Be careful — caramel mixture is very hot and will burn skin if splattered or spilled.*

Allow caramel popcorn to cool, then butter hands, shape popcorn into balls, and place popsicle sticks in middle. If desired, decorate caramel lollypops with candies of your choice.

*Makes 10 lollypops.*

# THE PUBLIC MARKET CANDY STORE

Colorful kites and wind socks in primary colors float from the rafters, the sugary smell of cotton candy hangs in the air, and children break into smiles at the Public Market Candy Store. This place is a step back in time for those of us old enough to remember penny candy, and even though Mary Janes, wax lips, licorice laces, candy cigarettes, and jawbreakers have succumbed to inflation, it's comforting to know they're still around.

The kids of today won't be disappointed either. They'll find Gummi Bears, all 40 flavors of Jelly Belly jelly beans, popcorn, and frozen slushies at the Public Market Candy Store, which is like the concession stands at a state fair midway all rolled into one place. It is located on the Market's Mezzanine Level, just down the staircase from the Main Arcade.

## *Jelly Bean Jumble*

### THE PUBLIC MARKET CANDY STORE

This is a great treat for children's birthday or slumber parties. Let your child be creative when deciding what jelly bean and cereal flavors to use. Although this recipe has lots of calories, it is very low-fat if you don't add the nuts, chocolate, peanuts, or butterscotch chips.

½ *cup your favorite flavor Jelly Belly jelly beans*

2 *cups presweetened cereal, such as Honey Nut Cheerios, Alpha-Bits, Cocoa Puffs, Trix, Froot Loops, Corn Pops, or Apple Jacks (coordinate with jelly bean flavor)*

1½ *cups miniature marshmallows (the colored kind make a beautiful mix)*

OPTIONAL ADDITIONS:

*Semisweet, milk, or white chocolate chips*

*Peanut butter or butterscotch chips*

*Dried fruits, such as dried apples, cherries, raisins, or apricots*

*Dry-roasted, unsalted peanuts*

Mix together all ingredients in a large bowl and serve.

*Makes 4 cups, 8 servings.*

# DAILY DOZEN DOUGHNUTS·

Located on Economy Row, Daily Dozen Doughnut Company is the place with the mechanical doughnut machine that pops out miniature (1½ ounces each) doughnuts, à la *Homer Price and the Doughnuts*, a story many of us read as children: "Doughnuts in the window, doughnuts piled high on the shelves, doughnuts stacked on plates, doughnuts lined up twelve deep all along the counter, and doughnuts still rolling down the little chute, just as regular as a clock can tick…Meanwhile, the rings of batter kept right on dropping into the hot fat, and an automatic gadget kept right on turning them over, and another automatic gadget kept right on giving them a little push, and the doughnuts kept right on rolling down the little chute, just as regular as a clock can tick."

Owner Barbara Elza explains that doughnuts themselves originated in Holland in the 1700s and took Europe by storm, although in a slightly different form than we take for granted today. It wasn't until the early 1900s, when doughnuts crossed the Atlantic to America, that some smart soul thought of putting holes in the middle to make them less doughy and improve their tex-ture. The idea caught on, and now even Europe has holes in its doughnuts.

# *Holiday Doughnut Trees*

### DAILY DOZEN DOUGHNUT COMPANY

This makes a pretty brunch dish for the holiday season and is fun for children to prepare. The extra five doughnuts called for in this recipe are for snacking, or if you make a mistake!

*25 to 30 Daily Dozen Doughnut miniature doughnuts, plain flavor*

*1 tube gel icing (available in the baking section of grocery stores)*

*Red and green sugar sprinkles*

*Chocolate (brown-colored) sprinkles*

Get out a large platter and arrange about 12 doughnuts in a triangle shape that looks like a pine tree.

Make circular designs with gel icing on top of 12 new doughnuts. Dip icing-side down into red and green sprinkles. Place decorated doughnuts on top of the first row of doughnuts.

Cut one remaining doughnut in half and place one of the halves at the base of the triangle to form the "trunk" of the "tree." Place gel icing over top of remaining half doughnut, then dip in chocolate sprinkles. Place over the half doughnut at the base.

If desired, sprinkle doughnut tree with multicolored sprinkles or nonpareils, or decorate with additional seasonal candies or maraschino cherries.

*Serves 6 to 8.*

# Breads

## Breads

Famous Garlic Bread

Sourdough Fresh Herb Bread

Focaccia Bread with Sun-Dried Tomatoes

Honey-Orange Rye Bread

Huckleberry/Pineapple/Zucchini Bread

Banana-Nut Bread/Cake

Strawberry-Nut Bread

Blueberry-Tarragon Pancakes

Oatmeal Breakfast Cookies

# CUCINA FRESCA

The scent of garlic lures you in; once inside you'll be tempted by dish after dish of Italian take-out specialties, such as *pollo al Toscano*, eggplant Parmesan, and *arancini*, Neapolitan herb rice balls with mozzarella centers. At this deliciously fragrant shop facing Pike Place (just past Le Panier), you'll also find fresh pastas (spinach-chive fettuccine, fresh egg linguine, and cilantro-sesame-scallion fettuccine) and sauces (smoked salmon cream cheese, Gorgonzola walnut, and roasted red pepper and goat cheese). Fresh pasta ends — red, green, and white pasta ribbons that swirl sinuously when cooked — are sometimes available and are not only thrifty and delicious but fun, especially for the kids.

Cucina Fresca's owners, Sue and Mike Tenore, focus on Neapolitan recipes (recipes typical of Naples) culled from Mike's side of the family, although the Tenores feature foods from every region of Italy. If they had one wish, Sue says it would be "to bottle the smells."

## *Famous Garlic Bread*

### CUCINA FRESCA

It's no typo that this recipe calls for four to six whole bulbs of garlic, but after roasting, garlic is surprisingly mild and wonderfully tasty, especially when mixed with the oils, butter, and parsley. This is a real treat.

*4 to 6 bulbs of garlic, peeled and chopped*

*⅓ cup canola oil*

*½ cup olive oil*

*½ cup canola oil*

*⅓ cup butter*

*¼ cup chopped fresh parsley*

*1 large baguette, cut in half lengthwise*

*½ cup freshly grated Parmesan cheese*

Preheat oven to 475°F. Get out a cookie sheet and set aside.

In a small oven-safe glass mixing bowl or dish, mix garlic with the ⅓ cup canola oil and place in oven until garlic is evenly and lightly browned, stirring occasionally, about 7 to 10 minutes. Heat the olive oil, the ½ cup canola oil, and the butter in a small saucepan over medium heat and add browned garlic and parsley.

Spread mixture over baguette halves, then sprinkle baguettes with Parmesan cheese. Place baguettes on cookie sheet and bake until edges begin to brown, about 7 to 10 minutes. Cut into serving-size slices before serving.

*Makes 12 slices.*

# CINNAMON WORKS

As you walk along Pike Place, the rich smell of cinnamon alerts you that another tray of mammoth cinnamon buns has just been hoisted from the ovens at Cinnamon Works. Customers jockey two and three deep in line to claim their share of the booty.

Under the guidance of owner Michael Ruegamer, an engaging man with the bluest eyes and the swagger of a salty sailor, Cinnamon Works is a natural foods bakery that uses real vanilla, maple syrup, butter, and eggs from free-running hens in its baked-on-the-premises goodies, and shuns all chemical additives and stabilizers.

Specialties include cinnamon buns of all varieties (whole wheat sticky buns are the best-selling favorite); whole grain breads; and *fragassa* (an Italian vegetable-cheese bread). Dessert specialties include oat bars made with seasonal fresh fruit; the seven-layer bars for chocolate lovers; pecan bars; no-flour peanut butter oatmeal cookies; and fresh-fruit, sugarless, whole wheat scones. Unbaked whole wheat pizza dough by the pound and a secret-formula granola are also available.

## Sourdough Fresh Herb Bread

### CINNAMON WORKS

Although it requires a little planning to prepare the sourdough starter a few days before you actually want to make this bread, it's worth it for the subtle sourdough/cheese taste and dense texture. You'll also be reliving a part of history — sourdough dates back to ancient Egypt and was an integral part of the diet of early American settlers, who enjoyed sourdough rolls, biscuits, and pancakes. You can purchase sourdough starter at Magnano Foods, MarketSpice, and Louie's on the Pike in the Pike Place Market. Be sure to use fresh herbs, not dried.

*1 package sourdough starter, prepared as package directs*

*2 packages active dry yeast*

*2¼ cups warm milk*

*2 tablespoons sugar*

*1 tablespoon butter, melted*

*6 cups unbleached white flour*

*2 teaspoons salt*

*2 tablespoons chopped fresh arugula*

*2 tablespoons chopped fresh sweet basil*

*3 cloves garlic, diced*

*1 cup grated Parmesan cheese*

*1 egg, beaten*

Grease four 5- by 9-inch loaf pans or 2 large cookie sheets, depending on whether you want loaves or rounds of bread.

In a large mixing bowl, whisk together 2½ cups of the prepared sourdough starter, the yeast, milk, and sugar and let stand until bubbly, about 2 minutes. Add butter and stir until mixed thoroughly. Add flour and salt and blend until a soft, smooth dough forms.

Add arugula, basil, garlic, and cheese to dough, and mix until well incorporated. Turn dough out onto a well-floured board and knead until smooth and satiny, about 5 minutes, adding additional flour if bread board or your hands become sticky.

Place dough in a lightly greased mixing bowl, turning once to grease surface. Cover with a dish towel and let rise in a warm place until doubled in size, about 1 to 1½ hours. Punch down dough, cut in fourths, and let rest 10 minutes. Shape loaves to fit in loaf pans, or form loaves into rounds and place on greased cookie sheets. Cover and let loaves rise again until doubled in size, about ½ to 1 hour. After 20 minutes, preheat oven to 350°F.

Brush loaves with egg wash (beaten egg). Place loaves in oven and bake until loaves color and bread pulls away from sides of loaf pan, about 30 to 40 minutes. To test rounds of bread for doneness, tap loaf; if it sounds hollow, it's done. Remove loaves from loaf pans or cookie sheet and place on a wire rack to cool. Slice and serve.

*Makes 4 loaves or rounds.*

*Note:* To make a warm place for dough to rise, fill a large baking pan with hot water, put on lowest rack in unheated oven, put covered dough in mixing bowl on oven rack above water, and close oven door.

Sourdough starter can be tricky to make. For best results, use a glass bowl to mix sourdough starter, and use a wooden or plastic spoon to stir it. Cover the glass bowl *loosely* with plastic wrap (do not use a snug-fitting lid, or the starter could die from lack of oxygen). Place sourdough starter in a warm, dark, draft-free area for about 2 days; I put mine in a little-used kitchen cupboard near the sink, where it will stay warm and undisturbed. When sourdough is ready, it will be thick, wispy, and cream-colored. Put to rest in refrigerator, loosely covered, but return to room temperature when ready to use. After you've used the amount you need, replenish the starter by adding ¾ cup flour, ¾ cup water, and 1 teaspoon sugar or honey, and return to a warm, dark, draft-free space for 24 hours. Then store in refrigerator. If you don't use starter within 10 days, add another 1 teaspoon sugar or honey; repeat every 10 days unless replenished.

# *Focaccia Bread with Sun-Dried Tomatoes*

## Sur La Table

Within the past few years, *focaccia* bread, a large, flat Italian bread sprinkled before baking with olive oil, salt, and herbs, has become popular at many Italian restaurants throughout the United States. This is an easy-to-prepare version you can whip up at home. The sun-dried tomatoes mixed in the dough really set it apart, and you can personalize it even further with your choice of fresh or dried herbs, garlic, or onions.

*4 cups flour, plus additional flour for bread board*

*2 teaspoons salt*

*2 packages quick-rise yeast*

*2 tablespoons olive oil*

*¼ cup chopped sun-dried tomatoes packed in oil*

*1¾ to 2¼ cups hot water*

*Olive oil*

*Fresh or dried herbs of your choice, such as oregano, rosemary, thyme, chives, parsley, basil, fresh garlic, onions, sautéed onions, or a mixture*

*Freshly ground pepper to taste*

Take out an 11- by 17-inch jelly-roll pan, grease lightly or spray with nonstick olive-oil spray, and set aside.

Place flour, salt, yeast, the 2 tablespoons olive oil, and sun-dried tomatoes in a large mixing bowl and stir with large spoon to mix ingredients. Add 1¾ cups hot water and stir well with large spoon. If dough seems too dry, add a bit more hot water until it forms a ball.

Flour bread board with additional flour and turn dough out onto board. Knead until smooth, adding the minimum amount of flour to keep dough from sticking to your hands and board (dough will be soft, almost the consistency of biscuit dough).

Place dough in a lightly greased mixing bowl, turning once to grease surface. Cover with a clean dish towel and let rise in a warm place for at least 30 minutes.

Preheat oven to 450°F. Flatten dough into jelly-roll pan until ¼ inch to ½ inch thick, cover dough with a clean dish cloth, and let rest in a warm place until puffed, about 20 minutes. Drizzle with olive oil and sprinkle top of dough with your choice of fresh or dried herbs. Sprinkle with freshly ground pepper to taste.

Bake until lightly browned and puffy, 12 to 15 minutes. Serve warm, cut into slabs, with additional olive oil or softened butter, if desired.

*Makes 16 to 20 slices.*

# Honey-Orange Rye Bread

### MECH APIARIES

Baking bread is so soothing and therapeutic — every time I make it, I wonder why I don't do it more often. And this dense, solid bread has a wonderful orange taste and a slight crunch from the rye grain. It's great for peanut-butter-and-jelly sandwiches, especially if you spread it with orange marmalade!

*2 packages active dry yeast*

*½ cup warm water*

*½ cup honey*

*½ cup molasses*

*2 tablespoons salt*

*½ cup vegetable oil*

*3 cups hot water*

*3 cups rye flour*

*¼ cup grated orange peel*

*8 to 9 cups unbleached white flour*

Grease four 4½- by 8½-inch loaf pans.

Soften the yeast in the ½ cup warm water. In a large mixing bowl, combine honey, molasses, salt, and oil. Stir in the 3 cups hot water, then stir in the rye flour and beat well. Add the softened yeast and the orange peel and mix well. Stir in enough of the unbleached white flour to make a soft dough. Cover with a dish towel and let rest for 10 minutes.

Turn dough out on a well-floured bread board and knead for 10 minutes, adding additional unbleached white flour if bread board or your hands get sticky. Place dough in a lightly greased mixing bowl, turning once to grease surface. Cover and let rise in a warm place until doubled (about 1½ hours), then punch down.

Turn dough out onto a lightly floured board, divide into four equal portions, and shape each into a smooth ball. Cover and let rest for 10 minutes, then shape into four loaves and place in loaf pans. Cover and return to warm place to rise until doubled (about 1 hour). Preheat oven to 375°F. Bake until golden brown, about 30 minutes, then cool on wire racks.

*Makes 4 loaves.*

*Note:* For a softer-crusted bread, brush with soft margarine or butter before baking.

Homebaked bread will slice well while still warm if you use an electric carving knife or a very sharp bread knife.

# THE GRANGER BERRY PATCH
In 1976, city folk Sandi and Ken Fein settled into their antique house and farm on Granger's Beam Road, named after the home's original owner. For years, the land had supported potato, apple, grape, and dairy farming, but the Feins left most of the ground in pasture, except for setting out 1,000 strawberry plants. When the strawberry plants proliferated and produced much more fruit than the Feins could eat, they converted the farm into a berry farm.

"Today we're a real berry museum," Sandi Fein explains. "We raise and make berry products from boysenberries, loganberries, marionberries, several kinds of blackberries, 12 varieties of red raspberries, golden raspberries, blackcaps (black raspberries), currants, red and black gooseberries, and many others."

The Feins enjoy the Market because the direct contact with the customer allows them to test-market new berries (such as black currants and golden raspberries) and new products. However, it does produce its funny moments. When customers see the golden raspberries for the first time, they often ask, "How did you make those yellow? Bleach them?"

## *Huckleberry/Pineapple/Zucchini Bread*

— THE GRANGER BERRY PATCH —

Huckleberries, also known as whortleberries and bilberries, are like small, tart blueberries, with a very limited season (mid-August through mid-September), but they're worth searching out as a great addition to this rich, moist bread. It freezes well, so make a double batch and freeze a couple of extra loaves for future enjoyment.

*3 eggs*

*1 cup light vegetable oil, such as canola, corn, or soy*

*2 cups sugar*

*2 teaspoons vanilla extract*

*2 cups unpeeled, grated zucchini*

*1 cup canned, crushed pineapple, well drained*

*3 cups flour*

*2 teaspoons baking soda*

*1 teaspoon salt*

*½ teaspoon baking powder*

*1½ teaspoons ground cinnamon*

*¼ teaspoon ground nutmeg*

*1 cup chopped nuts (optional)*

*1 cup huckleberries (fresh, frozen and defrosted, or dried)*

Preheat oven to 350°F. Take out two 5- by 9-inch loaf pans and grease lightly or spray with nonstick corn-oil spray.

In a large bowl beat together eggs, oil, sugar, and vanilla until foamy. Stir in zucchini and pineapple. Combine flour, baking soda, salt, baking powder, cinnamon, and nutmeg in a separate mixing bowl, then stir into creamed mixture. Add nuts (if used), and huckleberries.

Bake until toothpick inserted in middle comes out clean, 60 to 70 minutes. If top of bread starts to get too brown during baking, place a loose tent of aluminum foil over top during last 15 or 20 minutes of baking time.

Cool on a wire rack, turn out of loaf pans, and slice. Serve warm or cool with softened butter or margarine and berry spread, jelly, or jam, if desired.

*Makes 2 loaves.*

# Banana-Nut Bread/Cake

## SUR LA TABLE

This recipe is unlike any banana-nut bread I've ever tried. It can't seem to make up its mind — is it a cake masquerading as a bread, or a bread disguised as a cake? You decide, based on the type of pan you choose to bake it in. After you try it, you'll agree that whichever it is, it's rich, moist, and yummy.

½ *cup firmly packed brown sugar*

*1 cup granulated sugar*

*2 cups flour*

*1 teaspoon baking powder*

*2 eggs, beaten*

½ *cup buttermilk*

*1 teaspoon baking soda, dissolved in the buttermilk*

*1 teaspoon vanilla extract*

*3 or 4 ripe bananas, mashed*

*1 cup chopped walnuts*

Preheat oven to 350°F. Take out two 5- by 9-inch loaf pans or one 9- by 13-inch baking pan and grease lightly or spray with nonstick corn-oil spray.

In large mixing bowl, mix sugars, flour, and baking powder until well blended, and set aside. Mix eggs, baking soda dissolved in buttermilk, and vanilla in medium mixing bowl and blend thoroughly. Add bananas and nuts to wet ingredients and stir.

Make a well in center of dry ingredients and add wet ingredients, stirring just enough to moisten dry ingredients. Spoon batter into pan(s) of your choice.

Bake until bread/cake pulls away from sides of pan, turns golden brown on top, and a toothpick inserted in middle comes out almost clean (a few crumbs should remain), about 25 to 35 minutes, depending on baking pans used. Cool loaves on wire rack, turn out of loaf pans, slice, and serve. Cool cake pan on wire rack, and, if desired, frost cake with Cream-Cheese Icing (see German Apple Cake, page 166), slice, and serve.

*Makes 2 loaves or 1 cake, 12 servings.*

# BIRINGER FARM

Tucked back in the Post Alley Market, the Biringer Farm Bakery & Country Store is a good place to get away from the hustle and bustle of the Market and enjoy a fresh-baked pastry, light lunch, or berry shake.

Managed by Melody Biringer, a third-generation berry farmer, the store is an offshoot of the Biringer Farm U-Pick, run by Melody's parents Dianna and Mike Biringer in Marysville. The Pike Place Market store carries the complete line of Biringer farm products, including prize-winning berry jams, honeys, vinegars, and sauces. Their raspberry and strawberry cocoa mixes, red raspberry honey mustard, and berry and chocolate-fudge toppings make especially welcome gifts.

## *Strawberry-Nut Bread*

### BIRINGER FARM BAKERY & COUNTRY STORE

A light-brown nut bread bursting with cinnamon, this recipe is great to make around the Thanksgiving and Christmas holidays instead of banana-nut bread, and a good way to use up the extra strawberries you froze during the summer.

*3 cups sifted flour*

*1 teaspoon baking soda*

*1 teaspoon salt*

*1 tablespoon ground cinnamon*

*2 cups sugar*

*4 eggs, beaten*

*1¼ cups light vegetable oil, such as canola, corn, or soy*

*2 cups frozen, unsweetened strawberries, thawed and sliced*

*1¼ cups chopped pecans*

Preheat oven to 350°F. Take out two 5- by 9-inch loaf pans, lightly grease or spray with nonstick corn-oil spray, and set aside.

In large mixing bowl sift together flour, baking soda, salt, cinnamon, and sugar, then mix well with a large spoon or your hands until cinnamon is dispersed throughout flour. In separate large bowl combine eggs, oil, strawberries, and pecans, mixing well with fork.

Make a well in the center of the dry ingredients and add wet ingredients, stirring just enough to moisten dry ingredients. Divide batter between loaf pans and bake until a toothpick inserted in center comes out clean, about 1 hour.

Cool on wire rack. Turn out loaves, slice into 8 slices per loaf, and serve as desired (see hints for serving below).

*Makes 2 loaves.*

*Note:* I like to make this recipe in the spring or summer with fresh berries and toasted hazelnuts in place of the pecans. If you use fresh berries, make sure they are very ripe and juicy. Halve or quarter berries, then gently mash with fork to start juices flowing. Let berries sit at room temperature for

1 hour before adding to wet ingredients. You can also substitute frozen, sweetened berries, but reduce the 2 cups of sugar to 1½ cups.

Slices of Strawberry-Nut Bread make a scandalously rich base for strawberry short-cake or strawberry sundaes. Just put a slice in the bottom of a deep dish, and add a scoop of strawberry ice cream or frozen yogurt, additional sliced strawberries or strawberry syrup, whipped cream or whipped topping, and a whole strawberry on the top.

## Blueberry-Tarragon Pancakes

──────── RACHEL-DEE HERB FARM ────────

You'll enjoy this inventive recipe that's as healthful as it is delicious. And don't make it for breakfast only — hold the melted butter and serve for dessert at the height of blueberry season with a scoop of vanilla ice cream and a handful of additional blueberries or other fresh fruits.

*1 cup flour*

*2 teaspoons baking powder*

*¼ to ⅓ cup Rachel-Dee blueberry-tarragon jam*

*1 tablespoon light vegetable oil, such as canola, corn, or soy*

*⅔ cup milk*

*2 egg whites, beaten until stiff*

*¾ cup blueberries*

Preheat a lightly greased griddle over medium-high heat. Meanwhile, in a medium mixing bowl mix flour with baking powder. In another bowl combine jam, vegetable oil, and milk; fold in egg whites. Combine wet and dry ingredients, blend just until mixed, then fold in blueberries.

For each pancake ladle 2 tablespoons batter onto hot griddle. When edges turn dry and a few bubbles appear on surface of pancakes, turn with a spatula. Cook until second side turns golden brown.

Serve immediately with additional blueberry-tarragon jam and melted butter or margarine. If desired, add a small amount of water to additional blueberry-tarragon jam to form a syrup and pour over pancakes like maple syrup.

*Makes about 12 pancakes, 3 or 4 servings.*

# Oatmeal Breakfast Cookies

SUR LA TABLE

These hearty, fiber-full breakfast cookies are a sensible alternative for people on the run, or for those who normally don't eat breakfast. A couple of oatmeal breakfast cookies and a double latte with nonfat milk and you're set for the morning in a low-fat, low-calorie, delicious way. They also freeze well.

*1 cup margarine (Saffola brand preferred), softened*

*1 cup firmly packed brown sugar*

*1 whole egg, beaten*

*2 egg whites*

*1 teaspoon vanilla extract*

*1 tablespoon grated orange or lemon rind*

*1 cup flour*

*4 cups rolled oats (do not use instant oatmeal)*

*1 cup sunflower seed*

*½ cup sesame seed*

*¼ cup wheat germ*

*¼ cup raw bran flakes (use raw bran flakes, not Bran Flakes prepackaged cereal)*

*1 cup raisins*

*1 cup shredded coconut*

*1 cup chopped walnuts, pecans, or hazelnuts*

*½ cup granulated sugar*

*1 teaspoon ground cinnamon*

Preheat oven to 375°F. Take out two cookie sheets and set aside.

Mix together margarine and the brown sugar with a pastry blender or electric mixer. Add whole egg, egg whites, vanilla, and rind, and beat by hand or mix thoroughly with electric mixer.

Stir in flour and mix thoroughly, then add rolled oats, sunflower seed, sesame seed, wheat germ, and bran flakes, and blend well. Fold in raisins, coconut, and nuts. Make cinnamon/sugar mixture by blending the granulated sugar and the cinnamon in a small mixing bowl.

Scoop out dough with a tablespoon and roll into balls with your hands. Roll in sugar/cinnamon mixture, place on cookie sheet, and mash flat with the bottom of a glass. Bake until lightly browned, 8 to 10 minutes. Cool cookie sheets on wire racks 2 to 3 minutes, then remove cookies to wire racks to cool completely.

*Makes 4 dozen cookies.*

# Sauces, Relishes, and Dips

## Sauces, Relishes, and Dips

*Red Raspberry Chutney*

*Apricot-Pineapple Jam*

*Apricot Syrup*

*Poppy Seed Dressing with Honey*

*Deviled Fruit Vinegar Butter*

*Basic Vinaigrette with Fruit Vinegar*

*Fruity Vinegar Barbecue Sauce*

*Smoked Salmon Spread*

*Fresh Vegetable Sauce with Basil Vinegar*

*Basic Freezer Tomato Sauce and Variations*

*Basic Freezer Tomato Sauce with Lamb Shanks*

*Basic Freezer Tomato Sauce with Fish Fillets*

*Indo-Afro-Tex-Mex Culture-Shock Dip*

*Marinara Vegetable Sauce*

*Sassy Salsa*

# VALLEY PACKER FARMS

Since 1948 Tim Johannes's family has been in the frozen-fruit-processing business, selling frozen red raspberries, blueberries, and blackberries in retail and food-service sizes. "People love raspberries, but sometimes they don't realize the many varieties available," Tim explains. "Meekers are an all-round berry — large, firm, rich red in color with a high sugar content and excellent flavor. Chilcotins are sharp and acerbic, with a pecan tartness. Willamettes are large, deep-red berries with a slightly tart flavor. Chilliwacks, named after the town in British Columbia, are a big, hearty berry, very firm and sweet. Sumners are a small, round, bright berry, fairly firm, very sweet and delicious."

Valley Packer Farms is owned by Jim Johannes, Tim's father. Tim runs the branch of the company that picks fresh red raspberries each morning, trucks them to the Market from the farm in McMillan, and sells them in the North Arcade daily June through July.

## *Red Raspberry Chutney*

VALLEY PACKER FARMS

If you like chutney, you'll become as addicted to this hearty version as I have — serve it with meat or non-meat dishes; swordfish; Indian dishes; or on toast, crackers, biscuits, or crumpets. It would even be good on ice cream, frozen yogurt, or sherbet.

2 quarts red raspberries, Chilcotin or Willamette varieties preferred, although any variety will do

2¼ cups brown sugar

1 cup golden raisins

1 cup chopped unsulfured dried apricots

1 cup water (use less or eliminate completely if berries are very soft)

½ cup toasted, chopped almonds

¼ cup lemon juice, freshly squeezed

2 tablespoons lime juice, freshly squeezed

1 tablespoon of a mixture of grated lemon, lime, and orange rinds

1½ teaspoons salt (optional)

1 teaspoon grated yellow onion

¼ teaspoon ground cloves

Add all ingredients to a large saucepan and bring to a boil. Reduce heat to low and simmer, uncovered, until the mixture thickens and darkens, 1 to 2 hours, depending on flavor desired. (Taste after 1 hour and, if you desire a richer, heartier flavor and denser texture, continue cooking.) Chill and serve as desired. You can also increase or decrease any of the dried fruits or flavorings, depending on your taste and use for the chutney. It also freezes well and can be kept in the refrigerator for 1 to 2 weeks.

*Makes about 4 cups.*

# BICKFORD ORCHARD On weekends during July and August, you'll

find Penny and Monte Bickford handing out samples of their apricots, peaches, and cherries in the North Arcade. Penny says it's fun to see how the ultimate consumer reacts to their specialty fruits, although she always has to ask if they prefer their fruit sweet or tart because the flavors are so different.

Bing cherries are the traditional dark, sweet, rich fruit that everyone thinks of when they think of cherries. The Van cherries that Penny and Monte bring to the Market are similar to Bings, yet are normally seen only in local farmers' markets as they're perishable and don't ship well. They are best eaten fresh or used shortly after picking. The Rainier cherries that the Bickfords grow are premium sweet, yellow cherries with a red blush.

When it comes to apricots, Penny and Monte offer the Moorpark, an older variety with a mellow, sweet taste, best used to make fruit leather. Rivals are small and tart and make good drying apricots. The Perfection variety is a large, mildly tart, juicy variety of apricot good for eating fresh. Their Redhaven semi-cling peaches are sweet, juicy, and full of flavor, perfect to eat fresh or to freeze, but not to use for canning.

Penny and Monte's 10-acre orchard is located in Malaga, five miles downriver from Wenatchee on the banks of the Columbia River. They also grow five types of apples there — Erligold, Gala, Fuji, and Golden and Red Delicious — and often bring them to the Taste of Washington Farms event held every year in the Market over the Labor Day weekend.

# Apricot-Pineapple Jam

#### BICKFORD ORCHARD

Make Apricot-Pineapple Jam at the height of apricot season (July and August). Extra jars would make great Christmas gifts, if they're not long gone by December.

*2 pounds apricots, washed and pitted*

*1 tablespoon lemon juice*

*30 ounces canned, unsweetened, crushed pineapple (about 3¾ cups), undrained*

*1 package pectin, Slim Set brand preferred*

*4½ cups sugar*

Grind apricots and measure 3 cups of pulp. Add lemon juice and undrained pineapple and place in a 6- or 8-quart kettle. Add pectin and stir thoroughly until pectin is dissolved completely, scraping sides of pan often.

Place mixture over medium-high heat and bring to a boil, stirring constantly to prevent scorching. Add sugar, stir, and bring to a hard boil that cannot be stirred down. Boil hard exactly 1 minute, then remove pan from heat and skim off foam.

Pour jam into hot, sterile jars and process 10 minutes in boiling water bath. Check seals when cool.

*Makes 8 half-pint jars.*

# Apricot Syrup

#### BICKFORD ORCHARD

This original recipe was designed to use lots of fruit with a minimum of sugar, and the result is a syrup that is very fresh tasting — just like fresh apricots. It's great on pancakes or waffles, poured over fruit salad, or as a marinade for chicken or turkey when combined with fresh herbs of your choice.

*7 cups apricot purée, about 4 to 5 pounds of apricots that have been washed, seeded, and puréed in blender or food processor*

*2½ cups sugar*

*⅛ teaspoon lemon juice*

Bring apricot purée, sugar, and lemon juice to a boil in a large Dutch oven or stockpot, then turn down heat and simmer until slightly thick, about 1 hour.

Pour into hot, sterile pint jars and seal with two-piece canning lids. Process in boiling water bath 20 minutes. Begin timing when water returns to a boil. Remove from heat and let cool on towel-covered counter. Check seals. Store in a cool, dark place until ready to use.

After opening, refrigerate and use within two weeks.

*Makes about 3½ pints.*

# MECH APIARIES
Doris and Don Mech have been busy as bees since 1973, when they left their careers as a teacher and an electrical engineer, respectively, to begin Mech Apiaries, their honey farm in Maple Valley. Doris, a helpful, patient woman with wire-rimmed glasses perched on her nose, brings all the products of the beehive to the North Arcade every Saturday throughout the year.

Her stall is a visual knockout, with hand-carved beeswax sculptures of teddy bears, Christmas trees, bees in flight, and praying hands. Jars of 11 types of honey in shades from tan to brown march across her table in even rows from shortest to highest. You'll also find beeswax candles, bee pollen, honey taffy, and beautiful cut flowers, especially dahlias, Doris's specialty, from July until the first frost.

"Our honey is raw — pure and old-fashioned. As a result of simple straining and careful processing it comes to you with the original vitamins, minerals, enzymes, and pollen intact," Doris explains. "Many people don't realize that everything in the hive is useful, from bee pollen, to the sweet honeycomb, to the wax."

Like other types of farming, bee farming is seasonal and depends heavily on the presence or absence of rain. In May, the bees gather nectar from the flowers of broadleaf maple trees in Maple Valley to produce a robust-tasting honey. In June, the Mechs truck the beehives to Harstene Island, where the bees gather nectar from wild huckleberry bushes to produce a light amber honey in the middle range of flavor intensity. July sees the Mechs trucking the beehives back to the lowlands of the Green River Valley, where the bees feast on wild blackberries, which yield a light, delicate, slightly fruity honey.

Snowberry bushes blossom in August, when the Mechs move some of their bees over the Cascade Mountains to the farmland near Cle Elum and Ellensburg. Snowberry honey is mild, with a slight tang. Fireweed honey, a mild, pale honey, is produced in August, when the Mechs take their bees to the Cascade Mountains, near the foothills of Mount Rainier. Here black bears sometimes fight the Mechs for the rich honey.

In late summer, Doris and Don move the bees to the Kittitas Valley, where they feast on strawberry clover and produce a mild, delicate honey. "Since we have to move the hives at night in search of the finest nectars, during harvest season my husband and I are a lot like the worker bees — we never sleep!" Doris says.

# *Poppy Seed Dressing with Honey*

MECH APIARIES

This dressing is a delicious accompaniment to any tossed green salad or fruit salad. Try it with avocados, grapefruit slices, and apples on a bed of crisp romaine.

½ cup mild honey

1 teaspoon dry mustard

1 teaspoon salt

⅓ cup apple cider vinegar

1 tablespoon fresh onion purée

1 cup vegetable oil, soy oil preferred

1½ tablespoons poppy seed

Measure the honey, dry mustard, salt, and vinegar directly into blender or mixing bowl and process or whisk until smooth. Make the fresh onion purée by rubbing a sweet onion over the finest part of your hand grater, then add it to the dressing.

Start the blender, gradually add the oil in a slow stream, and process until thoroughly blended, or whisk oil in by hand, using a wire whisk. Stop the blender and sprinkle the poppy seed on top, then flip the blender on and off three or four times until the seeds are mixed in, or stir poppy seed in by hand.

Place in a serving bowl or small pitcher and let family and guests serve themselves.

*Makes just under 2 cups.*

# HARMONY FARMS

Mary Ann Norris is a fourth-generation farmer as well as a high school English and business teacher who describes herself as "a real country person with a great appreciation for Mother Earth." As owner of Harmony Farms in Silver Creek, she sells fresh strawberries, raspberries, blackberries, apples, Asian pears, gladiolus, and berry vinegars, syrups, and preserves on the weekends during the summer months in the North Arcade. "I'd rather go to the Market than anywhere else," she explains, "not only because it's so exciting, but because I like to learn from the other vendors. They have such a pride in their products; you can feel it."

## Deviled Fruit Vinegar Butter

### HARMONY FARMS

If you want a prettier presentation for this fruit vinegar butter, shape the softened butter into a log, refrigerate until well chilled, and then slice and place rounds on top of meat or fish just before serving.

¼ cup butter, softened to room temperature

2 tablespoons Harmony Farms fruit vinegar, any flavor

½ teaspoon dry mustard

2 teaspoons white Worcestershire sauce

¼ teaspoon salt

2 egg yolks

Place butter in small mixing bowl and stir well to soften completely. Add vinegar, mustard, Worcestershire sauce, salt, and egg yolks and mix well. If you have trouble incorporating the liquid into the butter, beat with an electric mixer at medium speed for 2 or 3 minutes.

Level off butter in bowl it was mixed in, then place in refrigerator until well chilled. Serve over grilled fish, poultry, or pork, using about 1 tablespoon per serving.

*Makes about ¼ cup; 4 servings.*

# Basic Vinaigrette with Fruit Vinegar

HARMONY FARMS

Although this dressing is wonderful as is, try adding tomato juice, mayonnaise, sour cream, yogurt, minced garlic or shallots, or crumbled blue cheese for variety.

3 tablespoons Harmony Farms fruit vinegar, any flavor

1 tablespoon Dijon or homemade mustard

½ cup olive oil, salad oil, or combination of the two

*Fresh herbs of your choice (optional)*

*Salt and pepper to taste*

With a whisk, combine fruit vinegar and mustard in a small glass mixing bowl. While whisking, add oil slowly. After mixture emulsifies, add herbs to enhance flavor, if desired, and salt and pepper to taste.

*Makes about ¾ cup.*

# Fruity Vinegar Barbecue Sauce

HARMONY FARMS

Barbecue sauces come in as many variations as there are cooks. This is a light, tangy/sweet version, perfect for chicken or fish.

1 tablespoon butter or margarine

¼ cup chopped onion

2 tablespoons firmly packed brown sugar

1 bottle (12 to 14 oz) tomato catsup

2 tablespoons drippings or light vegetable oil, such as canola, soy, or corn oil

½ cup Harmony Farms fruit vinegar, any flavor

Salt and pepper to taste

Heat butter or margarine in small skillet over medium heat and sauté onion until translucent. Remove from pan and place in medium glass mixing bowl. Add brown sugar, catsup, and drippings or fat. Whisk in fruit vinegar until well blended.

Cook chicken or fish as you normally would on a barbecue grill or by broiling or baking in the oven; to avoid bitterness, spread on barbecue sauce only during the last 15 minutes of cooking time. Salt and pepper to taste and serve.

*Makes about 2½ cups.*

# THE CRUMPET SHOP

Go into the Crumpet Shop, sit down at the counter, have a warm, buttered crumpet, and enjoy a view of First Avenue that's bound to teach you something about life if you keep your eyes and ears open.

Owners Nancy and Gary Lassater describe their signature item as "an unsweetened, yeasted English griddle cake." Kids drag their parents into the shop to watch the daily morning ritual as the baker pours crumpet batter into stainless steel crumpet rings that have been arranged on the griddle. The crumpets are "baked" on the stovetop until the bottoms are smooth and brown and the tops are riddled with tiny holes, much like English muffins. Once the crumpets are cool enough to handle, they're popped from their rings, the edges are snipped by hand, and they're ready to go.

Crumpets hail from the British Isles, and the Crumpet Shop opened in 1976 when Gary acquired a crumpet recipe from the owner of a bakery in Victoria, B.C., who had brought the recipe from England. Since then, the shop has gained fame throughout the United States and into Canada for its crumpets and scones.

Nancy Lassater is the quiet force that makes this place work. Whether she's up to her elbows kneading a batch of her famous Scottish groat bread, or sharing greetings with the gamut of people who make up her regular customer base, she shows a concern and caring that is all too rare.

With its tins of imported teas, a wide selection of Pacific Northwest preserves and honey, jars of imported jams and spreads, and a wonderful *Alice in Wonderland* mural on the back wall, the place offers a proper British atmosphere.

# Smoked Salmon Spread

— THE CRUMPET SHOP —

This is one of the easiest yet most satisfying recipes in the book, real Northwest comfort food. It's a wonderful light lunch or late-afternoon treat on a cold, cloudy day, and also makes elegant appetizers.

*½ cup lox*

*8 oz cream cheese, cut into ½-inch cubes*

*Crumpets or crackers of your choice*

*Garnishes: cucumber, tomato, and/or onion slices*

*Capers*

*Sprigs of fresh dill*

Blend lox in food processor until creamy. Add cream cheese, a few cubes at a time, until all cream cheese is processed and mixture is pale pink and smooth.

Spread on warm, buttered crumpets (as they do at the Crumpet Shop) and garnish with a cucumber, tomato, or onion slice. For appetizers, serve on crackers of your choice with cucumber, tomato, or onion slices, a few capers, and a sprig of fresh dill.

*Makes about 1½ cups, 8 servings as a light lunch, 24 appetizers.*

# Fresh Vegetable Sauce with Basil Vinegar

— SANDY'S ACRES —

Make this delicious sauce during basil season (June through October) and serve it over pasta or slices of crusty Italian bread.

*3 medium tomatoes or 1 basket cherry tomatoes, coarsely chopped*

*¼ cup chopped green onion*

*⅓ cup chopped fresh basil*

*½ cup Sandy's Acres basil vinegar or other herb vinegar*

*2 tablespoons mixed, minced fresh herbs of your choice, such as parsley, oregano, or thyme*

*Pinch of cayenne pepper*

*1 tablespoon walnut oil*

Gently mix tomatoes, green onion, basil, vinegar, herbs, and cayenne in a large mixing bowl. Drizzle the walnut oil over the vegetables and stir gently to mix. Serve as described above.

*Makes about 3 cups, 3 or 4 servings as a pasta entrée.*

# SUR LA TABLE

Sur La Table in the Seattle Garden Center Building is a foodie's delight. In this delightfully cluttered kitchen shop with a Continental feel and flair, you'll find items that literally aren't carried anywhere else in the United States, including cooks' tools, French copper cookware, direct imports from England and France, knives, table linens imported from China and India, dinnerware, glassware, and an extensive selection of baking equipment.

Among the more unusual offerings are asparagus tongs, Mickey Mouse waffle irons, olivewood nut crackers, pizza stones, British pan stands, and copper preserving pans. Their Sous Chef line of children's gear has become a nationwide hit, with mother/daughter and father/son apron and mitt sets, children's bake sets, and even child-sized chef's hats.

The staff is knowledgeable and ready to help, and the holiday catalog is always an event, as owner Shirley Collins describes the unique items she's gathered during her latest buying trips to Europe. In the July 1991 issue of *Atlantic Monthly*, senior editor and food writer Corby Kummer said, "Sur La Table is the best kitchen equipment store in the country," and the late James Beard proclaimed it one of the 10 best kitchen stores in America.

Founded in 1972, Sur La Table is located in a building that previously housed a St. Vincent de Paul thrift shop. After Sur La Table was granted the first change of use issued by the Historic Commission, the building was transformed into the gem it is today.

# Basic Freezer Tomato Sauce and Variations

SUR LA TABLE

At the height of tomato season, buy a couple of boxes of tomatoes to make into a basic sauce that can be frozen and used during the long winter months, when the only large tomatoes available look and taste like pink cotton balls. You can use this sauce in everything from pizza to appetizers, lamb shanks to fish fillets.

*4 large summer tomatoes*

Cut the tomatoes in half, core, cut into quarters, and place in a saucepan over medium heat. Cover the saucepan, reduce heat, and simmer, stirring every 10 minutes.

As the tomatoes become soft, mash them down into the liquid that accumulates in the pan. When all the tomatoes are cooked down, remove the lid and simmer to reduce sauce to the desired consistency. Remove from heat and allow to cool.

After the tomato mixture has cooled enough to handle safely, use a food mill to remove the seeds and skins. Place the sauce in a freezer-safe plastic bag or freezer container and freeze for later use.

*Makes about 4 cups sauce.*

*Note:* If you do not want to freeze your Basic Freezer Tomato Sauce or want to make fresh sauce, make as described above, and, when sauce is desired thickness, use as is or strain to remove seeds and skin.

If you want to make Basic Freezer Tomato Sauce during the winter months, use Roma tomatoes, as they have more flavor and maintain their shape and consistency better than the large tomatoes available then. As a rule of thumb, use one large summer or two-and-one-half Roma tomatoes per serving.

# *Basic Freezer Tomato Sauce with Lamb Shanks*

SUR LA TABLE

Braising lamb shanks in Basic Freezer Tomato Sauce will produce a tender cut of meat and a rich, delicious sauce. Serve with fresh pasta, brown rice, or any side dish that will help soak up the sauce.

*3 tablespoons olive oil*

*3 pounds lamb shanks (12 ounces per person)*

*1 large onion, chopped*

*1 cup dry red wine or water*

*Sprig of fresh oregano, minced, or 1 tablespoon dried*

*1 recipe Basic Freezer Tomato Sauce (about 4 cups), defrosted*

*2 or 3 cloves garlic, minced*

*Salt and pepper to taste*

*Minced fresh parsley*

*Grated Parmesan cheese*

Preheat oven to 200°F. Take out ovenproof plate and set aside.

Heat the olive oil in a large skillet over medium heat. Add lamb shanks and brown on all sides, then remove from pan and set aside. If needed, add a little more olive oil to pan, add onion, and cook for 5 minutes.

Add wine or water to pan and deglaze, scraping up the brown bits sticking to the bottom of the pan. Add oregano, tomato sauce, and garlic, place the lamb shanks on top, and cover the pan.

Cook over low heat until lamb shanks are done, 45 to 60 minutes. Remove the lamb shanks from the pan, place on ovenproof plate, and place in warm oven. Boil sauce until reduced to the desired consistency, and add salt and pepper to taste.

To serve, remove the meat from the lamb shanks and arrange on individual dinner plates or a large platter. Garnish with fresh parsley and serve the sauce over freshly cooked pasta or rice sprinkled with Parmesan cheese.

*Serves 4.*

# *Basic Freezer Tomato Sauce with Fish Fillets*

SUR LA TABLE

T his is a great dish to whip up after a hard day at work because it's fast and easy. I like to make it with tuna fillets and fresh basil for a light, healthy, Italian-style dinner.

*1 recipe Basic Freezer Tomato Sauce (about 4 cups), defrosted*

*½ cup dry white wine*

*6 tablespoons fresh herb of your choice (or a mixture), such as basil, tarragon, garlic, or chives*

*4 fish fillets of your choice (2 pounds), such as red snapper, flounder, sole, halibut, cod, or tuna*

*Minced fresh parsley*

Place sauce in large skillet and cook until reduced to a fairly thick consistency. Add white wine and herbs and mix well. Place fish fillets over tomato sauce and cover the pan. Cook 2 to 3 minutes and turn fish fillets. Continue to cook another 2 to 3 minutes until fillets are done.

Place fish fillets on four dinner plates and sprinkle with parsley. Place brown rice or fresh pasta beside fish fillets, spoon sauce over rice or pasta, sprinkle with parsley, and serve immediately.

*Serves 4.*

# WORLD CLASS CHILI

Joe Canavan, owner of World Class Chili*, jokingly claims that chili was invented by his Uncle Bill...one Saturday afternoon...in March...1863...near Butte, Montana. Regardless of who invented chili, Joe is reinventing it with his bubbling caldrons of Texas chili (made with beef), California-style chili (chicken), Cincinnati-style chili (pork and beef), and vegetarian chili, served straight or over your choice of rice, pinto or black beans, shell pasta, or any mixture of the four, with a side of oyster crackers, tortilla chips, or corn bread. It is also served in varying degrees of hotness (macho being the hottest). As Joe says, "It ain't the kind your mother used to make."

You can sling back a beer or a margarita at the L-shaped counter while you watch the ferryboats shuffle in and out, sit in the South Arcade and watch the people passing by, or order takeout chili to eat at home.

Joe, who's sometimes referred to as "the chili man," likes to tell of the time a worldly, well-traveled customer explained to him, "You understand life when you know why there's a hooker on the corner, a wind in the doorway, and, when you're in a re-ally good chili place, the waitress has dirt on her ankles."

 *Just outside of the Market Historic District.

# *Indo-Afro-Tex-Mex Culture-Shock Dip*

— WORLD CLASS CHILI —

Joe started cooking at the age of 14, when he was tending cattle and preparing his own meals. He devised this unusual yet delicious dip from recipes he learned in Cameroon, West Africa, where Indonesian and Arabian cuisines mix. He then merged these diverse cuisines with his own specialty: Tex-Mex. While in Cameroon (where he was visiting a niece, who was serving in the Peace Corps), he organized a chili cook-off!

*1 cup plain yogurt*

*1 cup smooth peanut butter, JIF brand preferred*

*8 mild green chile peppers, such as New Mexico or Anaheim, roasted, peeled, and chopped (you can substitute canned peppers, but the flavor won't be the same; see Techniques section for roasting instructions)*

*4 hot green chile peppers, such as jalapeños or serranos, roasted, peeled, and chopped (see Techniques section)*

*1 pickled chipotle pepper, chopped (these are sold in cans and are available at Mexican specialty markets, such as El Mercado Latino in the Pike Place Market)*

*Pinch of salt, or to taste*

*Pinch of sugar*

Combine all ingredients in food processor and blend until smooth. Chill overnight, then serve at room temperature as desired.

*Note:* You can use Indo-Afro-Tex-Mex Culture-Shock Dip in many ways. Serve with tortilla chips as a dip, or spread on squares of nine-grain bread for a quick lunch or onto quarters for easy-to-prepare appetizers. Add another chopped chipotle pepper to a few tablespoons of the dip and rub under the skin of a roasting chicken before placing in a hot (450°F) oven for a quick and delicious dinner. The dip is also good on grilled hamburgers served with hot mustard.

*Makes 2 cups.*

# LoPriore Bros. Pasta Bar & Eatery

The LoPriore brothers (Dave and Brian) come from a strong Italian background and use lots of family recipes at their pasta bar in the Post Alley Market. There's a casual atmosphere and sense of immediacy here — customers sit at the counter and watch as their selection is cooked right before their eyes. Fettuccine Alfredo, sausage sandwiches, and salads are specialties here, as is the first and only 30-ounce bowl of pasta in the Market.

## *Marinara Vegetable Sauce*

—————— LoPriore Bros. Pasta Bar & Eatery ——————

You'll enjoy this rich, garlic-filled sauce over fresh pasta cooked al dente. Add cooked shrimp, scallops, crab, and shellfish for a lusty version of seafood pasta.

*2 tablespoons olive oil*

*2 yellow onions, chopped*

*1 bulb garlic, cloves separated and minced*

*1 shallot, chopped*

*1 pound mushrooms, chopped*

*1 cup Burgundy wine or good-quality red table wine*

*¼ cup Worcestershire sauce*

*1 can (14½ oz) whole tomatoes, diced, plus their juice*

*1 can (12 oz) tomato paste*

*½ cup chopped fresh basil*

*1 cup chopped fresh cilantro*

*3 tablespoons granulated garlic*

*1 tablespoon ground black pepper*

*2 tablespoons dried oregano*

*2 to 3 cups water*

Place large Dutch oven or stockpot over medium heat and add olive oil. When oil is hot, add onion, garlic, and shallot, and sauté 1 or 2 minutes. Add mushrooms and sauté another 1 or 2 minutes. Add wine, Worcestershire sauce, tomatoes and their juice, and tomato paste and stir well.

Add basil, cilantro, granulated garlic, black pepper, and oregano and stir well. Add 2 cups water, stir well, cover, and simmer about 1 hour. If sauce gets too thick, add up to 1 cup more water during last 20 minutes of cooking time.

*Makes 8 cups.*

# RAIN GARDEN

"Many types of flowers are edible and add unique flavors and colorful garnishes to many dishes," according to Sharon Swoboda, who, with husband David, started Rain Garden in 1991. "Nasturtiums have a strong, peppery flavor. Violets are very floral. Borage adds a cucumber flavor. Chamomile is reminiscent of bitter apples. And squash and zucchini blossoms have a squashlike flavor."

Rain Garden is located on the last five acres of David's grandfather's farm about 40 miles from Seattle in Snohomish. The original home and farm buildings are still standing, and Sharon and David have about one acre planted, using herbs, companion planting, and ladybugs to control insects.

Sharon and David provide not only a large variety of organically grown edible flowers, but also fresh herbs, fresh herb mixes, and a salad mix featuring various lettuces, herbs, and edible flowers to their customers on Fridays, Saturdays, and Sundays April through November in the North Arcade. Sharon says she enjoys the people, scents, and music at the Market. "It's always fun to give samples of edible flowers, especially to children."

## *Sassy Salsa*

### — RAIN GARDEN —

This is a fresh-from-the-garden salsa that you'll want to serve with tortilla chips; over steamed potatoes or vegetables; as a side dish to grilled or roasted fish, chicken, or meat; or mixed with sour cream as a vegetable dip. You can adjust the hotness of the salsa by the amount of chili powder you add.

5 cloves garlic, minced

1 green, red, yellow, or purple bell pepper, diced

4 large, ripe tomatoes, cored, seeded, and diced

1 medium onion, diced

2 hot peppers, such as jalapeño or serrano, minced

1 bunch cilantro, chopped

5 green onions, sliced into ⅛-inch rings

¼ cup olive oil

⅛ cup red wine vinegar or herb vinegar

Juice of 1 lime

1 teaspoon freshly ground pepper

1 to 2 tablespoons chili powder

Dash of salt

In a medium mixing bowl with a cover stir together garlic, peppers, tomatoes, onion, hot peppers, cilantro, and green onions. In a small mixing bowl, whisk together olive oil, vinegar, lime juice, pepper, chili powder, and salt.

Pour dressing over vegetables and stir to mix completely. Cover and refrigerate several hours to let flavors meld, then return to room temperature before serving.

*Makes about 4 cups.*

# Beverages

## Beverages

Apricot Fizz

Continental Cooler Smoothie

A "Real" New York Egg Cream

Fresh Fruit Smoothie

Cider Pizzazz

The Perfect Cup of Coffee

Caffe Latte

Café Marrakech

Iced Café Crema

Indian-Style Chai (Yogi) Tea

Roasted Dandelion Root Coffee

The Perfect Pot of Tea

Menu for an Afternoon, Victorian, or Low Tea

# RANCH AT THE END OF THE ROAD

Vicky and Scott Williams grow Bing and Rainier cherries, apricots, Black Monukka grapes (black seedless table grapes), and Gewürtztraminer grapes at their farm, Ranch at the End of the Road, in Benton City, an area fast becoming known for its wine grapes.

"The Black Monukkas come into season from September through October, and, in a good year, they're as big as the top joint of your thumb and clusters weigh two or three pounds," Vicky says. "For the last few years, my son has known when the grapes are ripe before I do. If I can't find my child, I look for him under the grape canopy, often to find a smiling, purple-faced little boy with cheeks like a chipmunk's. Nothing's better!"

The Williamses like to sell their produce at the North Arcade during June through September because of the fast pace, the big crowds, and customers' surprised expressions when they taste Black Monukkas for the very first time.

## *Apricot Fizz*

### RANCH AT THE END OF THE ROAD

This is an extra thick and apricoty drink, bursting with Vitamin A. Enjoy it in July and August, the peak of the local apricot season.

*4 large or 8 small fresh, ripe apricots*

*1 cup sparkling water or soda water*

*2 teaspoons sugar or sugar substitute, or to taste (optional)*

*Fresh mint leaves, for garnish*

Wash apricots and remove pits. Purée in blender, then pour into an ice cube tray and freeze.

To serve place 6 apricot cubes, sparkling water or soda water, and sugar or sugar substitute (if used), into blender container. (You can vary the proportions according to your taste.) Blend to a slushy consistency, then pour into tall glasses. Garnish with fresh mint leaves, if desired, and serve immediately.

*Serves 1.*

# SCOTTY'S JUICERY

There really is a Scotty behind Scotty's Juicery, and you'll find him at his stand in the historic Triangle Building (built in 1910) facing Pike Place. Scotty Harris has been serving up fresh-squeezed juices, fresh fruit smoothies, and fresh-squeezed lemonade since 1977, which he claims makes his business Seattle's oldest full-service juice bar.

He enjoys recounting a story that shows the caring attitude of many customers at the Market. "My father needed a job to keep himself busy, but on the first day that he showed up, 10 minutes later I became sick with a life-threatening illness. My father was not trained and did not know how to operate the till or make the different products. So my customers told my father the prices and many times came behind the counter and prepared their own drinks. My customers trained my father to run and operate the business better than I could have!"

Scotty has since fought a successful battle against leukemia, including a bone-marrow transplant, and reports that the merchants, craftspeople, and artists provided great support and comfort during his three-year struggle.

## Continental Cooler Smoothie

SCOTTY'S JUICERY

*3 or 4 strawberries*

*Half a banana*

*3 or 4 chunks pineapple*

*1 cup orange juice, freshly squeezed, or apple juice*

*4 ice cubes*

*2 strawberries or 2 pineapple spears, for garnish*

Place all ingredients in blender and whip until smooth.

Pour into two tall glasses and garnish with a strawberry or pineapple spear.

*Makes about 4 cups, 2 servings.*

# DANNY'S WONDER FREEZE

Danny McCullem's the tanned, fit guy who runs around the Market in a red cap, red sports shirt, and khaki shorts. With a whistle swinging from his neck and clipboard in hand, he looks more like an athletic director than the owner of a hot dog stand, but that's what he is.

"The key thing here is hot dogs. I run Danny's Wonder Freeze like a New York hot dog stand," Danny explains. "I can tell what part of the United States a customer is from based on what condiments they ask for on their hot dog."

Danny explains that Southerners ask for "slaw" (coleslaw) on their dogs; those from New England ask for celery salt; those from New York like spicy New York red onion sauce, but not chili. No matter where you're from, mustard, relish, grilled onions, and sauerkraut are standard options at Danny's; homemade chili or cheese cost extra. Danny will also fix you a soft-serve vanilla ice cream cone ("vanilla's been the flavor of the day around here for 39 years"), a chocolate dipped cone with or without nuts, or a "real" New York egg cream. Danny's Wonder Freeze started out as The Wonder Freeze in 1952; Danny has owned it since 1986.

## A "Real" New York Egg Cream

### ———— DANNY'S WONDER FREEZE ————

Egg creams have been a favorite New York City soda fountain drink since the 1930s. They don't contain eggs; they're so named because the froth on the top looks like beaten egg whites. "There are 73 different ways to make an egg cream, and it all has to do with what neighborhood you grew up in," Danny explains. "When egg creams first began in New York City, you'd freeze whole milk, then chip it into chunks, add chocolate syrup, and 'fitzer' (soda) water, and stir. Nowadays, it's easier to add a touch of vanilla soft-serve ice cream. The key, though, is Fox's u-bet Chocolate Syrup, which is popular in the neighborhoods of Brooklyn. I'm one of only two people in Seattle who use it, and it makes quite a difference."

*Vanilla ice milk, frozen yogurt, or premium ice cream*

*Soda water*

*Chocolate syrup, Fox's u-bet brand preferred*

Place a couple of tablespoons of vanilla ice milk, frozen yogurt, or premium ice cream in the bottom of a large, tall glass. Fill glass almost to the top with soda water, and add a tablespoon or two of chocolate syrup. Stir, and serve immediately with a long spoon and a straw.

*Serves 1.*

# SHY GIANT FROZEN YOGURT

Shy Giant Frozen Yogurt started in 1976 and was the first frozen yogurt shop in the Pacific Northwest and only the second on the West Coast. Originally called Seattle's First Frozen Yogurt Shop, Inc., it was purchased by present owner Paul Billington in 1983. From his location in the Corner Market Building near Oriental Kitchenette and Quality Cheese, Paul serves custom-flavored frozen yogurts; nonfat yogurts; nondairy, sugarless products; and fresh fruit smoothies. If you're feeling more indulgent, you can order Dreyer's and Dankens premium ice creams by the scoop.

"The Market's a great attraction for locals and tourists alike," Paul, a blond, tanned, casual type of guy, says. "There's always lots of action, people from every cut of life, and all the good smells. The merchants are all such colorful characters, and the locals who patronize the Market or just hang out all add so much to make it what it is. Many of the aged locals are such landmarks."

## *Fresh Fruit Smoothie*

— SHY GIANT FROZEN YOGURT —

With its alternating layers of yogurt and fruit, this is a beautiful concoction, as well as a delicious, healthful treat.

*Half a fresh banana*

*1 cup fresh blueberries, raspberries, or strawberries*

*1 cup frozen yogurt of your choice*

*¼ cup low-fat milk or fruit juice of your choice*

In blender, purée fruits, pour into bowl, and set aside. In same blender, liquefy yogurt and milk or fruit juice.

Pour one-third of yogurt mixture into a tall glass. Pour half of fruit purée over yogurt. Repeat layers, ending with yogurt.

Serve with a straw and a long spoon, and enjoy.

*Serves 1.*

# WOODRING ORCHARDS

The Rankin family started coming to the Market in 1985, selling gallons of fresh cider (made entirely from crushed fresh apples) on the farm tables. Over the years Pat and Jim Rankin have expanded the scope of Woodring Orchards to include processed ciders; cider syrup, glazes, and chutney; and low-sugar jams, jellies, and apple butter. They're available seven days a week in the business's permanent space in the Main Arcade, where you can always try a free sample (or two, or three).

"We guarantee quality, not consistency," Jim says. "Because our products are prepared naturally and the fruit varies from year to year, this directly affects the texture, color, and sweetness in our juices and spreads. Customers have a hard time understanding this, but we never sell a product that doesn't taste good."

Everyone pitches in to keep this family-run business thriving. Pat and Jim run the orchard, with Jim also in charge of cider and apple production. Son Joel runs the store at the Market and the mail-order business; daughter Kathy develops and produces the processed products along with Pat; and another son, Larry, is the broker and packager. The business is named after John Woodring, an early settler on the Rankin's property, in the town of Cashmere.

## *Cider Pizzazz*

#### WOODRING ORCHARDS

A sweet punch, great for kids and adults alike, and you can make it lower in calories, if desired.

*½ gallon Woodring Orchards cider, chilled*

*4 cups regular or low-calorie cranberry juice cocktail, chilled*

*1 small can (6 oz) orange juice concentrate, not reconstituted*

*Regular or diet Sprite or 7-Up to taste, chilled*

Mix cider, cranberry juice, and orange juice concentrate together and stir well. Add Sprite or 7-Up to taste, and serve.

*Makes about 1 gallon, 32 servings.*

# SBC, Seattle's Best Coffee

Open since 1984, SBC, Seattle's Best Coffee, is an ideal Market meeting place because of its foamy lattes, indoor and outdoor seating, and relaxed, European atmosphere. The place attracts both locals and tourists alike, perhaps because of its welcoming neon coffee-cup sign, or perhaps because of its central location at Post Alley and Pine. If you get a seat at the back counter, you can take full advantage of Seattle's clean, bracing air, and get a good view of the sky, the tops of the Olympic Mountains, and the tips of the totem poles in nearby Victor Steinbrueck Park.

SBC traces its history back to 1968, to a young optometry student in Los Angeles who loved the smell but hated the taste and nerve-shattering effects of coffee. Nonetheless, Jim Stewart needed a job while attending school, so he went to work at a specialty coffee and tea shop, where he learned that high-quality coffees not only tasted good but contained less caffeine than tin-can coffees from the supermarket.

Today Jim is known as "Bwana Kahowa," or Mr. Coffee, in Africa, one of the many places he visits (along with Central and South America, the Caribbean, and Southeast Asia) in search of the highest-grade coffees. He likes to touch the raw beans, shake hands with the people who grow them, and witness how they're handled from picking basket to shipping bag to ensure the best-quality beans. "We look for the small producers who use the old methods and practice coffee handling as an art," Jim explains.

Once SBC beans find their way back to Seattle, they're roasted in small batches daily on Vashon Island in the "German-style northern European roast," a lighter roast than the full city roast favored by other coffee purveyors in town. SBC's Pike Place Market location, with its distinctive red bumbershoots hanging upside down from the ceiling, sells espresso drinks, whole-bean coffees, and an extensive line of coffee brewing, grinding, and serving accessories.

## The Perfect Cup of Coffee

— SBC, Seattle's Best Coffee —

Always use the correct grind of coffee for the particular brewing method you are using. Usually the faster the brewing method, the finer the grind.

Always start with fresh, cold tap water for brewing. Hot water tends to flatten taste.

Always measure water correctly according to the brewing system you have.

Never guess amounts. Recommended proportion for brewed coffee: 1 tablespoon ground coffee per one 6-ounce cup of water.

Never reheat coffee. Keep coffee warm in a thermos or vacuum container for best results.

# *Caffe Latte*

SBC, Seattle's Best Coffee

Pour one shot of espresso into a coffee mug. Steam milk by filling metal steaming pitcher halfway with cold milk. Insert steaming nozzle into milk, open valve on espresso machine, then lower the pitcher until the tip of the nozzle touches the surface of the milk and a smooth, hissing sound is heard. (If you have the nozzle too high above the milk, it will splatter. If the nozzle is too deep, there will be a dull rumble and the milk will only be heated, not steamed.)

Continue to lower the pitcher and keep the nozzle at the surface of the milk. When foaming is complete, lower nozzle into milk to finish heating milk. When pitcher is hot to the touch, steaming is complete. Turn off espresso machine. Fill your cup with steamed milk and top with foam.

*Serves 1.*

# STARBUCKS COFFEE CO.

The story of Starbucks Coffee Co. could be a chapter in a business-school casebook, and it all began in 1971 in the Pike Place Market, where three San Francisco area college graduates began selling roaster-fresh, whole-bean coffee to retail customers. Other branches opened, and the men started selling coffee wholesale to restaurants, other espresso houses, and coffee retailers throughout the United States. When espresso drinks were added in 1984, Starbucks helped launch Seattle's coffee culture, and a multimillion-dollar business was born.

Today Starbucks' Italian-style espresso bars stretch from the West Coast to Chicago. The three founders are no longer associated with the business, yet the Pike Place Market outlet remains a venerated touchstone. Market musicians like to set up just outside the door, and you'll often be treated to the strains of a string quartet or a folk song by blind street musician Jeanne Towne (a regular performer at the Market since 1978) while waiting for your latte.

Lisa McCrummen, Starbucks' Special Events Coordinator, adds, "We get such a wide variety of people at the Pike Place store — the more knowledgeable want to know from what estate we get our aged Java, or they order a double short almond *breve,* nonfat, of course! On the other hand, one gentleman who wasn't as sophisticated just couldn't understand why his grinder clogged up and why he had such bad coffee made from the chocolate-covered espresso beans he bought from us. (We sell them to *eat,* not brew!)"

In case you're wondering about the name, it's a siren motif, "intended as an invitation to a journey of discovery, exploring the world of exotic coffees which are shipped across the seven seas to our port city home."

## *Café Marrakech*

— STARBUCKS COFFEE CO. —

4 cups hot, strong coffee

2 cinnamon sticks (3 inches long each)

4 whole cloves

4 whole allspice berries

4 cardamom pods

Milk

Brown sugar

Brew coffee and pour directly into a glass carafe with all the spices at the bottom.

Allow to come to room temperature, strain, and store covered in the refrigerator.

Pour over ice in tall glasses and serve with milk and brown sugar, if desired (the addition of milk and sugar intensifies the spices, so taste as you go).

To make Café Rio, substitute 4 strips of orange peel, 4 strips lemon peel, and 8 whole cloves in place of the spices, and proceed as above.

*Serves 4 to 6.*

# Iced Café Crema

STARBUCKS COFFEE CO.

*1 cup chilled, strong coffee*

*½ cup half-and-half*

*2 rounded tablespoons confectioners' sugar*

*2 cups crushed ice*

Combine all ingredients in a blender and mix until creamy. Pour into tall glasses and serve at once.

For variety, add one of the following: 2 teaspoons malt powder, 1 teaspoon cinnamon, 1 teaspoon cocoa powder, or a garnish of whipped cream dusted with grated chocolate.

*Serves 4.*

*Note:* To make good iced coffee, start with your favorite coffee brewed double-strength to compensate for the dilution from the ice. (Starbucks recommends Caffé Verona Blend or other dark-roast blends because they produce a more flavorful iced coffee drink.) Use a filtered drip brewing method and 4 tablespoons coffee for every 8-ounce cup. Allow the coffee to cool, and use as soon as possible. Meanwhile, store in the refrigerator in a covered glass container to preserve the aroma and protect the flavor.

# TENZING MOMO INC.

Tenzing Momo Inc. is the kind of place where phrases like "heavy karma" and "good vibes" seem as at home as the antique glass jars of dried herbs and flowers that line its walls. Since 1977 this herbal apothecary has dispensed herbal alternatives to help people stop smoking, dull toothaches, and get over colds and flu. Indeed, their best-selling product is a cough, cold, and flu tea that you take when symptoms first appear, and which many Market merchants swear by to relieve the grippe.

Located in the Economy Market Atrium, Tenzing Momo was one of the first herbal apothecaries on the West Coast and is modeled after a Tibetan pharmacy. Its name means "illustrious food" and the focus is more old age than new age, with Tibetan Buddhism as a guide.

Here you'll find Chinese gecko balls (an age-old hangover cure made of ground gecko lizard and dried plants); snake vertebrae necklaces; tarot cards; crystals; incense and candles; and natural shampoos, soaps, and lotions. Floor-to-ceiling bookcases are filled with more than 500 volumes featuring theories from Tibetan, *ayurveda*, *Indra*, Hindu, Central and South American, Asian, European, and United States herbology.

"We try to keep the mood upbeat. Some of our customers are ill and using herbs as a last resort, so we enjoy every minute we have with them," says owner Jeffrey Gould, a vibrant man who sports a Muslim *kufti* cap over his strawberry-blond ponytail. "I can't promise cures and I suggest consulting traditional doctors, yet I also strongly advocate the secret ingredient — plants — from which the shop's herbal teas and oils are made."

# Indian-Style Chai (Yogi) Tea

TENZING MOMO INC.

This authentic, spicy tea is often served in Indian restaurants and would be great with any of the Indian recipes that appear in this book.

*12 ounces cassia chips (American cinnamon bark)*

*6 ounces ginger, cut and sifted*

*2 ounces whole cloves*

*2 ounces whole cardamom seeds*

*¾ ounce peppercorns*

*4 cups water*

*2 tablespoons black tea, such as Ceylon orange pekoe*

*6 cups whole or low-fat milk*

*Sugar or honey to taste*

Mix together cassia chips, ginger, cloves, cardamom seeds, and peppercorns to make Yogi Tea mix. Weigh 3 to 5 ounces of tea mix and simmer in the water for 45 minutes, covered. If desired, you can also buy the tea mix from Tenzing Momo already prepared and packaged.

Add black tea and steep for 5 minutes. Strain, add milk, and serve. Let your guests add sugar or honey to taste, if desired.

*Makes 3 cups tea; when prepared with milk, serves 18 (the proportion is 1 part tea to 2 parts milk).*

# Roasted Dandelion Root Coffee

TENZING MOMO INC.

This alternative to coffee has a deep, dark-roasted taste remarkably like that of real coffee.

*1 pound dried dandelion root*

*8 cups water*

Preheat oven to 200° to 250°F.

To roast dandelion root, spread dried dandelion root in thin layer on cookie sheet and roast for 2 to 3 hours. For a darker-roasted coffee, roast at higher temperature (250°F) for the shorter (2-hour) time.

In a coffee mill, grind ½ cup of the roasted dandelion root to a fine consistency. Place root in conventional, drip-style coffee maker, add the water, and brew as directed by manufacturer.

Add vanilla soy milk, royal bee jelly with honey, or plain honey for a sweet, latte-style drink.

*Makes 8 cups; 16 servings.*

*Note:* Stevia is a healthy sugar substitute made from plant material that contains no sugar or artificial sweeteners, is very sweet, and can be used in place of honey or sugar when brewing teas and coffees.

# THE PERENNIAL TEA ROOM

From its location on a narrow stretch of Post Alley, to the window-box planters filled with pansies out front, to the whimsical teapots that line its windows, the Perennial Tea Room looks like a shop straight out of England. The owners, Sue Zuege and Julee Rosanoff, teach classes on four-course teas, run a mail-order tea business (be sure to put your name on their mailing list), and are the authors of the self-published *The Perennial Tea Room Guide to Afternoon Tea*, a great little book that lists hotels, restaurants, and tea rooms in Washington State where one can "take" tea.

Here you'll find fine imported bulk teas, books on tea, tea towels imported from Britain and Ireland, sugar bowls and creamers, electric kettles, children's tea sets, automatic tea makers, handcrafted Japanese *washi* boxes to store tea, and all the necessities for afternoon tea, such as tea strainers and silver-plated serving trays. Several types of shortbread and tea biscuits, both imported (McVitie's from Britain) and domestic (Seattle's Own Shortbread from the Pastry Case in Wallingford) are offered, as are samples of two freshly brewed teas daily.

# The Perfect Pot of Tea

Bring fresh, cold water to a full boil. Place 1 level teaspoon of loose tea per cup directly into pot. Pour in water to fill, steep 3 minutes, then stir. Strain directly into cup or decant into serving pot. Use tea cozy only after leaves have been removed. Add milk or lemon and sugar or honey to taste and enjoy.

To decaffeinate tea, bring fresh, cold water to a full boil. Place 1 level teaspoon of loose tea per cup directly into pot. Pour in water to fill and steep caffeinated tea leaves of your choice for only 30 seconds. Pour off water in pot, then pour in fresh boiling water to fill, steep 3 minutes, and stir.

Strain directly into cup or decant into serving pot. Use tea cozy only after leaves have been removed. Add milk or lemon and sugar or honey to taste.

**For a perfect cup of tea,** bring fresh, cold water to a full boil. Place 1 level teaspoon of tea into strainer, infuser, or loose into a cup. Pour in water to fill, cover with saucer, and steep 3 minutes. Add milk or lemon and sugar or honey to taste.

# Menu for an Afternoon, Victorian, or Low Tea

Sandwiches are the introduction to the tea service, and can be light or substantial, plain or fancy, depending on your overall plan. Suggestions include boiled egg with chutney or cream cheese with chutney sandwiches, served with J. P. Morgan tea, a hearty black tea.

Scones are the basic ingredient of traditional teas, served with clotted cream and jam. Savory scones can also be used as the primary course in a luncheon or high tea. Hazelnut scones with butter, served with Ceylon orange pekoe tea, a basic black tea, would make a tempting choice.

The Light Course traditionally provides a break from the heavy dishes. It may include cheese and fruit, shortbread, or sorbet. It is also an excellent place to serve port or sherry. Cheddar teapots (slices of Cheddar cheese cut into teapot shapes with a sharp cookie cutter) with red grapes, served with Ceylon orange pekoe tea, is a good suggestion.

Variations on the Dessert Course are as plentiful as ideas. Fruitcake, English trifle, lemon squares, or anything else that will satiate your guests' sweet tooths will suffice. Apple-and-lemon-custard tart, served with almond tea, a delicately flavored black tea that refreshes without overpowering the palate, provides a sweet ending to an afternoon tea.

# Appendixes

# Appendixes
## Techniques
## Produce Availability Chart
## Mail Order Information

# TECHNIQUES

**To deglaze:** Add a liquid, such as wine, broth, or water, to the pan and heat on the stovetop over medium-high heat, scraping to loosen browned particles and crusted juices in order to make a sauce from the meat juices remaining in the pan after food has been roasted or sautéed.

**To make clarified butter (also referred to as *ghee*):** Melt butter in a skillet over low heat. As white foam rises to the top, skim and discard. The clarified butter is the heavy yellow liquid that remains in the bottom of the pan.

**To plump dried fruit, such as dried cherries, apricots, raisins, or apples:** Add fruit to a small saucepan and cover with water, stock, or liqueur. Bring to a boil, cover, then remove pan from heat. Allow to stand for 20 minutes, or until fruit is plumped. To plump fruit more quickly, put ½ cup water into a microwave-safe glass dish. Add fruit and microwave on high for 30 seconds. Stir and repeat. When fruit begins to plump, remove from microwave oven and cover. Let rest for 5 minutes, drain water, and add fruit to recipe.

**To roast or toast hazelnuts:** Put nuts on a cookie sheet in a single layer and place in a 375°F oven for 10 minutes. Remove from oven and allow to cool slightly. Place nuts between two rough terrycloth towels, and rub off as much of the nuts' brown skins as you can, or rub a handful of nuts between your palms, or a single difficult-to-skin nut between forefinger and thumb.

**To roast peppers:** Roast peppers in one of the following four ways. Char the outside of the peppers with a propane blowtorch until black; roast the peppers over a gas burner on high heat, turning frequently with kitchen tongs until well charred on all sides; broil the peppers under a hot broiler several inches from heat until brownish-black blisters form; or roast the peppers in a 400°F oven for 10 to 15 minutes until brownish-black blisters form. Put the roasted peppers in a paper or plastic bag, close the top, and let stand for 10 minutes. Remove the peppers from the bag and scrape off the skin, seeds, and ribs. Wipe away any remaining black particles with a damp cloth, then chop as described above. Use thin plastic or rubber gloves to protect your hands while preparing the peppers, or prepare them under cold, running water.

**To toast sesame seeds, almonds, walnuts, sunflower seeds, or other nuts or seeds:** Place seeds or nuts in a dry skillet over medium heat until they begin to turn light brown, about 3 to 5 minutes, shaking often. Remove from heat and add to recipe.

# PRODUCE AVAILABILITY CHART

| Produce | Jan | Feb | Mar | Apr | May | Jun | July | Aug | Sept | Oct | Nov | Dec |
|---|---|---|---|---|---|---|---|---|---|---|---|---|
| Apple cider (fresh) | ✦ | ✦ | ✦ | ✦ | ✦ | ✦ | ✦ | ✦ | ✦ | ✦ | ✦ | ✦ |
| Apples (fresh picked) | | | | | | | ✦ | ✦ | ✦ | ✦ | ✦ | ✦ |
| Apricots | | | | | | | ✦ | ✦ | | | | |
| Arugula | | | | | | | ✦ | ✦ | ✦ | | | |
| Asparagus | | | | ✦ | ✦ | | | | | | | |
| Basil | | | | | | ✦ | ✦ | ✦ | ✦ | ✦ | | |
| Beans, green | | | | | | | ✦ | ✦ | ✦ | | | |
| Beets | | | | | | ✦ | ✦ | ✦ | ✦ | ✦ | ✦ | ✦ |
| Blackberries | | | | | | | ✦ | ✦ | | | | |
| Blueberries | | | | | | | ✦ | ✦ | | | | |
| Bok choy | | | | | | ✦ | ✦ | ✦ | ✦ | ✦ | ✦ | |
| Boysenberries | | | | | | | ✦ | ✦ | | | | |
| Broccoli | | | | | | ✦ | ✦ | ✦ | ✦ | ✦ | ✦ | |
| Brussels sprouts | | | | | | | | | ✦ | ✦ | ✦ | |
| Cabbage, Chinese | | | | | | | ✦ | ✦ | ✦ | ✦ | | |
| Cabbage, green | | | | | | | ✦ | ✦ | ✦ | ✦ | ✦ | ✦ |
| Cabbage, red | | | | | | | ✦ | ✦ | ✦ | ✦ | ✦ | |
| Cabbage, Savoy | | | | | | | ✦ | ✦ | ✦ | ✦ | | |
| Carrots | | ✦ | ✦ | ✦ | ✦ | ✦ | ✦ | ✦ | ✦ | ✦ | ✦ | ✦ |
| Cauliflower | | ✦ | ✦ | | | | ✦ | ✦ | ✦ | ✦ | | |
| Celery | | | | | | | ✦ | ✦ | ✦ | ✦ | ✦ | |
| Chard | | | | | | | | | ✦ | ✦ | | |
| Cherries (pie) | | | | | | | ✦ | ✦ | | | | |
| Cherries (sweet) | | | | | | ✦ | ✦ | | | | | |
| Chile peppers | | | | | | | | | ✦ | ✦ | | |

| Produce | Jan | Feb | Mar | Apr | May | Jun | July | Aug | Sept | Oct | Nov | Dec |
|---|---|---|---|---|---|---|---|---|---|---|---|---|
| Collard greens | | | | | | | ❖ | ❖ | ❖ | ❖ | ❖ | |
| Corn | | | | | | | ❖ | ❖ | ❖ | ❖ | | |
| Cucumbers, pickling | | | | | | | ❖ | ❖ | ❖ | | | |
| Cucumbers, slicing | | | | | | | | ❖ | ❖ | | | |
| Currants | | | | | | ❖ | ❖ | ❖ | ❖ | | | |
| Daikon | | | | | | | ❖ | ❖ | ❖ | ❖ | ❖ | |
| Dill | | | | | | | ❖ | ❖ | ❖ | | | |
| Eggplant | | | | | | | | ❖ | ❖ | | | |
| Garlic | | | | | | | ❖ | ❖ | ❖ | ❖ | ❖ | ❖ |
| Gooseberries | | | | | | | ❖ | ❖ | ❖ | ❖ | | |
| Gourds, ornamental | | | | | | | | | ❖ | ❖ | ❖ | |
| Grapes | | | | | | | | | ❖ | ❖ | ❖ | |
| Herbs | | | | ❖ | ❖ | ❖ | ❖ | ❖ | ❖ | ❖ | | |
| Honey | ❖ | ❖ | ❖ | ❖ | ❖ | ❖ | ❖ | ❖ | ❖ | ❖ | ❖ | ❖ |
| Horseradish | | | | | | | | ❖ | | | | |
| Kale | | | | | | | | | ❖ | ❖ | ❖ | |
| Kohlrabi | | | | | | | ❖ | ❖ | ❖ | ❖ | ❖ | ❖ |
| Leeks | ❖ | ❖ | ❖ | | | | | | ❖ | ❖ | ❖ | ❖ |
| Lettuce, head | | | | | ❖ | ❖ | ❖ | ❖ | ❖ | ❖ | ❖ | |
| Lettuce, leaf | | | | | ❖ | ❖ | ❖ | ❖ | ❖ | ❖ | ❖ | |
| Loganberries | | | | | | | ❖ | ❖ | | | | |
| Marionberries | | | | | | | ❖ | ❖ | | | | |
| Melon, bitter | | | | | | | ❖ | ❖ | | | | |
| Melons | | | | | | | ❖ | ❖ | ❖ | | | |
| Mint | | | | | | ❖ | ❖ | ❖ | | | | |
| Mizuna | | | | ❖ | ❖ | ❖ | | | | | | |
| Mushrooms, wild | | | | | | | | | | ❖ | ❖ | |
| Mustard greens | | | | | ❖ | ❖ | ❖ | ❖ | ❖ | ❖ | ❖ | |
| Nectarines | | | | | | | ❖ | ❖ | ❖ | | | |
| Nuts | | | | | | | | | | ❖ | ❖ | |

| Produce | Jan | Feb | Mar | Apr | May | Jun | July | Aug | Sept | Oct | Nov | Dec |
|---|---|---|---|---|---|---|---|---|---|---|---|---|
| Onions, green | | | | ❖ | ❖ | ❖ | ❖ | ❖ | ❖ | ❖ | ❖ | |
| Onions, Walla Walla | | | | | | | ❖ | ❖ | ❖ | | | |
| Onions, yellow | | | | | | | ❖ | ❖ | ❖ | ❖ | ❖ | ❖ |
| Parsley | | | | | | | ❖ | ❖ | ❖ | | | |
| Peaches | | | | | | | ❖ | ❖ | ❖ | | | |
| Pears | | | | | | | | ❖ | ❖ | ❖ | | |
| Peas, green | | | | | ❖ | ❖ | ❖ | | | | | |
| Peas, snow | | | | | ❖ | ❖ | | | | | | |
| Peppers | | | | | | | ❖ | ❖ | ❖ | ❖ | ❖ | |
| Potatoes, Finnish | | | | | | | | ❖ | ❖ | ❖ | ❖ | |
| Potatoes, German | | | | | | | | | ❖ | ❖ | ❖ | |
| Potatoes, red | | | | | | | | | ❖ | ❖ | | |
| Pumpkins | | | | | | | | | ❖ | ❖ | | |
| Quince | | | | | | | | | | ❖ | | |
| Radishes | | | | | ❖ | ❖ | ❖ | ❖ | ❖ | | | |
| Raspberries | | | | | | ❖ | ❖ | ❖ | ❖ | | | |
| Rhubarb | | | | ❖ | ❖ | ❖ | | | | | | |
| Rutabaga | | | | | | | | | ❖ | ❖ | ❖ | ❖ |
| Shallots | | | | | | | | | ❖ | ❖ | ❖ | ❖ |
| Spinach | | | | ❖ | ❖ | ❖ | ❖ | ❖ | ❖ | ❖ | | |
| Sprouts (alfalfa, bean, etc.) | ❖ | ❖ | ❖ | ❖ | ❖ | ❖ | ❖ | ❖ | ❖ | ❖ | ❖ | ❖ |
| Squash, summer | | | | | | | ❖ | ❖ | ❖ | ❖ | | |
| Squash, winter | | | | | | | | ❖ | ❖ | ❖ | ❖ | ❖ |
| Strawberries | | | | | | ❖ | ❖ | | | | | |
| Tomatoes | | | | | | | ❖ | ❖ | ❖ | ❖ | | |
| Turnips | | | | | | | ❖ | ❖ | ❖ | ❖ | ❖ | ❖ |
| Watercress | | | | | | ❖ | ❖ | ❖ | ❖ | ❖ | | |
| Zucchini | | | | | | | ❖ | ❖ | ❖ | ❖ | | |

# Mail Order Information

Some of the recipes in the *Pike Place Market Cookbook* call for specialty products available only at the Pike Place Market. To make it easier for you to try the recipes, the following is a list of farmers and businesses that will send their products through the mail or via UPS. Some can transport only certain of their products (preserved items, such as herb vinegars, jams, and jellies); others will send fresh produce or foodstuffs. The businesses have varying policies on credit cards; some accept them, others will take only a check or money order, so inquire before placing your order.

**Alm Hill Gardens**
3550 Alm Rd.
Everson, WA 98247
(206) 966-4157

**Biringer Farm Bakery & Country Store**
1530 Post Alley #9
Seattle, WA 98101
(206) 623-0890
(800) 448-8212

**Canter-Berry Farms**
19102 S.E. Green Valley Rd.
Auburn, WA 98002
(206) 939-2706
(800) 548-8418

**Chukar Cherry Company**
P.O. Box 510
306 Wine Country Rd.
Prosser, WA 99350-0510
(509) 786-2055
(800) 624-9544

**Cucina Fresca**
1904 Pike Place
Seattle, WA 98101
(206) 448-4758

**DeLaurenti Specialty Food Markets**
1435 First Ave.
Seattle, WA 98101
(206) 622-0141

**Dilettante Chocolates**
5834 Sixth Ave. NW
Seattle, WA 98107
(800) 548-7766

**du jour** (gift baskets)
1919 First Ave.
Seattle, WA 98101
(206) 441-3354

**El Mercado Latino**
1514 Pike Place
Seattle, WA 98101
(206) 623-3240

**The Granger Berry Patch**
1731 Beam Rd.
Granger, WA 98932
(509) 854-1413
(800) 346-1417

**Harmony Farms**
630 Harmony Rd.
Silver Creek, WA 98585
(206) 983-3113

**Holmquist Hazelnut Orchard**
9821 Holmquist Rd.
Lynden, WA 98264
(206) 988-9240

**Kitchen Basics**
1514 Pike Place, #10
Seattle, WA 98101
(206) 622-2014

**Liberty Malt Supply Company/
Pike Place Brewery**
1418 Western Ave.
Seattle, WA 98101
(206) 622-1880

**Lina's Fruit & Produce**
Arcade #7
1521 Pike Place
Seattle, WA 98101
(206) 622-5952

**Louie's on the Pike**
1926 Pike Place
Seattle, WA 98101
(206) 443-1035

**Magnano Foods**
1501 Pike Place
Seattle, WA 98101
(206) 223-9582

**MarketSpice**
P.O. Box 2935
Redmond, WA 98073-2935
(206) 883-1220
(800) 735-7198

**Mech Apiaries**
P.O. Box 452
Maple Valley, WA 98038
(206) 432-3971

**Northwest Chestnuts**
265 Butts Rd.
Morton, WA 98356
(206) 496-3395

**The Perennial Tea Room**
1906 Post Alley
Seattle, WA 98101
(206) 448-4054

**Pike Place Fish**
86 Pike Place
Seattle, WA 98101
(206) 682-7181
(800) 542-7732

**The Pike Place Market Creamery**
(Unrefrigerated items only, such as jams,
jellies, honey, soy milk, and T-shirts)
1514 Pike Place #3
Seattle, WA 98101
(206) 622-5029

**Popcorner**
1530 Post Alley
Seattle, WA 98101
(206) 622-4240

**The Public Market Candy Store**
1501 Pike Place #502
Seattle, WA 98101
(206) 625-0420

**Pure Food Fish Market**
1511 Pike Place
Seattle, WA 98101
(206) 622-5765
(800) 392-3474

**Quillisascut Cheese Company**
2409 Pleasant Valley Road
Rice, WA 99167
(509) 738-2011

**Rachel-Dee Herb Farm**
40622 196th Ave. S.E.
Enumclaw, WA 98022
(206) 825-2797

**Sandy's Acres**
27716 71st Ave. N.E.
Arlington, WA 98223
(206) 435-0805

**SBC, Seattle's Best Coffee**
P.O. Box 1050
Vashon Island, WA 98070-9980
(800) 962-9659

**Silver Bay Herb Farm**
9151 Tracyton Blvd.
Bremerton, WA 98310
(206) 692-1340

**Snoqualmie Valley Honey Farm**
P.O. Box 529
North Bend, WA 98045
(206) 888-9021

**Sosio's Produce**
1527 Pike Place
Seattle, WA 98101
(206) 622-1370

**The Souk**
1916 Pike Place
Seattle, WA 98101
(206) 441-1666

**Stackhouse Brothers' Orchards**
13501 Cogswell Rd.
Hickman, CA 95323
(209) 883-2663

**Starbucks Coffee Co.**
2203 Airport Way S.
P.O. Box 34510
Seattle, WA 98124
(800) 445-3428

**Sur La Table**
84 Pine St.
Seattle, WA 98101
(206) 448-2244
(800) 243-0852

**Totem Smokehouse**
1906 Pike Place
Seattle, WA 98101
(206) 443-1710
(800) 972-5666

**Vashon's Old-Fashioned Nursery**
P.O. Box 5042
Dockton, WA 98070
(206) 463-3760

**Verdi's Farm-Fresh Produce**
10325 Airport Way
Snohomish, WA 98290
(206) 568-0319

**Woodring Orchards**
5420 Woodring Canyon Rd.
Cashmere, WA 98815
(509) 782-2868
(800) 548-5740

# INDEX

Spencer Johnson

# ABOUT THE AUTHOR

Braiden Rex-Johnson is a freelance
writer who lives a stone's throw from
Seattle's Pike Place Market. She has
coordinated cooking demonstrations at
the Market, has won awards at cooking
contests, and writes for a variety of
regional and national publications.
Her husband, Spencer Johnson, is an
architect and the illustrator for
*Pike Place Market Cookbook*.

IN MEMORIAM
*Rachel the Pig*
*1980–1991*